The Vestry Book
OF
Stratton Major Parish

West end—South side   THE "UPPER CHURCH" OF STRATTON MAJOR PARISH   *South side—East end*
Photographs taken July 4, 1931, by The Editor

THE VESTRY BOOK

OF

STRATTON MAJOR PARISH

KING AND QUEEN COUNTY, VIRGINIA

1729-1783

TRANSCRIBED, ANNOTATED AND INDEXED
BY
C. G. CHAMBERLAYNE

CLEARFIELD

Originally published
Richmond, Virginia, 1931

Reprinted for
Clearfield Company, Inc. by
Genealogical Publishing Co., Inc.
Baltimore, Maryland
1999

International Standard Book Number: 0-8063-4846-1

Made in the United States of America

Introductory Note

The parish records of Colonial Virginia (the vestry books and the registers) are among the most valuable records, both from an historical and a genealogical point of view, that have come down to us. Very few, relatively, are, so far as known, in existence, the great majority of them having, unfortunately, been burned in the houses of custodians or lost. It is estimated that there are probably forty-eight of these records that can now be located. It is barely possible that others may yet be found.

Thirteen of these records have been printed, three by the Colonial Dames of America in the State of Virginia and the others by individuals, the motive being in each case a patriotic one, since the sale of the printed books, however well advertised, is bound to be so limited that no money can be made from their publication.

Dr. Churchill Gibson Chamberlayne, who had already published three of these records, as a labor of love, suggested to Dr. Lyon G. Tyler, Chairman of the Library Board, that the publication of the volumes should be undertaken by the Board, offering at the same time to see through the press a volume that he had already prepared.

This offer being accepted, the present volume, The Vestry Book of Stratton Major Parish, is the result. It is hoped that other volumes in this series may also be published.

                                        H. R. McILWAINE,
                                                 State Librarian.

Richmond, August 4, 1931.

Preface

The MS. volume hereinafter reproduced contains the earliest consecutive record of Stratton Major Parish known to be in existence. There are, however, references to the parish in *Hening* and other sources which antedate this record by many years, going back indeed to the year the parish was established; i. e., to 1654-5.

The old Vestry Book is a folio 16 by $10\frac{1}{4}$ inches in size, and contains at present 89 leaves (178 pages) of heavy laid paper, the water-marks being two: the Roman numeral IV ($\frac{1}{2}$ inch by 1 inch) and a fleur-de-lis on a shield, surmounted by a crown, the whole over the monogram WR ($2\frac{3}{4}$ inches by $5\frac{5}{8}$ inches). Formerly the volume contained more pages than at present; for there is a fragment of a leaf preceding what is now page 1 of the MS., and evidently one leaf is missing between what are now pages 6 and 7. The last twenty-seven pages in the book (152 to 178, inclusive) are blank. The record as it now stands covers—except for the eleven months between May 10, 1731 and April 11, 1732, where one leaf is missing from the MS.—the period from April 8, 1729 to Dec. 13, 1783, or fifty-four years and eight months.

This old book is one of twenty-five or more Virginia Colonial Church records in the possesion of the Library of the Theological Seminary in Virginia, at Alexandria. It was one of those made use of by Bishop Meade when preparing his *Old Churches, Ministers and Families of Virginia*. Permission to transcribe and publish it was given the undersigned by the Rt. Rev. H. St. George Tucker, D. D., President of the Board of Trustees of the Seminary.

The history of Stratton Major Parish prior to the date at which the present record begins is painfully scanty and fragmentary. As far as the present editor has been able to discover, it is as follows:

The parish was established by the General Assembly at the session beginning March 24, 1655—the 6th session under the Commonwealth. The entry in *Hening* [Vol. I, page 404] recording this action of the General Assembly reads: "Ordered, that from Poropotank to Mattapony upward (vizt) on the north side of Yorke river be a distinct parish by the name of Stratton Major." It is to be noted here that in the above entry the boundaries of the parish on but two sides are given; on the south-east, Poropotank Creek, and on the south-west, York River and the Mattapony. What the boundary line on the northeast was can only be conjectured. It was probably the same as that of the newly created County of New Kent, of which Stratton Major Parish formed a part [*Hening*, Vol. I, p. 388 under date of Nov., 1654—5th session under the Commonwealth—reads: "It is ordered that the upper part of York county shall be a distinct county called New Kent, from the west side of Scimino Creek to the heads of Pomunkey and Mattaponie river, and down to the head of the wist side of Poropotanke Creek."] As to the northwest boundary of the new parish, it is impossible to say definitely whether or not there was one. If, as seems to the present editor most unlikely, the parish of St. Stephen's was established the same year as Stratton Major, then the south-east boundary of St. Stephen's was the north-west boundary line of Stratton Major. Otherwise, until the establishment of St. Stephen's Parish, the parish of Stratton Major extended toward the north-west *theoretically* to a line drawn between the head springs of the Pamunkey (South Anna) and the Mattapony, and *actually* to the point to which settlement had reached. The whole question as to what and where the north-western boundary of Stratton Major Parish at the date of its establishment was depends entirely upon the date of the establishment of St. Stephen's Parish, its next door neighbor to the north-west. Bishop Meade [*Old Churches,* etc., Vol. I, p. 379] gave 1691 as the probable date. This date is, however, certainly too late; for in the Public Record Office in London there is a document [C. O. 1. Vol. 45 No. 27] dated 1680 June 30, and entitled *A list of the Parishes in Virginia,* in which occurs the item:

"New Kent South side { St Peters
Blissland parish } ....
North side { St Stephen's parish
Stratton Maj: } { M^r. Tho: Taylor
Mr Wm Williams
Mr Robt Carr"

At the present time, 1680 is the earliest date in the history of St. Stephen's Parish that has been established, but it is obvious that the parish must have been established at least a few years earlier than that, and the present editor's guess is that it was established between 1660 and 1675. At all events, by the year 1680 the north-west boundary of Stratton Major Parish was, as it ever after remained, the same as the south-east boundary of St. Stephen's parish, i. e., a line running from the Mattapony river to the Dragon Swamp (the boundary between the present counties of King and Queen and Middlesex) some few—two or three—miles south east of the present King and Queen Court House.

In 1680 the Rev. Mr. Robert Carr was the minister of Stratton Major Parish. In 1702 the minister was the Rev. Edward Portlock [Public Record Office. C. O. 5 1312. N°. 38^{11}; Document headed "1702 Tabulated List of parishes, ministers and tithables &c. in Virginia. Sent home by Secretary Jennings 18 July 1702"]

On March 13, 1705 the Church Wardens and Vestry of Stratton Major Parish wrote the following letter to Governor Francis Nicholson:

To His Excell:^ry^ ffrancis Nicholson Esqr her Majesty's Lieu^t^ Govver^r^ Gen^ll^ of Virg^a^:
May it Please yor Excell^ry^

Wee the Churchwardens and Vestrymen of Stratton Major ⅌ish in the County of King & Queen Virg^a^ having had three years experience of the Good life and Doctrine of the Reverend Mr Edward Portlock do (upon your Excell^rys^ Motion for the Induction of Ministers by presentacon) hearby present the said Rever^d^ Mr Edward Portlock to be Inducted into the Said parish, and accordingly we the Said Churchwardens & Vestrymen (being the undoubted patrons of the Said parish of Straton Major) do hearby request your Excell^ry^ to Issue out Instruments for Inducting the said Mr Edward Portlock according to Law and Agreeable to the usuall form and method in that case, In Testimony whereof wee have Sett our hands and Seals this the thirtieth day of March Anno Dom one thousand Seven hundred & four

	John Story } Churchward^s^
	Wm Orrill }
Rich Roy	Rich Anderson
Nich° Ware	Jn° Major
James Erico	Wm Jones
Edward Lewis	Th° Turner
	Wm Hunt

[P. R. O. C. O. 5. Vol. 1314. N°. 63 ^xvii^]

In August, 1705 the Rev. Mr. Portlock, Minister of Stratton Major Parish, was one of a large number of clergymen (a large majority of all the clergymen holding parishes in the Colony) who signed various papers in a controversy between them and the Bishop of London's Commissary in Virginia, the Reverend James Blair [*Papers relating to the History of the Church in Virginia, A. D. 1650-1776, Edited by William Stevens Perry, D. D., 1870,* pp. 141 to 178.]

In 1724 the Rev. John Skaife, who had been Minister of Stratton Major Parish since 1710 [See *The Official Letters of Alexander Spottswood*, Richmond, 1882, Vol. I, pp. 2 and 4; also *Papers relating to the History of the Church in Virginia, A. D. 1650-1776*, p. 320 Letter of Mr. Commissary Blair to the Bishop of London, dated July 17th, 1724] answered the "Queries to be Answered by every Minister" [*Papers relating to the History of the Church in Virginia A. D. 1650-1776.*] From these answers it appears that the parish was about 18 miles in length and 8 in breadth, and contained between 190 and 200 families; that Divine Service was performed every Sunday, in fair weather about 300 persons and upwards attending it; that the Sacrament of the Lord's Supper was administered four times a year to about 220 communicants; that during Lent the youth of the parish were catechised; that all things were duly disposed and provided in the church for the decent and orderly performance of Divine Service except a font; that the value of the living was about £80 sterling; that there was a Glebe, which was occupied by the minister and kept in repair by the parish; and that there was no public school in the parish and no library. As to the means used for the conversion of negroes, Mr. Skaife reported: "Generally negroes are unbaptised; they that desire it have it, the Church is open to them all."

Of references to subsequent happenings in or connected with the history of Stratton Major Parish, other than those recorded in the Vestry Book, the following may be cited: *An Act to empower the Vestry of the Parish of Stratton Major, in the county of King and Queen, to sell the glebe of the said parish; and to purchase a more convenient glebe, in lieu thereof* [*Hening*, Vol. 5, p. 251, September, 1744]; *An Act to enable the Parish of Stratton Major, in the County of King and Queen, to sell their Glebe, and for other purposes therein mentioned* [*Hening*, Vol. 7, p. 147, April, 1757]; a letter of the Rev. William Robinson, Minister of Stratton Major Parish, to the Bishop of ————, Dated Nov. 20, 1760, and letters of the same, now Commissary of the Bishop of London, to the Bishop of London, dated, respectively, 1763; Aug. 17, 1764; May 23, 1765; Aug. 12, 1765; June 6, 1766; and Oct. 16, 1767 —all dealing with, among other things, the complaints of the clergy relative to the Act of the General Assembly, passed on the 12th of October, 1758, entitled *"An Act to enable the inhabitants of this Colony to discharge their public dues, officers fees, and other tobacco debts, in money, for the ensuing year* [Papers relating to the History of the Church in Virginia, pp. 463 to 529]; An act for the dissolving the vestries of several parishes: "WHEREAS it hath been represented to this general assembly, that ———————— there are such divisions among the vestry of the parish of Stratton Major, in the county of King and Queen, that the affairs of the said parish have been some time neglected: *Be it therefore enacted by the General Assembly,* That the vestries of the said parishes shall be, and the same are hereby dissolved." [*Hening*, Vol. 9, p. 317, May, 1777—1st year of the Commonwealth.]

Following the history notes just given, a word or two on the geography of Stratton Major Parish will not be out of place here. Stratton Major Parish, which from the year of its establishment until 1691 was in New Kent County and after that date in King and Queen County, of which it forms the south-eastern third, is bounded on the southeast by Poropotank Creek (which separates King and Queen from Gloucester), on the south-west by York River (which separates King and Queen from New Kent) and the Mattapony (which separates King and Queen from King William), on the north east by the Dragon Run (which separates King and Queen from Middlesex), and on the north-west by the south-east line of St. Stephen's Parish. The territory embraced within the limits of Stratton Major Parish is strictly rural in character, there being no towns at all and few villages of any considerable size.

There are many water courses, of which the majority empty into either the Mattapony or the York.

Of the nine creeks or swamps referred to by name in the Stratton Major Parish Vestry Book (i. e., Portopotank Creek, Matasip Swamp, Pepetico Swamp, Arracaco Creek, the Monack Swamp, Burgess's Swamp, Tarsatyan Swamp, Great Heartquake Swamp, and Little Hartquake Swamp) only three appear by name on the Fry & Jefferson map of 1775 (i. e., Portopotank, Pepetico, and Hartquip) and three on the United States, Department of the Interior, Geological Survey Maps of 1906 and 1919 (i. e., Poropotank Creek, Tastine Swamp, and Heartquake Creek).

The most casual reading of the Stratton Major Parish record, or any other of the Colonial Vestry Books, is enough to prove to any serious student of social history that until all the colonial parish records now in existence have been published, the complete story of daily life in Colonial Virginia cannot be told. Up to the present time thirteen of these records have appeared in print. They are, in the order of their publication, the following:

1. The Vestry Book of Henrico Parish, Virginia, 1730-1773 . . . Edited by Dr. R. A. Brock. Richmond, 1874. Wynne's Historical Documents from the Old Dominion, No. 5.

2. Register Containing the Baptisms Made in the Church of the French Refugees at Mannikintown in Virginia, in the Parish of King William, 1721-1754. Translated from the French and Edited by Dr. R. A. Brock in his *Huguenot Emigration to Virginia.* Collections of the Virginia Historical Society, *New Series,* Vol. V. 1888.

3. The Parish Register of Christ Church, Middlesex County, Virginia, from 1653 to 1812. Published by the National Society of the Colonial Dames of America in the State of Virginia. Richmond, 1897. (The last paragraph of

the introduction is as follows: "The copy here printed was made by one of the Virginia Dames, Mrs. Sally Nelson Robins, of Richmond, and compared with the original, and verified by Messrs. Edward W. James and William G. Stanard.")

4. The Vestry Book and Register of Bristol Parish, Virginia, 1720-1789. Transcribed and Published by C. G. Chamberlayne. Richmond, 1898.

5. The Parish Register of Overwharton Parish, Virginia, 1720-1760. Published by William F. Boogher, 1899.

6. The Register of St. Peter's Parish, New Kent County, Virginia, 1680-1787. Published by the National Society of the Colonial Dames of America in the State of Virginia. Richmond, 1904. (The name of the person who did the copying of this book is not given in the introduction.)

7. The Vestry Book of St. Peter's Parish, New Kent County, Virginia, 1682-1758. Published by the National Society of the Colonial Dames of America in the State of Virginia. Richmond, 1905. (Editor's name not given.)

8. The Vestry Book of King William Parish, Virginia, 1707-1750. Translated and Published in the Virginia Magazine of History and Biography, Vols. XI, XII, & XIII (1913, 1914 & 1915).

9. The Vestry Book of Christ Church Parish, Middlesex County, Virginia, 1663-1767. Transcribed, Annotated, and Indexed by C. G. Chamberlayne. 1927. Old Dominion Press, Richmond, Virginia.

10. The Douglas Register (St. James Northam Parish, Goochland County, Virginia, and King William Parish, Virginia), 1750-1797. Published by W. Mac Jones, Richmond, Virginia, 1928. (This book is not exactly a Parish Register, but is a record of births, marriages, and deaths as kept by the Rev. William Douglas, and put into alphabetical order by the editor, Mr. Jones, with other material.

11. The Vestry Book of Kingston Parish, Mathews County, Virginia (until May 1, 1791, Gloucester County),

1679-1796. Transcribed, Annotated, and Indexed by C. G. Chamberlayne. 1929. Old Dominion Press, Richmond, Virginia.
12. Cumberland Parish, Lunenburg County, Virginia, 1746-1816. Vestry Book, 1746-1816. By Landon C. Bell. 1930. The William Byrd Press, Inc., Printers, Richmond, Virginia.
13. The Vestry Book of Stratton Major Parish, King and Queen County, Virginia, 1729-1783.

Among the Colonial Virginia parish record books known to be in existence, but which as yet remain unpublished, are the following:

1. Abingdon Parish, Gloucester County, Virginia. Register, 1678-1761. Original lost when "Rosewell," Gloucester County, Va., was destroyed by fire. Two transcripts exist; one in the possession of Dr. Lyon G. Tyler, Holdcroft, Va., the other in the custody of the Virginia Historical Society, Richmond, Va.
2. Albemarle Parish, Surry and Sussex Counties, Virginia. Vestry Book, 1742-1788. Original in the Library of the Theological Seminary in Virginia, Alexandria, Va.
3. Albemarle Parish, Surry and Sussex Counties, Virginia. Register, 1739-1778. Original in the Library of the Virginia Historical Society, Richmond, Va.
4. Antrim Parish, Halifax County, Virginia. Vestry Book, 1752-1817. Original—consisting of three books bound up in one volume—in the Library of the Theological Seminary in Virginia, Alexandria, Va.
5. Blisland Parish, New Kent County, Virginia. Vestry Books, 1721-1786. Original in the Library of the Theological Seminary in Virginia, Alexandria, Va.
6. Cambden Parish, Pittsylvania County, Virginia. Vestry Book, 1767-1852. Original in the possession of Mrs. N. E. Clement, Chatham, Va.

7. Charles Parish, York County, Virginia. Register, 1618-1789. Original in the Library of the Theological Seminary in Virginia, Alexandria, Va.

8. Christ Church Parish, Lancaster County, Virginia. Vestry Book, 1739-1788. [The earlier pages record proceedings of the Vestry of St. Mary's White Chapel. St. Mary's White Chapel and Christ Church united in 1752, and in a short time the united parish came to be called Christ Church.] Original in the Library of the Theological Seminary in Virginia, Alexandria, Va.

9. Dettingen Parish, Prince William County, Virginia. Vestry Book, 1745-1802. Original in the Library of the Theological Seminary in Virginia, Alexandria, Va.

10. Frederick Parish, Frederick County, Virginia. Vestry Book, 1764-1818. Original in the Library of the Theological Seminary in Virginia, Alexandria, Va.

11. Fredericksville Parish, Louisa County, Virginia. Vestry Book, 1742-1787. Original in the Library of the Theological Seminary in Virginia, Alexandria, Va.

12. Fredericksville Parish, Louisa County, Virginia. Record of Indentures and Processioning Returns, 1742-1787. Original in the Library of the Theological Seminary in Virginia, Alexandria, Va.

13. Hanover Parish, King George County, Virginia. Vestry Book, 1779-1796. Original (bound up with the Fredericksville Parish Record of Indentures and Processioning Returns) in the Library of the Theological Seminary in Virginia, Alexandria, Va.

14. Kingston Parish, Mathews County, Virginia. Register, 1755-1776. Original in the Library of the Theological Seminary in Virginia, Alexandria, Va.

15. Lexington Parish, Amherst County, Virginia. Vestry Book, 1779-1880. Original in the Library of the Theological Seminary in Virginia, Alexandria, Va.

16. Lunenburg Parish, Richmond County, Virginia. Register, 1790-1800. [Strictly speaking, not a Colonial

record.] Original in the Library of the Theological Seminary in Virginia, Alexandria, Va.

17. Lynnhaven Parish, Princess Anne County, Virginia. Vestry Book, 1723-1892. Original in possession of Judge B. D. White, Lynnhaven, Va.

18. Newport Parish, (the Upper Parish of) Isle of Wight County, Virginia. Vestry Book, 1724-1772. [Called simply "the Upper Parish" until 1734.] Original in the custody of the Clerk of the Court of Isle of Wight County, Virginia.

19. North Farnham Parish, Richmond County, Virginia. Register, 1672-1800. Original in possession of the Circuit Court of Richmond County, Warsaw, Va.

20. Overwharton Parish, Stafford County, Virginia. Register, 1724/5-1774. Original in the Library of the Theological Seminary in Virginia, Alexandria, Va.

21. Petsworth (until about 1730 commonly called Petsoe) Parish, Gloucester County, Virginia. Vestry Book, 1677-1793. Original in possession of the Vestry of Abingdon and Ware Parishes, Gloucester County, Va.

22. St. Andrew's Parish, Brunswick County, Virginia. Vestry Book, 1732-1797. Original in the custody of the Clerk of the Circuit Court of Brunswick County, Lawrenceville, Va.

23. St. James Northam Parish, Goochland County, Virginia. Vestry Book, 1744-1860. Original in the Library of the Theological Seminary in Virginia, Alexandria, Va.

24. St. Mark's Parish, Culpeper County, Virginia. Vestry Book, 1730-1785. Original in the possession of the Vestry of the Parish.

25. St. Mark's Parish, Culpeper County, Virginia. Register, 1794-1797. [Strictly speaking, not a Colonial record.] Original in the possession of the Vestry of the Parish.

26. St. Patrick's Parish, Prince Edward County, Virginia. Vestry Book, 1755-1774. Original in the Library of the Theological Seminary in Virginia, Alexandria, Va.

27. St. Paul's Parish, Hanover County, Virginia. Vestry Book, 1705-1785. Original in the Library of the Theological Seminary in Virginia, Alexandria, Va.

28. St. Paul's Parish, King George County (until 1776-7, Stafford County), Virginia. Register, 1716-1793. Original in the possession of Mr. G. C. Stuart, Episcopal High School, Alexandria, Va.

29. Shelburne Parish, Loudoun County, Virginia. Vestry Book, 1771-1805. Original in the Library of the Theological Seminary in Virginia, Alexandria, Va.

30. Southam Parish, Powhatan County, Virginia. Vestry Book, 1745-1791. Original in the custody of the Clerk of the Circuit Court of Powhatan County, Powhatan Court House, Va.

31. South Farnham Parish, Essex County, Virginia. Processioning Book, 1739-1779. Original in the custody of the Rev. G. MacLaren Brydon, D. D., Registrar of the Diocese of Virginia, 110 W. Franklin St., Richmond, Va.

32. Suffolk Parish, Nansemond County, Virginia. Vestry Book, 1749-1784. Original in the possession of Judge Robert R. Prentiss, Supreme Court of Appeals, Richmond, Va.

33. Upper Nansemond Parish, Nansemond County, Virginia. Vestry Book, 1743-1793. Original in the Library of the Theological Seminary in Virginia, Alexandria, Va.

34. Wicomico Parish, Northumberland County, Virginia. Vestry Book, 1703-1795. Original in the Library of the Theological Seminary in Virginia, Alexandria, Va., on loan from the Rector and Vestry of the Parish.

35. The Rev. John Cameron's Marriage Register, 1784-1815. [Strictly speaking, not a Colonial record.] The (erroneous) binder's-title of this volume is: *Marriage Register, Bristol Parish*. Original in the Library of the Theological Seminary in Virginia, Alexandria, Va., on loan from Mrs. Robert G. Thornton, 1819 Monument Avenue, Richmond, Va.

The two views of the "Upper Church," appearing as a frontispiece, were taken July 4, 1931 by the editor. This old building, which must have been erected prior to 1729, is mentioned casually some four or five times in the Rev. Dr. Alfred Bagby's *King and Queen County, Virginia,* [The Neale Publishing Company, 1908]; the character of the references, however, is sufficient to show that with the lapse of time and under changed conditions interest in ancient landmarks can die out and the essential facts with regard to their history be completely forgotten. Three of those references are as follows:

(Page 60.) 'The so-called "Old Church" still stands some two miles below Little Plymouth and is used by the Methodists.'

(Page 83.) "The Old Church, a half-mile below Plymouth, was built in Colonial times. This house is about nine miles below the Courthouse."

(Page 290.) 'The lower portion of the county was comprised in Stratton Major parish, and the leading church in that parish was Stratton Major Church, the site of which, I have no doubt, has been located where the ruins of a church are still visible on the Milford estate, the home place of the late P. Thornton Pollard, and now owned and occupied by his granddaughter, Mrs. H. J. Dudley. When or how that church was destroyed we are unable to ascertain. A church house was built near by, but a few miles up the country, and called "The New Church," presumably to take the place of the one which had been destroyed. I suppose the church house now used by the Methodists, and known as "The Old Church" to be the same as the New Church above referred to.'

Now as to the supposition that "The Old Church" now used by the Methodists is the same as "The New Church" of Stratton Major Parish, a comparison of the present building with the specifications of the "New Church" (page 131 of the present volume) shows that it is incorrect; there is scarcely a detail given in the specifications that fits the present building. Moreover the records show conclusively that there was an Upper Church in existence in 1729, and that it was in constant and regular use until 1768, when an order appears for its abandonment as a place of worship by the parish (page 175, pres. vol.). If anything more were needed to prove that the present "Old Church" was not the "New Church" (built in 1760-1763), the style of architecture of the present building, which is that of the period between 1700 and 1750, might be cited, and also the facts that while there was an Upper Church in existence in 1729, the records, which are practically complete for the period between 1729 and 1783, are silent as to any rebuilding of that church, and that while the "New Church" was being built, the meetings of the Vestry were regularly held at the "Upper Church." The present "Old Church," used by the Methodists, is the old "Upper Church" of Stratton Major Parish, and was built prior to 1729.

The specimen pages of the MS. used to illustrate the volume are reproductions of photographs made from the original. Blanks in the MS., which were left by the Clerk to be filled in later, but were never filled in, are indicated in the printed volume by blank spaces. Gaps in the MS. resulting from tearing, rubbing, or other kinds of intentional or unintentional mutilation are indicated by blank spaces enclosed in brackets. Unintentional omissions in the MS. and all mistakes of whatever kind are, as far as was found possible, reproduced in the printed volume as made. Pages in the MS. are indicated in the printed volume by Arabic numerals enclosed in brackets. In the indexes the number of times a name or a topic occurs on a page is indicated by a small Arabic numeral above, and to the right of, the numeral indicating the number of the page.

Although the editor has read the proof several times, each time using the original MS. as his guide, he is well aware of the fact that in work of this kind some mistakes are inevitable. He hopes, however, that the number of such mistakes in this volume is small. One mistake, at least, he is already aware of: "the Wid". Gramskill," on page 33, should have been "the Wid". Gramshill." Any one wishing to check up on the work can do so by comparing the printed volume with the original MS. (in the Library of the Theological Seminary in Virginia, Alexandria, Va.) or with the photostat copy of the original on file in the Archives Department of the Virginia State Library in Richmond.

That the present volume may contribute to awaken interest in the preservation and reproduction in print of the parish records of Colonial Virginia is the hope of

THE EDITOR.

Richmond, Virginia,
July 30, 1931.

The Vestry Book
...of...
Stratton Major Parish

King and Queen County, Virginia, 1729-1783

At a Vestry held for Stratton Major Parish at yᵉ G[   ] the 8ᵗʰ of April 1729.

Pʳſent The Revᵈ Mʳ Skaife
 Mʳ. Richd Roy Mʳ Tho: Foſter
 Capᵗ. Richd Johnſon Capᵗ. Robᵗ Dudley
 Capᵗ. Heñ Hickman Mʳ. John Collier
 Mʳ Edwᵈ: Ware

It is ordered that Capᵗ Dudley do pay to Henry Gaines [   ] money toward railing yᵉ Church yards, to Capᵗ Johnſon [   ] Tarring yᵉ uper Church & Mʳ. Shipton three pounds f[   ] the Comunion Table in yᵉ lower Church all to be paid out of [   ] in his hands.

It is agreed by this vestry that yᵉ Glebe houſe be put in [   ] following, to be wether boarded wᵗʰ feather edged quarte[   ] poplar nine inches broad & one inch thick put on at s[   ] the window frames to be new Silled & bevelled off & that [   ] well covered wᵗʰ good Shingles & Coll Corbin Capᵗ Johnſ[   ] are requeſted & Impowered to agree wᵗʰ Some work [   ] Same & to build a hen houſe of twenty foot long & [   ] boarded with good Sypruſs boards, & other repairs ab[   ] reffered for futher conſideration.

     Teſt John Skaif[   ]
   Truly regiſtered ℔ John Pig[   ]

At a Veſtry held for Stratton Major Pariſh at the lower Ch[   ] of June 1729.

     The Rev^d: Mr Skaife
P^rſent Maj^r: Richd Johnson M^r R[   ]
   Coll Gawin Corbin M^r T[   ]
   Mr Valent. Ware Capt. J[   ]
   Capt. Heñ Hickman M^r. R[   ]
   M^r. Edward Ware Maj [   ]
     Mr John Coll[   ]

[   ] Anderson & [   ]

[2]
[   ]¹. Orrill are appointed to Number all ye Tob^o. plants in their [   ] order'd to perform the Same according to law.
[   ]ll & Tho: Jones are appointed to number all the Tob^o. plants in their [   ] nct & order'd to perform the Same according to law.
[   ]nes & Wm Alcock are appointed to number all ye Tob^o plants [   ]er p^rſinct & order'd to perform the Same according to law.
[   ] & Danl. Hayſe are appointed to number all ye Tob^o. plants in their [   ]nct & order'd to perform the Same according to law.
[   ] Ware & Humphry Garrett are appointed to number all y^e Tob^o [   ] heir former p^rſinct & order'd to perform the Same according to law.
        Ex^t: ℔ John Skaife
               Rector
 Truly regiſtred
    ℔ John Pigg Cl Veſt.

[   ] Veſtry held for ſtratton Major pariſh at the uper Church on Mun=[   ]he 13ᵗʰ of October 1729.

The Revᵈ. Mʳ Skaife

[ ]ʳ Richd Roy
Mʳ. Valent. Ware
Majʳ Richd Johnſon
Capᵗ. Heñ Hickman
Mʳ. Roger Gregory

Mʳ. Tho: Foster
Capᵗ. Robᵗ. Dudley
Mʳ. John Collier

The Pariſh   is   Dʳ

[   ]kaife   16000
[   ]g Clk of the Veſtry   800
[   ]kford reader of the lower Church   1200
[   ] office of Sexton of yᵉ lower Church   600
[   ] twice Waſhing the Surpliſs   100
[   ]ell reader of the uper Church   1200
[   ]for Office of Sexton of yᵉ uper Church   600
[   ] for Worke done at yᵉ Glebe   5000
[   ] Church Wardin   [   ]
[   ]ox one yea[   ]
[   ] one ye[   ]

[3]

To Coll Corbin for four times providing for the Sacramᵗ   240
To Henry Gaines by Accoᵗ.   510
To Majʳ. Johnson for making two Dorment windows for the Glebe houſe   400
To Arthur Pryor Conſtable for one levy overcharged laſt year   35½
To Mʳ. Blackgrove for charges aboᵗ. a Sick woman a Stranger   200
To Danˡ. Guthrie for charges of keeping Richd Skelton in his Sickneſs   200
To Mʳ: Charles Collier for keeping Mark Barkley 4 [ ]
To Cask & Sall of 29557ˡᵇ of Tobᵒ at 18 ℔ Cent   53 [ ]

The levy being Settled is found to amount (for this present year) to y⁰ Sum [   ] 34878ᶫᵇ Tob⁰. which being levied on 862 Tithables is 40½ᶫᵇ Tob⁰. ℔ pole & [   ] remaines a fraction of 33ᶫᵇ Tob⁰. & the laſt years fraction 28, the Col[   ] is to pay to the pariſh at the next levy 61ᶫᵇ Tob⁰.

Memorandᵐ. Charles Forget & Francis Bayly are Set levy free & [   ] upon them

Mʳ Valent. Ware & Mʳ. Thomas Foster are appointed C[   ] for the enſuing year.

Ordered that the Church Wardens bind Elinor Lankford Orp[   ] Lankford to William Morris her Grandfather according to [   ]

Ordered that yᵉ Church Wardens bind Mary Bartlet to Some f[   ] according to law.

Ordered that the Church Wardens take care & provide for Rich[   ] a poor man in his Sickneſs.

Charles Forget & Francis Bayly are exempted paying pariſh levy [   ] the future by reaſon of their great age & impotency.

Capᵗ. Robert Dudley is appointed Collector for the preſent levy.

Majʳ. Robison is requeſted & Impowered to appear & defend yᵉ Suite in Chancery brought by Henry Cary againſt this Veſtry in the Genˡˡ. Court.

The Revᵈ. Mʳ. Skaife Majʳ. Johnson Capᵗ. Dudley & Mʳ. Colli[   ] appointed to Settle the levy on Munday next.

[4]
Majʳ. Johnson & Majʳ Robison are requeſted to treat with Mʳ. Henry Cary about the Suit at law brought by him

againſt this Veſtry & pay him according to the Settlem'
at Coll Corbins if he will take that

Order'd that Majʳ Johnſon Capᵗ. Dudley & Mʳ. Collier
View the plaſtering and Glaſing of the Glebe Houſe &
agree with Some workman to repair them

Examᵈ: ℔ John Skaife Rector

Truly regiſtred ℔ John Pigg Cl Veſt.

[   ]try held for Stratton Major pariſh at yᵉ
lower Church on wednesday [   ] October 1730

The Revᵈ. Mʳ Skaife
Mʳ Valent. Ware   Mʳ Thom Foster
Majʳ Richd Johnson   Mʳ Richd Anderson
Coll Gawin Corbin   Majʳ John Robison
Capᵗ. Henry Hickman   Mʳ John Collierᵢ
Mʳ Roger Gregory

[   ] agreed & ordered that a Barn be built at
yᵉ Glebe of Thirty Two foot long [   ]enty foot
wide Ten foot pitch underpined Three bricks high with
brick and [   ]ick & half broad to be Shingled
wᵗʰ good Cyprus Shingles, fourteen foot [   ] yᵉ
length & the whole breadth to be floored wᵗʰ good white
oake plank of Inch [   ] half thick, the Studs
Rafters Winbeams and braces to be Sawed & to be weather
boarded wᵗʰ good Oake boads, one folding door & one
Single one oppoſite, And a Dary of Twelve foot Square
with eighteen Inches Jett & to be underpined as the Barn
& floored with brick Shingled as the Barn & latticed as
uſual, the Studs Rafters braces & winbeams to be Sawed
weather boarded wᵗʰ [   ]od Oake boards, the maner houſe
& hen houſe to be Tarred on the Covers [   ]d three
planks high of the weather boards of the great houſe &
the two front [   ]ndows to be glaſed wᵗʰ Square glaſs,

And Coll Corbin Majʳ Robison Mʳ [ ]oſter & Mʳ Collier or any two of them are impowered to agree wᵗʰ Some [ ]dertaker to do all the aforesᵈ. worke & to meet at yᵉ Glebe the second Tueſ[ ]y in September for that purpoſe:

[5]
Mʳ. Benjᵃ. Needler is appointed a Veſtryman in the room of Mʳ Roy deced.

Teſt John Skaife Rector

Truly Regiſtred ℔ John Pigg Cl Veſt.

At a Veſtry held for Stratton Major pariſh at the uper Church on the 10ᵗʰ of October 1730

	The Revᵈ. Mʳ John Skaife	
Pʳſent	Mʳ Valent. Ware	Mʳ. Tho: Foster
	Coll Gawin Corbin	Mʳ. Richd Anderſon
	Capᵗ. Henry Hickman	
	Mʳ Edward Ware	

The Parish is Dʳ

To Mʳ Skaife	16000
To John Pigg Clerke of yᵉ Veſtry	700
To Tho: Lankford reader of yᵉ lower Church	1200
To Gabˡ. Mitchell reader of the uper Church	1200
To Anne Clear Sexton of the lower Church	600
To Grace Soward Sexton of the uper Church	600
To Majʳ. Johnson in part toward the Glebe worke	20‖00‖0
To Mʳ. Valent. Ware Church Warden by accoᵗ	471
To Mʳ: Foster by accoᵗ	240
	ll s d.
To Mʳ John Collier by accoᵗ	1‖ 2‖ 0
To James Muire for worke done at the Glebe	7‖13‖ 4
To Mʳ. Shipton for the Pedeſtile for the Font	2‖00‖ 0

To Majʳ. Johnson for lead glaſs & soder for
y° Glebe 1‖19‖10
To Charles Collier for keeping Suſana Fox one year 600
To Anne Clear for four times waſhing the Surplis 200
To John Grameil for keeping Richd Skelton 4 weeks 240
To Tob° levied to defray the above money debts 7000
To Caſk & Sall of 29051ˡᵇ Tob° at 18 ℔ Cᵗ. 5229

34280

The levy being Settled for this preſent year is found to amount [ ] forty [6] pounds of Tob°. ℔ poll 34280ˡᵇ of Tob°. being levyed upon 855 Tithables & there remaines a fraction of 80ˡᵇ of Tob°. to be allowed to the Collecter at laying the next levy.

It is agreed & ordered that the Church Wardins & Mʳ. Foster or any two of them do Sell the Seven thouſand pounds of Tob°. levied for defraying the money debts for Caſh at the beſt money price they can get.

Whereas Coll Gawin Corbin out of a pious deſigne for the deſent Adminiſtration of Baptiſm is pleaſed to give a Marble Font to the uper Church of this pariſh it is ordered that it there remain for the uſe of the pariſh.

Mʳ. Benjᵃ. Needler perſuant to order of the Veſtry at their laſt Sitting came in & took the Oaths &c & is Added to this Veſtry.

I promiſe that I will conform to the doctrine & discipline of the Church of England as by law Eſtabliſhed
        Benjᵃ. Needler

Mʳ. Edward Ware & Mʳ. Benjᵃ. Needler are appointed Church Wardins for the Enſuing year & Mʳ. Tho: Foſter is appointed Collector.
     Exᵃ. ℔ John Skaife Rector
  Truly Regiſtered ℔ John Pigg Cl Veſt.

At a Veſtry for Stratton Major pariſh at the lower Church on Munday the 10ᵗʰ of May 1731

Pʳſent
        The Revᵈ. Mʳ. Skaife
   Mʳ. Valent. Ware   Capᵗ. Robᵗ. Dudley
   Coll Gawin Corbin   Mʳ. Thomas Foster
   Majʳ. Richd Johnſon Mʳ. Richd Anderſon
   Capᵗ. Henry Hickman Mʳ. John Collier
                            Mʳ. Benjᵃ. Needler

It appearing that there's four pounds Seventeen Shillings due to Majʳ Johnſon on accoᵗ. of Mʳ Cary (Carpenter) & fifty Shillings for a Lawyer's fee in the Suite brought by the said Cary againſt this Veſtry, it is ordered that the Same be paid out of the money raiſed by the Tobᵒ. levied for defraying money debts.

Mʳ. John Livingston offering eleven Shillings ℔ Cent. for the Six thouſand pounds of Tobᵒ. yet unsold of the Seven thouſand pounds of Tobᵒ. levyed for defraying money debts it is ordered that he have the said Tobᵒ. paying alſo three Shillings ℔ hogshd. for each Caſk.

It is agreed that Mʳ. John Livingston be added to this Veſtry Mʳ. Gregory being dead.

[7]
It is order'd that Samˡ. Orrill Jnᵒ: Norman & Tho: Lankford do meet on the fourth Munday in November & go in proceſsion of & Se every perſons land between the Southern & Weſtern branches of Arracaca Swamp plainly markt continuing their proceedings in all Suitable Wether till the whole ℔ſinct be finiſhed & that all yᵉ Inhabitants of yᵉ sᵈ ℔ſinct do attend the sᵈ proceſsioners according to law & the sᵈ proceſsioners are further ordered to make & return to this Veſtry at their next Sitting after yᵉ laſt of March next a true accoᵗ. of what lands proceſsioned what

not yᵉ reaſons in caſe of failure & what pʳſons preſent in their whole proceedings

It is order'd that Gabˡ. Mitchell Tho: Collins & William Bruſhwood do meet on yᵉ firſt munday in December next & go in proceſsion of & Se every perſons land from Burges field to the branch next above Mʳ. Hunt's plainly markt continuing their proceedings in all Suitable wether till the whole preſinct be finiſhed & that all yᵉ Inhabitants of the sᵈ. pʳſinct do attend the sᵈ pʳceſsioners according to law, and the sᵈ pʳceſsioners are further ordered to make & return to this Veſtry at their next Sitting after the laſt of march next a true accoᵗ. of what lands proceſsion what not the reaſons in caſe of failure & what pʳſons pʳſent in their whole proceedings.

It is ordered that Robert Garret John Ware & Tho: Borne do meet on the third Munday in November next & go in proceſsion of & Se every perſons land between Tarſatyans & little Harquip Swamps plainly marked continuing their proceedings in all Suitable weather till yᵉ whole pʳſinct be finiſhed, & that all the Inhabitants of the sᵈ. pʳſinct do attend the said proceſsioners according to law, And the Said proceſsioners are required to make & return to this Veſtry at their next Sitting after the laſt of March next a true accoᵗ. of what lands proceſsioned what not yᵉ reaſons in caſe of failure and what perſons preſent in their whole proceedings.

It's order'd that Mʳ. Valent. Ware Humphry Garret & John Smith do meet on the fourth Thurſday in November next & go in proceſsion of & Se every perticular perſons land between little Harquip & great Harquip Swamps plainly markt continuing their proceedings in all Suitable weather till the whole preſinct be finiſhed, & that all the Inhabitants of the Said pʳſincts do attend the Said proceſsioners according to law, And the sᵈ. proceſsioners are hereby further required to make & return to this Veſtry at their next Sitting after the laſt of March next a true acco^t. of what lands proceſsioned what not the reaſons in caſe of failure & what perſons preſent in their whole proceedings.

It is order'd that Danl. King Thomas Cardwell & Thomas Hallier do meet on the firſt munday in Feb^{ry} next and go in proceſsion of & See all & every perticular perſons land between the branch next above M^r. Hunts & ye Extent of the pariſh upward planly marked continuing their proceedings in all Suitable weather till the whole preſinct be finiſhed. And that all the Inhabitants of the s^d. ℘ſinct do attend the said proceſs^{rs}. according to law, And the s^d. proceſsioners are further order'd to make & return to this Veſtry at the next Sitting after the laſt of March next a true acco^t. of what lands proceſsioned [8] what not the reaſons in caſe of failure & what perſons preſons preſent in their whole proceedings

It is order'd that Capt. Gaines Richd Shackelford & *[   ] Turemon do meet on the Second Munday in December next & go in proceſsion of & See every perticular perſons land between the weſtern branch of Arracaca Swamp & Tarſsatyans Swamp plainly markt continuing their proceedings in all Suitable weather til the whole ℘sinct be finiſhed & that all the Inhabitants of the s^d ℘ſinct do attend the Said proceſs^{rs} according to law and the s^d proceſs^{rs} are hereby further ordered to make & return to this Veſtry at their next Sitting after the laſt of march next a true acco^t. of what lands ℘ceſsioned what not, the reaſons in caſe of failure & what perſons preſent in their whole proceedings.

It is order'd that the Church Wardens do bind William Sprigg als Wilſon to M^r. John Collier according to law.

---

*First name illegible. It looks like Ignce.—C. G. C.

Cap⁰. Henry Hickman & Mʳ. John Livingston are appointed Church Wardens for this pʳſent year & Capᵗ. Hickman is appointed Collector & order'd to give bond & Security according to law.

Order'd that the Chur Wardˢ pay Mʳ Needler forty pounds of Tob⁰ omitted in yᵉ levy

Exᵗ. ℔ John Skaife Rector
Truly regiſtred ℔ John Pigg Cl Veſt.

At a Veſtry held for Stratton Major pariſh at yᵉ lower Church on the 11ᵗʰ of April 1732 being Tueſday in Eaſter Week

Pʳſent
  The Revᵈ. Mʳ. Skaife
  Coll Gawin Corbin Capᵗ. Robᵗ. Dudley
  Capᵗ. Henry Hickman Mʳ. John Collier
  Mʳ. Thomas Foster Mʳ. John Livingston

Order'd that the three Thouſand pounds of Tob⁰. levied to raiſe the Money due to Majʳ Johnſon & the two hundred ninty one yᵉ ball of the Fraction be Sold by Coll Corbin & Capᵗ. Hickman for Currᵗ. money & that they pay Majʳ. Johnſon fifteen pounds Currᵗ. money out of the produce.

Maj Johnſon Majʳ Robiſon & Mʳ Needler added

It's agreed & order'd that Mʳ. John Collier do build a houſe of twelve foot wide & Sixteen foot long upon his own land for the uſe of Alice Daniell during her life the sᵈ Mʳ Collier agreeing thereto & to find all & do all for fifty Shillˢ. & it's order'd that Mʳ. Foster pay him yᵉ forty nine Shillˢ. in his hands

[9]

It is agreed between this Veſtry & Henry Gaines that the sᵈ. Gaines Shall new Shingle yᵉ back gutter of this Church with good Cyprus Shingles & Tarr the Same well

& plaiſter & whitewaſh what is broaken down on the inſide & the said Gaines Obliges himſelf yᵗ the Same Shall hold Tite the Space of Seven Years for which he is to be paid Seven hundred pounds of Tobº. in the next levy

Samuel Guthry now refuſing to have Dorathy Holliday bound to him the Church wardens are hereby Impower'd & order'd to bind her to John Pigg or any other perſon whom they Shall think fitt.

Capᵗ: Phillip Roots is appointed a Veſtryman in the room of Mʳ. Valent. Ware deced.

Teſt John Skaife Rector
Truly regiſtred ℥ John Pigg Cl Veſt.

At a Veſtry held for Stratton Major pariſh at the uper Church on Tuesday the 10ᵗʰ of October 1732

Pʳſent   The Revᵈ. Mʳ. Skaife
     Majʳ. Richᵈ Johnson   Mʳ Richd Anderſon
     Coll Gawin Corbin   Maj John Robison
     Capᵗ. Henry Hickman   Mʳ. John Collier
     Mʳ. Thomas Foster   Mʳ. John Livingston
     Capᵗ. Robᵗ. Dudley

The Parish is Dʳ.

To Mʳ. Skaife	16000
To Tho: Lankford reader of the lower Church	1200
To Anne Clare Sextonˢ. of yᵉ Same	600
To Gabˡ. Mitchell reader of the uper Church	1200
To Grace Soward Sextonˢ. of yᵉ Same	600
To John Pigg Clk of the Vestry	700
To Capᵗ. Henry Hickman Collector on ball of Accoᵗˢ.	595
To Geo: Major for Sumoning Elizᵃ. Dowlin	15
To Mʳ. John Livingston by accoᵗ	640
To Henry Gaines by accoᵗ.	800

To Anne Clare for three times waſhing the Surpliſs	150
To James Muire by accoᵗ.	80
To Charles Collier decd his order for Keeping Suſan Fox	600
To David Edwards for his wifes nursing Suſana Barker's baſtard Child nine months	600

To

[10]

To Cask at 4 ℔ Cᵗ. of 23780	951
To 4 ℔ Cᵗ. of 24731 for Collector	989
To 10 ℔ Cᵗ. of 25720	2572
To Majʳ. Robison for a Copy of the liſts	40
	28332
To the fraction raiſed	143
	28475

Capᵗ. Robᵗ. Gaines is appointed a Veſtry man in the room of Mʳ. Edᵈ: Ware deced.

Capᵗ. Philip Roots & Capᵗ. Robᵗ. Gaines came in & took the oaths appointed & Signed to conform to the Church of England as by law Eſtabliſhed, & were added to this Veſtry.

The levy being setled for this preſent year is found to amount to Thirty three pounds & one half pound of Tob⁰ ℔ poll 28475ᵗᵇ of Tob⁰ being levied upon 850 Tithables & there remaines a fraction of 143 in the Collector's hands.

Capᵗ. Robᵗ. Dudley & Capᵗ. Philip Roots are appointed Church Wardens and Capᵗ. Dudley is appointed Collector.

Teſt John Skaife Rector

Truly Regiſtred ℔ John Pigg Cl Vest.

14   VESTRY BOOK OF STRATTON MAJOR PARISH

At a Vestry held for Stratton Major parish at the lower Church on Wedneſday the 10ᵗʰ of Octobʳ 1733

Pʳſent
The Revᵈ. Mʳ. Skaife
Majʳ Richd Johnson   Majʳ John Robinson
Mʳ Thomas Foster   Mʳ. John Collier
Capᵗ. Robᵗ. Dudley   Capᵗ. Phil. Roots
Mʳ. Richd Anderson   Capᵗ. Robᵗ. Gaines
Vestry Men

The Pariſh is	Dʳ
To Mʳ. Skaife	16000
To John Pigg Clk Vestry	700
To Gabˡ. Mitchell reader of the uper Church	1200
To Grace Soward Sexton of the Same	600
To Tho: Lankford reader of the lower Church	1200

[11]

To Ann Clare Sexton of Same	600
To Capᵗ. Dudley Collectʳ. by Accoᵗ.	407
To Capᵗ. Roots Chur Wardin by Accoᵗ.	240
To Henry Gaines by Accoᵗ.	40
To Majʳ. Robinſon for Copys of the liſts	40
To Ann Clare for thrice Waſhing the Surpliſs	150
To David Edwards for keeping Frances Barker one year	800
To Grace Soward by Accoᵗ	150
To Majʳ: Johnſon for Glaſing & Shutters to yᵉ Windows & hanging two pew doors at the uper Church	100
To Mʳ. John Collier for 5 buſhells of Lime	30
To Caſk of 22257ˡᵇ Tobᵒ at 4 ℔ Cᵗ.	890
To Convenience at 10 ℔ Cᵗ.	2407
To 4 ℔ Cᵗ. of 23147ˡᵇ Tobᵒ ℔ Collectʳ	926
	26480

	Crd^t
By Capt. Dudley for laſt years fraction	143
To the fraction raiſed	273

The Levy being Settled for this p^{r}ſent year is found to amount to thirty pounds of Tob°. ℔ poll — 26610^{lb} of Tob° being levied upon 887 Tithables & there remaines a fraction of 273^{lb} Tob° due to the pariſh

M^r. Richd Anderſon & Capt. Robt. Gaines are appointed Church Ward^s. for the enſuing year & M^r. Anderſon is appointed Collector

Order'd that the Church Wardins demand the five pounds five Shillings which is due from Capt. Hickman's Eſtate upon Acco^t. of fines in his hands laſt year and in caſe the Executor refuſes paym^t. to bring Suit.

Order'd that the Chur. Wardins pay Alice Daniell forty Shillings in Such Neceſsaries as are most needfull.

Order'd that the Chur Ward^s. bind John the baſtard Son of Sarah Morris deced to Thomas Burnet & Eliz^a his wife till he comes to age by law.

Order'd that Frances Barker the Baſtard daughter of Suſanna Barker deced. be bound to David Edwards till She comes to age by law.

Order'd that Robert the Son of Robt. Graves be bound to Thomas Collier till he comes to age by law.

Order'd that the Church Ward^s. provide for Suſana Fox one woollin petticoate & waſtcoate two corſe aprons & a quarter of a pound of brown thred, & twenty Shillings to Owen Dayly in neceſarys.

Order'd that the Church Ward⁵. pay Mʳ. John Collier Ten Shillings out of the fines being for worke done to Alice Daniel's houſe more than was agreed for

Teſt John Skaife Rector

Truly registered ℔ John Pigg Cl Veſt.

[12]
At a Veſtry held for Stratton Majʳ pariſh at the uper Church on Tueſday the 16ᵗʰ of April 1734, being Eaſter week.

The Revᵈ. Mʳ. Skaife

Pʳſent   Capᵗ. Robᵗ. Dudley   Mʳ. John Collier
       Mʳ. Richard Anderſon   Capᵗ. Phil Roots
       Majʳ John Robinſon   Capᵗ. Robᵗ. Gaines

Vestry Men

Mʳ. John Ware & Mʳ. Richard Shackelford are appointed Vestrymen to Supply the present vacancies.

It is Order'd that Mʳ. John Livingston do pay to Mʳ. Richd Anderson two pounds five Shillings the ball of fines in his hands & that Capᵗ. Roots alſo pay to Capᵗ. Gaines one pound Six Shillˢ. & nine pence of like ball in his hands.

Order'd that the Chur Wardin let Richd Webb have four barrels of Corn & Make the accoᵗ of fines debter for the Same.

₋t is agreed that Ann Edwards be paid two hundred pounds of Tobº. at laying the next levy for maintaining Frances Baker from this day to that time.

It is order'd that Capᵗ. Roots & his family do Sit (in Church) in that Pew Majʳ. Robinson Sits in.

Capᵗ. Robᵗ. Gains & his wife Mʳ. Richd Shackelford & his wife Mʳ. Wᵐ Lyne & his & Mʳ. John Ware are appointed to Sit in the pew next above the pulpit & that M^r. John Smith & his wife Sit with his mother.

Test John Skaife Rector
Truly registered ℔ John Pigg Cl Vest.

At a Vestry held for Stratton Major Parish at y^e: Lower Church on Thursday y^e: 10th: of October 1734

P^rſent
    The Reverd: M^r: Skaife   M^r: Richd Anderson
    Collo: Gawin Corbin   M^r: John Collier
    M^r: Thomas Foster   Capt: Phil: Roots
    Capt Robt: Dudley   Capt Robt: Gaynes
Vestry-Men

The Parish is	D^r:
To M^r. Skaife	16000
To Thomas Lankford Reader of the Lower Church	1200
To Ann Clare Sexton of the Same	600
To John Pigg Clk: of y^e: Vestry	700
To Gab^l: Michel's Exect:s for his Service reader of the Upper Church nine Months	900
To Grace Soward Sexton of the Upper Church	600
To Arthur Herring for his wife's Keeping Susan: Fox two Years	1003½
To Anne Clare for 3 times Washing the Surplice	150
To Capt Gaynes by acct	240
To M^r: Richd Anderson by acc^t: on Ball^e:	
To Henry Brown Reader of the Upper Church 3 Months	300
To M^r: Richd Anderson for 3 Levies of M^r: Vernons not paid	
To d^o: for 4 times Providing for ye Sacramt:	240
To Major Robinson for Copies of the Lists	40
[13]	
To Cask of 21933^lb: of Tobo at 4 ℔^r: C^t:	877

To Sall: of 22810ᵇ: of Tobᵒ: at 4 ⅌ʳ: Cᵗ: 912
To Geo: Major ⅌ʳ: Arrest. Capᵗ: Hickmˢ: Executˢ.   54

The Levies being Settled for this ⅌sent Year is found to amount to twenty Nine Pounds of Tobᵒ: ⅌ʳ: Poll to 24012ᵇ: of Tobᵒ: being Levied upon 828 Titheabˢ: and there remains a fraction of one hundred Ninty Six in yᵉ: Collect:ˢ hands to be paid to Job Jackson

Order'd yᵗ: the Church Wardˢ: Bind Frances Barker & James Roberson Barker Bastard Children of Susˢ: Barker to Job Jackson According to Law.

Capᵗ: John Collier & Mʳ: Richd Shackelford are appointed Church Wardens & Capt Collier is Collector for yᵉ Ensuing Year.

Mʳ: Richd Shackelford & Mʳ: John Ware Came in & took yᵉ oaths as Usual & Sign'd yᵉ Test & are added to this Vestry.

Order'd yᵗ: Capᵗ: Dudley Pay Alice Daniel forty Shill: in Corn & Meat.

Order'd yᵗ: the Church Wardˢ: bind John the Son of Mary Evans by Indenture to Wᵐ: Guthrey according to Law—

Order'd yᵗ: Capt Gaynes Let Owin Daly have two bro: Lin: Shirts and a kersey Jacket for yᵉ: ball in yᵉ: Sᵈ: Capt Gaines's hand, being twenty one Shillings & Nine pence.

Test: John Skaife
Rector

Truly registred ⅌ʳ: Henry Hill C:l: Vest.

At a Vestry held for Stratton Major Parish at the Upper Church on Tuesday the 8:ᵗʰ day of Apl: 1735.

Prſent　The Revd: M:ʳ Skaife　　Mʳ: Richᵈ Anderson
　　　　Collo: Gawin Corbin　　Cap:ᵗ Phil Roots
　　　　Mʳ: Thomas Foster　　　Capt Robᵗ: Gaynes
　　　　Capᵗ: Robᵗ: Dudley　　　Mʳ: Jno Livingston
　　　　　　　　　　　　　　　Mʳ: Richd Shackelford
　　　　　　　　　　　　　　　Mʳ. John Ware

Vestry Men

Mʳ William Taliaferro is appointed Vestry Man in Stead of Mʳ: John Collier Deceas'd

Mʳ: Richd Shackelford is appointed Collector in the room of Mʳ: John Collier Deceas'd

Henry Hill is appointed Clerck of the Vestry

Order'd yᵗ: Richd Philip Underwood is to be bound to Thomas Collins provided the Sᵈ Collins give Sufficient Security to keep the Parish Undamnified till the Child Come to age & yᵗ: for yᵉ: Sd Collins Shall be Levied 800ᵗᵇ: of Tobᵒ: for yᵉ: Same

[14]
Order'd yᵗ: the Ball due of Capᵗ. Hickmans Estate Shall be given by the Church Warden to Richd Webb to buy him Corn & Meat

Order'd that yᵉ: Balle in Capᵗ: Dudley's hands Shall be paid by the Church Warden to the Widow Mary Crouch

Order'd yᵗ: the Church Warden take away from Job Jackson Frances Barker & James Roberson Barker both Bastard Children of Susa Barker & to bind out the Sd Children to Such persons as the Church Warden Shall Approve off.

　　　　　　　　　　　Test:　John Skaife
　　　　　　　　　　　　　　　　　Rector
　　　　Truly registred ℔ʳ: H: Hill C:k. Vest.

At a Vestry held for Strattⁿ: Majʳ: ℔rish at the Lower Church on Friday the 10th day of 8bʳ 1735

Presᵗ:
The Revᵈ: Mʳ: Skaife
Mʳ: Thomˢ: Foster
Capt Robᵗ Dudley

Vestry Men

Mʳ Richd Anderson
Majʳ Jno Robinson
Capᵗ: Philip Roots
Mʳ: Jno. Levingston
Capᵗ: Robᵗ: Gaynes
Mʳ: Jno Ware

The Parish is Dʳ

To Mʳ: Skaife	16000
To Thomˢ: Lankford Reader of yᵉ: Lower Church	1200
To Anne Clair Sexton of the Same	600
To Henry Hill Clk of the Vestry	600
To Henry Brown Reader of yᵉ: Upper Church	1200
To Grace Soward Sexton of yᵉ: Same	600
To Mʳ: Richd Shackelford Ch Wardⁿ:	286
To Mʳˢ: Anne Collier	60
To Grace Sowards Last Years accᵗ: for Washing yᵉ: Surplus	150
To Dᵒ: for Washing yᵉ: Surplus this Year	150
To Anne Clair for Washing yᵉ Surplus this Year	150
To Job Jackson for Taking Care of Barkers Bas-⎞ tard Children for 6 mths: & a before Ballᵉ ⎠	404
To Mʳˢ: Jane Pigg	100
To James Muir	60
To Anne Clair for Keeping Susa: Fox	600
To 4 ℔ʳ: Cᵗ upon 22160 for Cask	886½
To 4 ℔ʳ: Ct for Collectg 23046½ Tobᵒ	922
To Major Jno Robinson	52
To Levied for yᵉ: poor of the ℔rish 351 ⎫	
To yᵉ 4 ℔ʳ Cᵗ: upon yᵉ Sd. Tobᵒ: for Cask 14 ⎬	380
To Dᵒ: ℔ʳ Cᵗ: upon 365 lb Tobᵒ. Collt: 15 ⎭	
	24400

The Levies for This ⅌Sent Year being Settled are found to Amount to Thirty and an half pd Tob: pʳ: poll is 24400 lb of Tob°: being Levied upon 800 Titheables.

Ordered yᵗ Mʳ: Shakelford pay to Owen Daily in the Store Twenty Shillings

Ordered that This present Ch-Warden buy for Owen Daily 200 Wᵗ: of Porck.

[15]
Ordered yᵗ: Mʳ: Shakelford pay Susª: Fox Eight Shill. in The Store.

Ordered yᵗ: Mʳ: Shakelford pay to Alice Daniel in yᵉ Store Sixteen Shill.

Ordered yᵗ: the Church Warden pay to Alice Daniel Thirty five Shill. to buy her Self Meat and Corn.

Ordered yᵗ: the Ch-Wardⁿ: Agree with Workmen to repair both Ch's and yᵉ. Steps with 2 Inch oak plank.

Mʳ. Foſter and Mʳ: Jno: Ware are appointed Ch-Wardens

Mʳ: Thomˢ Foster is appointed Collectʳ: of the ⅌rish Dues.

Order'd yᵗ: Mʳ: Jno Smith & his wife be mov'd to the Pew above yᵉ: Pulpit in the Upper Church.

Ordered That Mʳ: Taliaferro & his Wife be Mov'd to the Right-hand pew by the Communion Table.

Test: John Skaife Rect:

Truly regis'td ⅌ʳ: H: Hill C:k: Vest:

At a Vestry held for Strattⁿ: Major ⅌rish at the Upper Church on Thursday the 13th of 9br: 1735

Pres.ᵗ

The Revᵈ: Mʳ: Skaife
Collo: Gawin Corbin   Majʳ Jno Robinson
Mʳ: Thomas Foster   Mʳ: Jno Levingston
Capt. Robᵗ: Dudley   Mʳ. Benja Nedler
Mʳ: Richard Anderſon Capᵗ: Robᵗ. Gaynes.
                      Mʳ: Jno. Ware

It's Ordered yᵗ: Mʳ: Richd Anderson, Mʳ: Jno Livingston & Jno Shackelford do meet on yᵉ: first Monday in Xbr Next and go in proceſsion of & See all & every persons Land between Portopotank Creek and Matasip Swamp plainly mark'd Continuing their proceedings in all Suitable weather till the whole precinct be finished, and yᵗ: all yᵉ: Inhabitants of yᵉ: Said precinct do attend the Sᵈ: proceſsioners according to Law and the ſd proceſsioners are further ordered to make & return to this Vestry at their next Sitting after yᵉ: Last of March Next a true accᵗ: of what Lands proceſsioned What not, yᵉ: reasons in Case of failure and what persons present in theire whole proceedings

It is Ordered yᵗ Mʳ: Wᵐ: Taliaferro, Jno Waller & Jno Berry do Meet on the first Wednesday in Xbr next and go in proceſsion of and See all & every persons Land between Matasip & Pepetico Swamps plainly Mark'd, Continuing their proceedings in all Suitable Weather till the whole precinct be finished and yᵗ all the Inhabitants of the Sd precinct do attend the Said proceſsioners according to Law & the Sd proceſsioners are further ordered to make & return to this Vestry at their Next Sitting after y Last of March Next a true acct of what Lands proceſsioned what not yᵉ: reason in Case of failure and what persons ꝑsent in their whole proceedings.

[16]

It is Ordered yᵗ Mʳ: Thomas Foster, Nichoˢ: Dillard & Henry Collier do Meet on the first friday in Xbʳ: Next, and go in ₱rocesſion of & See all & every persons Land between Pepetico Swamp & yᵉ: Southern Branch of Arracacoe plainly Mark'd Continuing their proceedings in all Suitable weather till yᵉ: whole precinct be finished. & yᵗ: all the Inhabitants of the Sd precinct do attend yᵉ: Sd proceſsioners according to Law & the Sd proceſsioners are further ordered to make & return to this Vestry at their Next Sitting after the Last of March Next a true account of What Lands proceſsioned What not, the reasons in Case of failure and What persons ₱sent in theire Whole proceedings

It is Ordered yᵗ: Jno Walden Senʳ:, Thomˢ: Lankford & Thomˢ: Dillard do meet on the 2d: Monday in Xbr: Next and go in proceſsion of & See all & every persons Land between the Southern & Western Branches of Arracacoe Swamp plainly Mark'd, Continuing theire proceedings in all Suitable Weather till yᵉ: Whole precinct be finished & that all the Inhabitants of the Sd precinct Do attend yᵉ: Sd proceſsioners according to Law and the Sd proceſsioners are further ordered to Make & return to this Vestry at their Next Sitting after the Last of March next, a true accᵗ: of what lands proceſsion'd What not the reasons in Case of failure & wᵗ: p:ſons pſent in their whole proceedings.

It's Ordered that Jno Collins, Thom s Collins & Edward Spencer do Meet on the Second Wednesday in Xbr Next and go in proceſsion of & See all and every persons Land from Burgesſ field to the Branch Next above Mʳ: Hunts plainly Mark'd Continuing their proceedings in all Suitable Weather till the Whole precinct be finish'd & yᵗ: all the Inhabitants of the Sd presinct do attend the Sd proceſsioners according to Law & the Sd proceſsioners are further ordered to Make & return to this Vestry at their Next Sitting after the Last of March Next a true accᵗ: of what lands proceſsion'd What not the reasons in Case of failure & what persons ₱ſent in theire Whole proceedings

It is Order'd that Jno Ware, Thom^s: Soward & Thom^s: Bourn do meet on the 2d: friday in Xbr Next & go in proceſsion of & See all & every persons Land between Tarsatyans & little Hartquip Swamps plainly Mark'd Continuing their proceedings in all Suitable Weather till the whole presinct be finished & y^t: all the Inhabitants of the Sd presinct do attend the Sd proceſsioners according to Law, & y^e: Sd proceſsioners are further order'd to Make & return to this Vestry at their Next Sitting after y^e: Last of March Next a true acc^t: of what Lands proceſsion'd, What not, y^e: reasons in Case of failure & what persons present in their Whole proceedings

It is Order'd y^t: W^m: Mackarty, Thom^s: Burk & Humphrey Garret do meet on the 3d Monday in Xbr: Next & go in proceſsion of & See all & every persons Land between little Hartquip & great Hartquip Swamps plainly Mark'd, Continuing their proceedings in all Suitable Weather till the Whole precinct be finish'd, & y^t: all the Inhabitants of the Sd presinct do attend the Sd proceſsioners according to Law & the Sd proceſsioners are further ordered to Make & return to this Vestry at their Next Sitting after the Last of March Next a true acc^t: of What Lands proceſsion'd What not the reasons in Case of failure and What persons present in their whole proceedings

[17]
It is Ordered y^t: Daniel King & Thomas Cardwell & W^m: Ware do Meet on the 3d: Wednesday in Xbr Next and go in proceſsion of & See all & every persons Land between y^e: Branch Next above M^r: Hunt's & y^e: Extent of y^e: ℘rish upward plainly Mark'd Continuing their proceedings in all Suitable Weather till the Whole presinct be finish'd, & y^t: all the Inhabitants of the Sd presinct do attend the Sd proceſsioners according to Law, & the Sd proceſsioners are further order'd to make & return to this

Vestry at their Next Sitting after the Last of March Next a true acc⁺: of What Lands procefsioned, What not the reasons in Case of failure & What persons ⅌sent in their whole proceedings.

It is Order'd that Capt Gaynes, William Lyne & Jno Thack do Meet on the 3d: friday in Xbr Next and go in procefsion of & See all & every persons Land between the Western Branch of Arracacoe Swamp & Tarsatyans Swamp plainly Mark'd Continuing their proceedings in all Suitable Weather till the whole presinct be finish'd, & yᵗ: all the Inhabitants of the Said presinct do attend the Sd procefsioners according to Law, & the Said procefsioners are further ordered to Make & return to this Vestry at their next Sitting after the Last of March Next a true accᵗ: of What Lands procefsion'd, What not, the reasons in Case of failure & What persons Present in their whole proceedings

Teste John Skaife Rector

Truly registred ⅌ʳ: Henry Hill Clk Vest.

At a Vestry held for Strattⁿ: Major Prish at the Lower Church on tuesday the 27th of April 1736

Present: The Reverᵈ: Mʳ: Skaife
    Collo Gawin Corbin   Major John Robinson
    Mʳ: Thomas Foster   Capᵗ: Robᵗ: Gaynes
    Capt Robᵗ: Dudley   Mʳ: Jno Ware
    Mʳ: Richard Anderson   Mʳ: William Taliaferro
                                  Mʳ: Jno Levingston

Mʳ: Wᵐ: Taliaferro took the Oaths & Subscrib'd to be Conformable to the Church of England as by Law Established & was added to this Vestry

Capᵗ: Robᵗ: Gayns, Wᵐ: Lyne & John Thack procefsioners returnd their report & it was ordered to be registred

Mr Richard Anderson, Mr: Jno Livingston & Jno: Shackelford procefsioners return'd their report and it was ordered to be registred

Daniel King, Thomˢ: Cardwell and Wᵐ: Ware procefsioners return'd their report and it was ordered to be registred

[18]
Mr: William Taliaferro, Jno Waller & Jno Berry Procefsioners, returnd their report and it was ordered to be registred

Mr: Jno Ware, Thomas Sword & Thomˢ: Bourn Procefsioners returnd their report & it was order'd to be registred

It is ordered that Mr: Thomas Foster Lett Richd: Webb have three Barrils of Indian Corn

Mr: Jno Strachey is Appointed Vestry Man in the room of Mr: Benja Nedler

*Teste John Skaife Rectr

*Truly register'd ℞: Henry Hill Clk Vest.

Mr: Thomas Foster, Henry Collier & Nicho Dillard procefsioners return'd their report & it was orderd to be registred

Thomas Lankford, Thomas Dillard & Jno Walden Senr: procefsioners return'd their report & it was order'd to be registred

Teste John Skaife Rectr.

Truly register'd ℞: Henry Hill C:k Vest

---

*These lines were scratched over in the original but are still legible.—C. G. C.

At a Vestry held for Stratton Major Parish at the Upper Church on Monday the Eleventh of 8b^r: 1736.

Collo: Gawin Corbin
Pres^{ts}: M^r: Thos: Foster   Capt: Robt: Gaynes
Capt: Robt: Dudley   M^r: Richd Shackelford
M^r: Richd: Anderson   M^r: Jno: Ware
Maj^r: Jno Robinson   M^r: W^m: Taliaferro
Capt: Philip Rootes   M^r: Jno: Strachey
Vestry-Men

The Parish is D^r.

To M^r. Skaife	16000
To Thom^s: Lankford Reader of the Lower Church	1200
To Henry Brown Reader of the Upper Church	1200
To Henry Hill Ck: of the Vestry	700
To Grace Sword Sexton of the upper Church	600
To d^o: for washing of the Surplus 3 times	150
To Anne Clair Sexton of the Lower Church	600
To d^o: for washing of the Surplus 3 times	150
To d^o: for board: Susa: Fox	600
[19]	
To Thomas Collins	800
To Maj^r: John Robinson	171
To Capt: Robt Gaynes	1600
To Saml: Guthrey	200
To M^r: Thom^s: Foster	240
To M^rs: Mitchel for Keeping Jam^s: Satterwite from the 1st of May Last till now	400
	24611
To Cask upon 24440 at 4 ℔^{r} C:^{t}	977½
To 4 ℔^{r} C:^{t} for Collect^r: 25417½	1016½
	26605

The Levie being Settled for this present Year is found to amount to Twenty Six thousand Six hundred & five pounds of Tobo: it being Levied upon 790 Thiteables at 34 lb ℔ʳ: Poll and there remains a fraction of 255 in the Collectors hands, whereof he pay to Mʳ John Ware 120 lb & Cask & to Edward Ware 50 for mending yᵉ: Benches.

Mʳ: Wᵐ: Taliaferro is appointed Collector for this Year

Mʳ: Jno Strachey took the Oats and Subscribd to be Conformable to the Church of England as by Law Established and was added to this Vestry

It is order'd that the Church-Warden pay Alice Daniel forty Shillings out of the fines

It is order'd that the Ch-Warden pay Owen Daily 30 S for pork Shirts & a pair of Breeches.

It is order'd yᵗ: Collo Corbin pay Mʳ: Nedler 20 S for his Fee agˢᵗ: Hickmans Executʳ:

It is order'd that yᵉ: Widʷ: Mictchel do keep Jamˢ: Satterwite this Ensuing Year for 800 wᵗ: Tobᵒ: to be levied at yᵉ: Laying of the next Levies

Teste G: Corbin

Truly registered ℔ʳ: Henry Hill Ck: Vest:

At a Vestry held for Stratton Major Parish at the Lower Church on Monday the fifteenth of 9bʳ: 1736

Presᵗˢ
Mʳ: Thoˢ: Foster	Capᵗ: Philip Rootes
Capᵗ: Robᵗ: Dudley	Capᵗ: Robᵗ: Gaynes
Mʳ: Richd Anderson	Mʳ: Richd Shackelford
Majʳ: Jno: Robinson	Mʳ: Jno: Ware
Mʳ: Jno Livinston	Mʳ: Wᵐ: Taliaferro
	Mʳ: Jno Strachey

The Gentlemen of this Vestry have Agreed to receive the Rev[d]: Jno Reade as Minister of this Parish

Teste: Thom[s]: Foster
Truly Registred ⅌[r]: Henry Hill Ck: Vest

[20]
At a Vestry held for Stratt[n]: Major Parish at the Upper Church on Monday the 7th: of March 1736/7

The Rev[d]: M[r]: Reade

Pres[ts]
Collo Gaw: Corbin
M[r]: Tho: Foster
Cap[t]: Rob[t]: Dudley
M[r]: Rich[d]: Anderson
Major Jno Robinson
M[r]: Jno Livingston

Major Phil: Rootes
Cap[t]: Rob[t]: Gaynes
M[r]: Richd Shackelford
M[r]: W[m]: Taliaferro
M[r]. Jno Strachey

M[r]: William Lyne is appointed Vestry-man in the room of M[r]: Jno Ware

It is order'd that the Church-Wardens provide a Font for the Lower Church

It is agreed that M[r]: Reade is to buy Cushions for the Communion Table and three Books at the ⅌rish Charge

Teste John Reade
Truly registred ⅌[r]: Henry Hill C:k: Vest.

At a Vestry held for Stratt[n]: Major Parish at the Lower Church on Monday the 10th. of 8b[r]: 1737

The Rev[d]: John Reade

Pres[ts]
Collo. Corbin
M[r]: Foster
Cap[t]: Dudley
M[r]: Anderson
M[r]: Livingston
M[r]: Roots

Cap[t]: Gaynes
M[r]: Shackelford
M[r]: Taliaferro
M[r]. Strachey
M[r]: Lyne

The Parish is D':
To M': Reade for 11 Mths Salary	14666
To Thom*. Lankford Reader of the Lower Church	1200
To Ann Clair Sexton & her washing the Surplice and boarding Sus*: Fox the Year	1350
To Henry Hill Ck. of the Vst.	700
To Henry Brown Reader of the Upper Church	1200
To Grace Sword Sexton o' the Upp': Ch & washing y* Surplice	750
To Dorothy Mitchel for keeping Ja: Satterwite y*: Year	800

To Cap': Gaynes for work done at y*: Glebe 4 £
To Geo Tureman for Coffin & gll: rum. Owin Daly =: 15

[21]

To Cap': Taliaferro's Balle 4 S and 308
To Alice Daniel 2
To Wid*. Webb for Corn 2 = 10 S
 ———
 9 = 9 S

To Edward Didlake	34
To Collo Corbin for finding Elemts for y* Communion	240
To Tob°: Rais'd to pay ℔rish Charges 1512 / 1310	2822
To Collo Robinson's Copy	40
To M': Jno Strachey	300
	24410
To 4 ℔ C:' for Collectg. 24410 Tob°.	976
To 4 ℔' C': ℔' Cask upon D°.	976
	26362
To a fract". rais'd	203
	26565

The Levies being Settled for this ⅌st. Yʳ. are found to amount to twenty Six thousand five hundred and Sixty five pounds of Tobº. it being Levied upon 805 Titheables at 33 lb pʳ. pole and there remains a fraction of 203 lb of Tobº. in the Collectˢ. hands

Mʳ. Wᵐ. Lyne took the Oaths and Subscrib'd to be Conformable to the Ch. of England and was added to this Vestry.

Mʳ. Lyne & Mʳ: Jno Strachey are Appointed Ch-Wardens and Mʳ: Lyne Appointed Collector for this present Year

Order'd yᵗ: the Ch. Wardens do Bind James Satterwite to Dorothy Mitchel provided the Sd Dorothy Mitchel give Bond and Security to keep the ⅌rish Undamnified till the Child's of age and for the Sd. Dorothy Mitchel to be Levied 800 Wᵗ .of Tobº. at the Laying of the Next Levies

Order'd yᵗ the Ch. Wardens pay 50 S in Corn to Widʷ. Webb.

Order'd yᵗ the Ch-Wardens pay to alice Daniel 40 S for Meat & Corn.

Order'd yᵗ. the Ch-Wardens Agree With Workmen for to dig & brick a Well at the glebe and for paling in yᵉ. garden and Yard

       Teste John Reade

    Truely registred ⅌ʳ. H: Hill Ck. Vest.

[22]
    At a Vestry held for stratton

At a Vestry held for Strattⁿ: Major Parish at the Lower Church on Monday the Ninth day of 8bʳ. 1738

Prest: The Rev.ᵈ: Mʳ. Reade
Mʳ. Thomˢ Foster   Majʳ. Rootes
Capᵗ. Robᵗ. Dudley   Capᵗ. Gaynes
Mʳ Anderson   Mʳ. Shackelford
Collo. Robinson   Mʳ. Taliaferro
Mʳ. Livingstone   Mʳ. Strachey
  Mʳ. Lyne

The Parish is Dʳ

To Mʳ. Reade	16000
To Thomˢ. Lankford Reader of the Lower Church	1200
To Anne Clair Sexton of the Same & her washing the Sirplice and boarding Susa Fox	1350
To Henry Brown Reader of the Upper Church	1200
To Henry Hill Ck o' the Vest.	700
To Grace Seward Sexton of the Upper Church & washg: Surplice	750
To Mʳ. Wᵐ. Lyne	178
To Widow Mitchel for Satterwite the Year	800
To Geo: Pigg for a horse-Block	150
To Geo Tureman for Work done	270
To Mʳˢ. Anne Collier	350
To James Muirs accᵗ	250
To Dʳ. Strachey	1040
To Collo Robinson's List	40
To Collo Robinson's Fees	146
To James Muir	600
	25024
To Tobᵒ. to Defray Charges	4000
	29024
To 4 ℔ʳ C.ᵗ pʳ. Cask upon 29024 lb Tobo	1160
To 4 ℔ʳ C:ᵗ pʳ Collectⁿ. of 30185 lb Tobᵒ.	1208
	31392

The Levies being Settled this pſent Year are found to Amount to 31274 lb of Tobº. it being levied upon 823 Titheables at 38 lb per Poll and there remains a fraction due to the Collectʳ. of 118 lb to Make up the 31392 lb to the parish.

Collo: Robinson & Mʳ. Livingston are Appointed Ch-Wardens this pſent Year and Collo Robinson Appointed Collector

Ordered that the Ch-Wardens bind Mary Mansfield to the Widʷ. Gramskill till She attains to age according to Law

Ordered that Joseph Simcoe take Susa Fox for the Year and for her board to have Tobº. Levied as before at the Laying of the Next Levies

Ordered that the Ch-Wardens bind to Dʳ. Strachey Anne Devenport's Bastard Child according to Law

Teste. John Reade

Truly register'd pʳ. Henry Hill Ck Vest.

[23]
At a Vestry held for Strattⁿ: Major Parish at the Upper Church on Wednesday the 25th day of July 1739:

Prestˢ.   The Revᵈ: Mʳ. Reade
   Mʳ. Foster   Capᵗ. Gaynes
   Capᵗ. Dudley   Mʳ. Shackelford
   Collo. Robinson   Mʳ. Taliaferro
   Mʳ. Livingstone   Mʳ. Strachey
   Major Rootes   Mʳ. Lyne

It is ordered yᵗ. Mʳ. Richard Anderson, Mʳ. Jno Livingston & John Shackelford or any two of them do Meet on the first Monday in Xbr. Next and go in proceſsion off & See all and every persons Land between Portopotank Creek and Mataſsip Swamp plainly Marked Continuing their proceeding in all Suitable Weather, till yᵉ. Whole precinct be finished and that all the Inhabitants of yᵉ. Sd. precincts do attend the Said proceſsioners according to Law, and yᵉ. Sd. proceſsioners are further ordered to Make and return to this Vestry at their Next Sitting after the last of March Next a true acct: of What Lands proceſsioned What not, the reasons in Case of failure and What persons present in their whole proceedings

It is Ordered that Samuel Shapard, William Richards and William Berry or any two of them, do Meet on the first Wednesday in Xbʳ. Next and go in proceſsion of and See all and every persons Land between Mataſsip & Pepetico Swamp plainly Mark'd Continuing their proceeding in all Suitable Weather till the Whole precinct be finish'd, and that all the Inhabitants of the Said precincts do attend the Sd. proceſsioners according to Law, and the Said proceſsioners are further ordered to Make and return to this Vestry at their Next Sitting after the last of March Next a true accᵗ. of What lands proceſsioned what not the reasons in case of failure, and what persons present in their whole proceedings

It's Ordered that Mʳ. Thomas Foster, Nicho Dillard & Mʳ. Gregory Smith or any two of them do Meet on the first friday in Xbʳ. Next and go in proceſsion off and See all and every persons land Xtween Pepettico Swamp and the Southern Branch of Arracacoe plainly Marked, Continuing their proceedings in all Suitable Weather till the whole precinct be finished and that all yᵉ. Inhabitants of the Sd. precinct do attend the Said proceſsioners according to Law, and the Said proceſsioners are further ordered to Make & return to this Vestry at their Next Sitting after the last of March Next a true acct. of what lands proceſsioned what not the reasons in caſe of failure and what persons present in their whole proceedings.

[24]

It's Ordered that Charles Roane, Thomas Lankford & Tho⁸. Dillard or any two of them do Meet on the 2d Monday in Xbʳ. Next and go in procefsion off and See all and every persons land Between yᵉ. Southern and Western Branch of Arracacoe Swamp plainly Marked Continuing their proceedings in all Suitable Weather till the Whole precinct be finished and that all the Inhabitants of the Said precinct do attend the Said procefsioners according to Law, and the Said procefsioners are further ordered to Make and return to this Vestry at their Next Sitting after the Last of March Next a true acct. of what Lands procefsioned What Not, the reasons in Case of failure and what persons present in their Whole proceedings

Ordered that Thomas Collins, Edward Trice & Edward Spencer or any two of them do Meet on the 2d Wednesday in Xbʳ. Next and go in procefsion off and See all and every persons Land from Burgefs's Swamp to the Branch Next above Mʳ. Hunts plainly Marked, Continuing their proceedings in all Suitable Weather till the whole precinct be finish'd, and that all the Inhabitants of yᵉ. Sd. precinct do attend the Said procefsioners according to Law, and the Said procefsioners are further ordered to Make and return to this Vestry at their Next Sitting after the last of March Next a true acct. of What lands procefsioned, What not, the reasons in cafe of failure & what persons present in their whole proceedings

It's Ordered yᵗ. Mʳ. Thomas Thorpe, Thomas Seward & Thomas Bourn or any two of 'em do Meet on the 2d. Friday in Xbʳ. Next and go in procefsion off & See all & every persons land Between Tarsatyans and little Hartquip Swamp plainly Mark'd, Continuing their proceedings in all Suitable Weather till the whole precinct be finished and that all the Inhabitants of the Said precinct do attend the Said proceſsioners according to Law. and the Said proceſsioners are further ordered to Make & return to this Vestry at their Next Sitting after the last of March Next a true acct. of what lands proceſsioned what not, the reasons in Caſe of failure & what persons present in their whole proceedings.

It's Ordered yᵗ. William Mcarty Thomas Burch & Richard Garret or any two of them do meet on the 3d. Monday in Xbʳ. Next and go in proceſsion off & See all & every persons land Between little Hartquip & great Hartquip Swamp plainly Marked Continuing their proceedings in all Suitable Weather, till the whole precinct be finished, and that all the Inhabitants of yᵉ. Sd precinct do attend the Sd proceſsioners according to Law and the ſaid proceſsioners are further ordered to Make and return to this Vestry at their Next Sitting after the last of March Next a true acct of what lands proceſsioned what not the reasons in Caſe of failure & what persons present in their whole proceedings

It's Ordered that Robert Ware, Thomas Cardwell & William Ware or any two of them do Meet on the 3d Wedesday in Xbʳ. Next and go in proceſsion off and See all and every persons land Between the Branch Next above Mʳ. Hunt's & the Extent upwards plainly Marked, Continuing their proceedings in all Suitable Weather, untill the whole precinct be finished, and that all the Inhabitants of the Said precinct do attend the Said proceſsioners according to Law and the Sd proceſsioners are further ordered to Make & return to this Vestry at their Next Sitting after the last of March Next a true accᵗ. of what Lands proceſsioned, what not the reasons in Caſe of failure, and what persons present in their whole proceedings

It's Order'd that Capᵗ. Gaynes, Mʳ. Wᵐ. Lyne & John Thack or any two of them do meet on the 3d friday in Xbʳ. Next and go in proceſsion off and See all & every persons land Between the Western Branch of Arracacoe Swamp & Tarsatyans Swamp plainly mark'd Continuing their proceedings in all Suitable weather untill the whole precinct be finish'd, and that all the Inhabitants of the Said precinct do attend the Said proceſsioners according to Law, and the Said proceſsioners are [25] further ordered to Make and return to this Vestry at their Next Sitting after the Last of March Next a true acct. of what Lands proceſsioned, What Not the reasons in Caſe of Failure and What persons present in their Whole proceedings

Teste John Reade

Truely register'd ⅌ʳ. Henry Hill Clk Vst.

At a Vestry held for Stratton Major Parish at the Lower Church on Wednesday the 10th day of 8bʳ. 1739

Presᵗ.
The Revᵈ. Mʳ. Reade
Mʳ. Thomas Foster   Capᵗ. Gaynes
Capᵗ. Robᵗ. Dudley   Mʳ. Shackelford
Mʳ. Anderson   Capᵗ. Taliaferro
Collº. Robinson   Mʳ. John Strachey
Mʳ. Wᵐ. Lyne

The   Parish   is   Dʳ.

To Mʳ. Reade	16000
To Thomˢ. Lankford Reader of the Lower Church	1200
To Henry Brown Reader of the Upper Church	1200
To Anne Clair Sexton of the Lower Church	750
To Grace Seward Sexton of the Upper Church	750
To Henry Hill Ck. of the Vestry	700
To Collo John Robinson Ch-Warden o' the Upper Church	240
To Mʳ. John Livingston Ch-Warden o' the Lower Church	620
To Joseph Simcoe for Susᵃ Fox	400

To Capt. Robert Gaynes	120
To M^r. Thom^s. Shipton	40
To Mr Tunstall	40
To Levied to be Sold for Money	7000
	29060
To 4 ₽^{r}. C:^{t} p^r. Cask on 29060	1162½
	30222½
To 4 ₽^{r} C.^{t} for Collect^r: 30222½	1208½
	31431

The Levies being Settled this ₽Sent Year are found to amount to 31431 lb of Tob^o. it being Levied upon 835 Titheables at 38 lb p^r. Poll and there remains a fraction in the Collectors hands of 299 lb of Tobo.

Capt. Robt. Dudley and Maj^r. Philip Rootes are Appointed Church-Wardens this present Year & Maj^r. Rootes appointed Collector.

Order'd that Collo. Robinson and M^r. Livingston the late Church-Wardens acc^t. with the present Church-Wardens and pay the Balle of the Money in their hands to them

[26] £ S d
Order'd that the Church-Wardens pay Doct^r.
Strachey   2 19 8

Order'd that the Collector pay Ja. Carter 35 £ for repairing y^e. Low^r. Church

Order'd that the Ch-Wardens do provide for Chls: Mcarty.

Order'd that the Ch-Wardens give Eliz^a. Rollins Such cloaths as they find Neceſsary for her

Order'd that the Collector do Sell the 7000 lb of Tob°. at ſome Convenient time at or before July Court next

Orderd that the Ch-Wardens do agree With Workmen to Build a Convenient Gallery in the Upper Church

Teste John Reade

Truly registered ⅌ʳ. Henry Hill Ck Vst

At a Vestry held for Strattⁿ: Major Parish at the Upper Church on Friday yᵉ 10th of October 1740

The Revᵈ. Jno Reade

Presᵗ:
Mʳ. Thomas Foster Capᵗ. Robᵗ. Gaines
Capᵗ. Robᵗ. Dudley Mʳ. Richd Shackelford
Mʳ. Richᵈ: Anderson Capᵗ. Wᵐ. Taliaferro
Collo Jno Robinson Mʳ. Jno Strachey
Majʳ. Rootes Mʳ. Wᵐ. Lyne

Strattⁿ: Majʳ. Parish is Dʳ

To Mʳ. Reade	16000
To Thoˢ. Lankford Reader of the Lower Church	1200
To Anne Clare Sexton & for washing the Surplice	750
To Henry Brown reader of the Upper Church	1200
To Grace Seward Sexton & for washing the Surplice	750
To Henry Hill Ck of the Vst:	700
To Major Philip Rootes	202
To Capᵗ. Dudley	390
To Jno Hooker for Keeping Jane Willis's child	250
To Tob°. Levied to be Sold	5000
	26442
To 4 pʳ C.ᵗ for Cask upon 26442	1057
	27499
To 4 pʳ Cᵗ for Collecting 27499	1100
	28599

The Levies being Settled this ⅌Sent Year are found to amount to 28866 lb of Tobo it being Levied upon 849 Titheables at 34 lb pʳ Poll and there remains a Fraction of 267 lb of Tobo. in the Collectors hands for yᵉ. Parish

[27]
Mʳ. Richd Anderson and Capᵗ. Robᵗ. Gaines are Appointed Church Wardens and Mʳ. Anderson is Appointed Collector for this ⅌Sent Year

Ordered that the Church Wardens do Sell the aforeſaid 5000 Wt of Tobo at or before July Court Next

Ordered yᵗ: the Church-Wardens do pay to Mʳ. Reade 4 £ 18 S 9½d.

Ordered yᵗ. the Church-Warden do pay to Capᵗ. Gaines 23 £ 18 S.

Ordered yᵗ. Jno Camel keep Cha. MCarty and for him to be Levied at the Next Levies 600 W.ᵗ of Tobᵒ.

Mʳ. Rich'd Anderſon Mʳ. Jno Levingston & Jno Shackelford proceſsioners return'd their report & it was order'd to be register'd.

Samˡ. Shapard, William Berry & William Richards Proceſsioners return'd their report & it was order'd to be register'd.

Mʳ. Thomas Foster, Nicho Dillard & Gregory Smith Proceſsioners return'd their report & it was order'd to be register'd.

Charles Roane, Thomas Lankford & Thomas Dillard proceſsioners return'd their report & it was order'd to be register'd.

Thomas Collins, Edward Trice & Edward Spencer Proceſsioners return'd their report and it was order'd to be register'd.

Thomas Thorpe, Thomas Seward & Thomas Bourn proceſsioners returnd their report & it was order'd to be register'd.

Wᵐ. MCarty, Thomas Burch & Richard Garret proceſsioners return'd their report & it was order'd to be register'd.

Robᵗ. Ware, Thomas Cardwell & Wᵐ. Ware proceſsioners return'd their report and it was order'd to be register'd.

Capᵗ. Robert Gaines, Mʳ. Wᵐ. Lyne & Jno Thack proceſsioners return'd their report and it was order'd to be register'd.

Teste John Reade

Truely register'd pʳ Henry Hill Ck Vst.

At a Vestry held for Strattⁿ. Major Parish at the Lower Church on Friday the 10ᵗʰ of April 1741 To Distribute Fines.

Capᵗ. Robᵗ. Dudley

	Mʳ. Richard Anderson	Capᵗ. Wᵐ. Taliaferro
Presᵗ:	Capᵗ. Robᵗ. Gaines	Mʳ. John Strachey
	Mʳ. Richᵈ. Shackelford	Capᵗ. Wᵐ. Lyne

Ordered that Capᵗ. Dudley pay to Dʳ. Jno Strachey five pound & Eight pence for taking care of John Lankford Deceas'd

[28]
Ordered that Capᵗ. Dudley pay to Thomas Bowden 20 S for the Schooling of his Children

Ordered that Mʳ. Livingston pay Jno. Walden Senʳ. 2£ 1 S Towards the Clothing of his Children

Ordered that Capᵗ. Gaynes pay Thomas Garrett 1 £ 6 S as pʳ Accᵗ.

Ordered that Cap⁴. Gaynes pay to Mary Walden 1 £ 3 S 8d Towards the Support of her Family.

Ordered that Cap⁴. Dudley pay to Cap⁴. Gaynes 4 S 4d

Ordered that Major Rootes pay Cap⁴. Gaynes 9 S

Ordered that the Church-Wardens do bind Wᵐ Kettle Bagwell to Samuel Cristy to learn the Blacksmiths Trade and the Said Samˡ. Cristy to give him Educãon according to Law Untill he attains to Age.

Ordered that Mʳ. Cha. Collier be Appointed Vestry-Man in the room of Mʳ. Thomas Foster Deceas'd.

Teste Robert Dudley

Truly registered ℔ʳ: Henry Hill Ck Vst.

At a Vestry held for Strattⁿ. Major Parish at the Upper Church on Saturday the 10ᵗʰ. of 8bʳ. 1741.

	Collo. Gawin Corbin	
	Cap⁴. Dudley	Cap⁴. Taliaferro
Presᵗ.	Mʳ. Anderson	Mʳ. Strachey
	Cap⁴. Gaines	Cap⁴. Lyne
	Mʳ. Shackelford	Mʳ. Collier

The Parish is Dʳ.

To Mʳ Reade	16000
To Thoˢ. Lankford Reader of the Lower Church	1200
To Henry Brown Reader of the Upper Church	1200
To Anne Clare Sexton & for Washing yᵉ. Surplice	750
To Grace Seward Sexton & for Washing yᵉ. Surplice	750
To Henry Hill Ck. of the Vst.	700
To Jno Camel for Keeping Cha. Mcarty	600
To Mʳ. Richᵈ. Tunstal Ck Cᵗ.	146
To Cap⁴. Gaines	490

To Mʳ. Anderson	240
To Mʳ. Garret	300

                                            22376
To 4 ℔ᵣ Cᵗ. for Casq upon 22376   895

                                            23271
To 4 ℔ᵣ. Cᵗ. for Collectᵣ. 23271   931

                                            24202

[29]

    The Levies being Settled this ℔Sent Year are found to Amt. to 24424½ lb Tob°. it being Levied upon 857 Titheables at 28½ lb. ℔ʳ. Poll and the remains a fraction in the Collectors hand of 222½ lb Tob°. due to the Parish

    Mʳ. Cha. Collier took the Oaths and Subscrib'd to be conformable to the Church of England as by Law Establish'd & was Added to yᵉ. Vestry

    Order'd yᵗ. the Church-Wardens pay Mʳ. Shipton two Pound.

    Order'd yᵗ. Capᵗ. Gaines pay Major Rootes one £. Nine S. & 4 d.

    Order'd yᵗ. Capᵗ. Gaines pay Dʳ. Strachey 10 S 4 d.

    Order'd yᵗ. Capᵗ Gaines pay Jno Camel 10 S

    Hannah Hodkins by Agreemt of this Vestry is Exempted of paying Parish Levies for the future by reason of her Impotency

    Order'd yᵗ. the Collector pay Harry Gaines 8 S.

    Order'd yᵗ. the Ch-Wardens take in poſseſsion the Estate of Elizᵃ. Rollins and to pay to Majʳ. Rootes 1 £ 6 S 1¾.

Orderd that the Ch-Wardens pay Capt. Dudley for Mending y^e. Glebe Windows with Lead & glaſs out of y^e. hands of Major Rootes

Order'd y^t. the Present Ch-Wardens Settle With Capt. Gaines for what balle is in his hands

Order'd y^t. the Ch-Wardens board out Eliz^a. Rollins for y^e. Ensuing Year at Jno Camels for 600 w^t. Tob^o. & Casq to be Levied at y^e. Laying o' the Next Levies

Order'd y^t. Major Rootes pay Capt. Dudley 6 £ 5 S o' y^e. Money in's hands

Orderd y^t. the Ch-Wardens bind Rich^d. Ray to Rich^d. Bray According to Law

Order'd y^t. Robt. Garret Keep Eliz^a. Brown daughter of Robert Brown for 700 w^t. Tob^o. & Casq this Ensuing Year

Order'd y^t. the Ch-Wardens bind Anne Devenport Bastard Child of Anne Devenport to D^r. Jno Strachey According to Law.

Ordered y^t. the present Ch-Wardens do Acc^t. with the late Ch-Wardens for y^e. fraction of 267 lb Tob^o.

Collo Corbin & M^r. Cha. Collier rec Appointed Ch-Wardens & Capt. Wm Lyne Appointed Collector for this Present Year.

      Teste Gawin Corbin

    Truly regist'd ℔^{r}. Henry Hill Ck. Vst.

[30]
At a Vestry held for Stratton Major Parish at the Lower Church on Tuesday the 20th. of Apl. 1742. for Distributing y^e. Fines

KING AND QUEEN COUNTY, VIRGINIA, 1729-1783 45

⹋S⁸:
    The Rev⁴. Jno Reade
  Cap'. Rob'. Dudley   Cap'. Wᵐ. Taliaferro
  Mʳ. Richᵈ. Anderson   Mʳ. Jnº. Strachey
  Mʳ. Jno Livingstone   Cap'. Wᵐ. Lyne
  Cap'. Rob'. Gaines   Mʳ. Cha. Collier

Order'd that Majʳ. Rootęs pay 3 £ to Mʳ. Cha. Collier of the money in his hands

Order'd that Mʳ. Anderson pay to Mʳ. Collier 1 £ 10 S for the last Years fraction of 267 Wᵗ. o' Tobº.

Order'd that Mʳ. Anderson pay to Mʳ. Collier 2 £ 5 S.

Order'd that Capᵗ. Gaines pay to Mʳ. Collier 9 S.

Order'd that Mʳ. Cha. Collier Distribute 7 £ 4 S. in Corn to theſe following persons in yᵉ following proportions Viz To Jno Green 1 £ 6 S to Jno Walden 1 £ 6 S to Patrick Mallion 1 £ 4 S to Jane Mackendree 10 S To Mos. Shumack 1 £ 4 S To Widʷ. Birch 1 £ 4 S to Jno Hooker 10 S

        Teste John Reade
   Truely Register'd pʳ. Henry Hill Ck. Vst.

At a Vestry held for Stratton Major Parish at yᵉ. Upper Church on Monday the 11ᵗʰ. of 8bʳ. 1742.

⹋Ses
  Collº. Corbin   Capᵗ. Gaines
  Capᵗ. Dudley   Capᵗ. Taliaferro
  Mʳ. Anderson   Mʳ. Jno Strachey
  Collº. Robinson   Capᵗ. Lyne
  Mʳ. Jno Livingston   Mʳ. Cha. Collier
  Mjʳ. Rootes   Mʳ. Tho. Thorpe

  The Parish is Dʳ

To the Rev'd Mʳ. Reade   16000
To Tho Lankford reader of the Lower Church   1200

To Henry Brown reader of the Upper Church	1200
To Anne Clair Sexton & for washing the Surplice	750
To Grace Seward Sexton & for washing the Surplice	750
To Henry Hill Ck V.ſt	700
To Robᵗ. Garret for Keeping Elizᵃ. Brown	700
To Jno Camel for Keeping Elizᵃ. Rollens & Burying her	416
To Capᵗ. Tunstal for 2 Copies of List of Titheables	40
To Collᵒ. Corbin pʳ. Order of Jno Bray	600
To Henry Brown for reading over Elizᵃ. Rollens	40
To Mʳ. Cha Collier for providing a Copy of the Law ℔r Hen. Hill	40
To Job Jackson for Keeping Mary Jones's Bastard Child John	600
To Mʳ. Cha Collier for 3 Times providing for the Communion	180
To Collo Corbin for 3 Times providing for the Communion	180
To Mʳ. Jno Livingston	50
To Capᵗ. Lyne pʳ. 3 Delinqᵗˢ. at 28½	85½
[31]	
To Elizᵃ. MCarty	400
To Tobᵒ. Levied for the Uſe of Dennis MCandree's wife	500
To Dᵒ. Levied for Mʳ. Cha Collier to pay off charges	880
To Dᵒ. Levied for repairing the Glebe	7018
	32329½
To 4 ℔ʳ Cᵗ. for Casq upon 32329½ lb o' Tobᵒ	1293½
	33623
To Collect. of 33623 Wᵗ. of Tobᵒ. at p ℔ʳ Cᵗ.	2017
	35640

The Levies being Settled this ⅌sent year are found to Am*. to Thirty five Thousand Six hundred & forty Wᵗ. of Tob°. at 40 lb pʳ. Poll it being Levied upon 891 Titheables

Mʳ. Thomˢ. Thorpe took the Oaths and subscrib'd to be Conformable to the Church of England as by Law Establish'd & was added to this Vestry

Order'd yᵗ. Robᵗ. Garret keep Elizˢ. Brown this ensuing Year for 700 wᵗ. Tob°. and Casq to be Levied at y°. Laying of the Next Levies

Order'd yᵗ. Job Jackson Keep Mary Jones's Child John this Ensuing Year for 800 Wᵗ. Tob°. & Casq & to clothe it & the Tob°. to be Levied the Laying of the Next Levies

Order'd That Thomas Collins Keep Bridget Costula's Child Lucy as from the 22'd of Agᵗ Last till 8br y° 10ᵗʰ. Next & Clothe it to receive at y°. rate of 800 Wᵗ. of Tob°. & Casq pʳ. annum to be Levied at y°. Laying of the Next Levies

Order'd yᵗ. Moses Shumack be exempted from paying any more ⅌rish Levies

Order'd yᵗ. Henry Brown keep Cha MCarty this Ensuing Year for 800 Wᵗ Tobo & Casq to be Levied at the Laying of the Next Levies

Capᵗ. Taliaferro & Mʳ. Thomas Thorpe are Appointed Church-Wardens and Capᵗ. Taliaferro Appointed Collector for this ⅌sent Year

Order'd yᵗ. Capᵗ. Lyne Late Collector pay to the ⅌sent Church-Wardens the Last years fraction of 222½ lb of Tob°

Order'd that the Church-Wardens Sell the Said 7018 Wᵗ. of Tob° and out of the Said Money pay for what repairs are done to the Glebe

Order'd that Capt. Gaines be paid by M^r. Thorpe 17 S 3 d.

Order'd that M^r. Thorpe pay 4 S 4 d to Coll^o. Corbin

Teste Gawin Corbin
Truely Registred ℞^{r} Henry Hill Ck V.ſ.t.

[32]

At a Vestry held for Stratt^n. Major Parish at the Lower Church on Wednesday the Third Day of August 1743

Preſent Col^o. Gawin Corbin   M^r. Thos. Thorpe
Maj^r. Philip Rootes   M^r. Jno. Strachey
Capt. Robt. Dudley   M^r. Jno: Livingston
Capt. Robt. Gaines   M^r. Chas: Collier
Capt. Willm. Lyne   Capt. W^m. Taliaferro
M^r. Rich^d. Anderson

Vestry Men

Ordered that Francis Gaines be Clark of this Vestry

Pursuant to an Order of King & Queen County Court, dated the 12th Day of July 1743. requiring the Several Vestries in each respective Parish in this County to divide their Parishes into precincts for proceſsioning every Person's Land therein as by the Law in that Case is directed—

Ordered that the inhabitants of the Several Precincts hereafter Mentioned do go in Proceſsion of the Lands as followeth Viz^t.

Ordered that George Pigg Willm. Livingston & John Shackelford or any two of them do meet on the first Monday in Decem^r. next & go in Proceſsion of & see all & every Persons Land between Portopotank Creek & Mattaſip Swamp, plainly Marked; continuing their proceedings in all Suitable weather, till the whole precinct be finished & all the inhabitants thereof are required to Attend y^e. Said Proceſsioners according to Law & the said Proceſsioners are farther Order^d: to make & return to this Vestry at their next sitting after the laſt of March next a true Accoᵗ of every Persons Land they have Proceſsioned, & of the Persons present at the same, and of what Lands they have not proceſsioned & yᵉ ℘ticular Reason of such failure—

Ordered that Samuel Shepherd Willᵐ: Richards & Willᵐ: Berry or any two of them do meet on the first Wedneſday in Xber next & go in Proceſsion of & see all & every Persons Land between Mattaſip swamp & pepetico Swamp, plainly Marked continuing their proceedings in all Suitable weather, till the whole Precinct be finished, & all the inhabitants thereof are required to Attend yᵉ. said Proceſsioners According to Law, & the said Proceſsioners are farther Ordᵈ. to make and return to this Vestry at their next sitting after the last of March next a true Accoᵗ of Every ℘sons Land they have Proceſsioned, & of the Persons ℘sent at the same, & of what Lands they have not Proceſsioned & the ℘ticular Reason of such failure—

[33]
Ordered that Gregory Smith John Foster & Nicho: Dillard or any two of them do meet on the first Fryday in Xber next & go in proceſsion of & see all & every Persons Land between pepetico Swamp and the Southern Branch of Arracacoe plainly Marked continuing their proceedings in all Suitable weather, till the whole precinct be finished & all the inhabitants thereof are required to attend the Said Proceſsioners according to Law, & the Said Proceſsioners are farther Ordᵈ: to make & return to this Vestry at their next Sitting after yᵉ. laſt of March next a true Accoᵗ. of every Persons Land they have Proceſsioned, & of the Persons ℘sent at the Same, & of what Lands they have not Proceſsioned, & the ℘ticular Reason of such failure—

Orderd that Thomas Dillard Thomas Lankford & Chaˢ: Roan or any two of them do meet on the 2ᵈ. Monday in

Xber next & go in Proceſsion off & see all & every Persons Land Between the Southern & Western Branch of Arracacoe Swamp, Plainly Marked, continuing their proceedings in all Suitable weather, till the whole precinct be finished & all the inhabitants thereof are required to attend the Said Proceſsioners according to Law, & the Said Proceſsioners are farther Order'd to make & return to this Vestry at their next sitting after the last of March next a true Acco^t. of every Persons Land they have Proceſsioned, & of the Persons ꝑsent at the same, & of what Lands they have not Proceſsioned, & the ꝑticular Reason of such failure—

Ordered that Thos. Collins Ed: Trice & James Trice or any two of them do meet on the 2^d. Wedneſsday in Xber next & go in Proceſsion off & see all & every Persons Land between Burgeses swamp & the Monack Swamp to Morgan Myry's Corner, thence a Strait Course to a Gum Stand^s. between W^m. Brushwoods & Jno. Overstreets decd, thence a strait course to Taſatian swamp between Doct^r. Joyeux, & Mary Hollinger, Plainly Marked, continuing their proceedings in all Suitable weather, till the whole precinct be finished, & all the inhabitants thereof are required to attend the said proceſsioners according to Law, & the said Proceſsioners are farther Ord^d. to make & return to this Vestry at their next Sitting after the last of March next a true Acco^t. of every Persons Land. they have Proceſsioned, & the Persons ꝑsent at the same, & of what Lands they have not Proceſsioned, & the ꝑticular Reason of such failure

Ord^d. that Willm. Hunt, Robt. Didlake & Ed: Spencer or any two of them do meet on the 3^d. Wedneſday in Xber next, & go in Proceſsion off & see all & every Persons Land between the monack Swamp & the Branch next above M^r. Hunts, Plainly Marked; continuing their Proceedings in all Suitable Weather, till ye whole precinct be finished, & all the inhabitants thereof are required to Attend the said Proceſsioners according to Law, & the Said Proceſsioners are farther Ord⁴. to make & return to this Vestry at their next Sitting after the laſt of March next a true Accoᵗ. of Every Persons Land they have Proceſsioned [34] and of the ℞sons Present at the same & of what Lands they have not Proceſsion'd and the ℞ticular Reason of such Failure—

Ord⁴. that Robert Garrett Tho˚. Bourn & Tho˚. Soward or any two of them do meet on the 2ᵈ. Fryday in Xber next & go in Proceſsion off & see all & every Persons Land Between Tarſatian Swamp & little Hartquake swamp, plainly Marked; continuing their proceedings in all Suitable Weather till the whole precinct be finish'd and all the inhabitants thereof are required to attend the said Proceſsioners according to Law. and the Said Proceſsʳˢ. are farther Ord⁴. to make & return to this Vestry at their next Sitting after the last of March next a true Accoᵗ. of every Perſons Land they have Proceſsion'd, & of the Persons ℞sent at yᵉ. same, & of what Lands they not Proceſsion'd, & the ℞ticular Reason of such failure—

Ord⁴. that Tho˚. Burk, Edward Dugliſs & Tho˚. Garrett juʳ. or any two of them do meet on the 3ᵈ. Monday in Xber next & go in Proceſsion off and see all and every Persons Land Between little Hartquake & great Hartquake swamps plainly Marked; Continuing their proceedings in all Suitable Weather till the whole precinct be finished, and all the Inhabitants thereof are required to attend the sᵈ. Proceſsʳˢ. according to Law, & the sᵈ. Proceſsʳˢ. are farther Ord⁴. to make & return to this Vestry at their Next Sitting after the laſt of March Next a true Accoᵗ. of every Persons Land they have Proceſion'd & of the ℞ersons ℞sent at the same, & of what Land they have not proceſsion'd. & the ℞ticular Reason of such failure—

Order'd that Robᵗ Ware Tho˚. Cardwell & Will. Ware or any two of them do meet on the 3ᵈ. Wednesday in Xbʳ.

Next, & go in Procefsion off & see all & every Persons Land Between the Branch Next above M͟r. Hunts, & the Extent Upwards plainly Mark'd, Continuing their Proceedings in all Suitable Weather till the whole precinct be finish'd & all the Inhabitants thereof are required to Attend the said Procefsioners according to Law & the said Procefsioners are farther Ord͟d. to make & return to this Vestry at their Sitting after the laſt of March Next a true Acco͟t. of every Persons Land they have Procefsion'd, & of the Persons Present at yͤ. same, & of what Lands they have not Procefsion'd & the Perticular Reason of such failure—

Order'd that Capt Gaines Capt Lyne & Richard Wyatt or any two of them do meet on the 3͟d. Fryday in Xber, & go in Procefsion off & see all & every Persons Land between the Western Branch of Arracacoe Swamp & Tarfatyan Swamp plainly Mark'd, Continuing their proceedings in all Suitable Weather till the whole precinct be finish'd; & the Inhabitants thereof are requir'd to attend the Said Procefsioners according to Law & the Said Procefsioners are farther Ord͟d. to make & return to this Vestry at their Next Sitting after the laſt of March Next a true Acco͟t. of every Persons Land they have Procefsion'd, of the Persons Present at the same, & of what Land they have not Procefsion'd, & the ꝑticular Reason of such failure—

Teſt Gawin Corbin
Truely registred ꝑ Fr. Gaines

[35]

At a Vestry held for Straton Major Parish at the Upper Church on Monday the 10ᵗʰ day o 8ber 1743

The Rever͟d: M͟r. Reade

Preſent	Col͟o. Corbin	Capt. Gaines
	Capt. Dudley	Capt. Taliaferro
	M͟r. Anderson	M͟r. Strachey
	Col͟o. Robinson	Capt. Lyne
	M͟r. Livingston	M͟r. Collier
	Major Rootes	M͟r. Thorpe

The Parish	D⁀.
To the Rever⁀. M⁀. Reade	16000
To Thomas Lankford reader of the Lower Church	1200
To Henry Brown reader of the Uper Church	1200
To Anne Clear Sexton of the Lower Church & Wash⁀. y⁀ Surplice	750
To Grace Soward Sexton of the Uper Church & D⁀	750
To Rob⁀. Garretts Estate for Keeping Eliz⁀. Brown	700
To Job Jackson for Keeping Mary Joness Child John	800
To Tho⁀. Collins for Keeping Bridget Costulas's Child Lucey From the 22⁀. Aug⁀⁀. 42 to the 10⁀. 8ber 43. at 800⁀. Tob⁀. ℔ Annum	900
To Henry Brown for Keeping Cha⁀: McCarty	800
To Capt. Tunstall for 2 Cop'ys of Lists Tiths 40⁀ & Cop'y Thaches Bond. 10⁀	50
To Tho⁀. Guthrie for putting up Benches at y⁀ Lower Church	100
To Capt. Taliaferro for Providing for y⁀. Commu. Delinq⁀⁀. &⁀.	309
To Henry Hills Widow for Part of Clks Fee	350
To Francis Gaines Clk	350
To M⁀. Thorpe for Providing 3 Times for y⁀. Commu.	180
To D⁀. for Work done at y⁀. Uper Church	100
To John Guthrie for keeping Jos⁀: Moore 8 Months	800
To Job Jackson for keeping Jane McKendree	182
To Sam. Shepherd for keeping & Burying M⁀. Lanktra	250
	25771
To 4 ℔ C⁀. for Cask on 25771⁀ Tob⁀.	1031
	26802

To 6 ℔ Cᵗ. for Collecting 26802ᵇ. Tobº.   1608

                                                      28410

Levied to be Sold   6160

To 4 ℔ Cᵗ. on Dº. for Cask   246
To 6 ℔ Cᵗ. for Collecting 6406ᵇ Tobº.   384

                                                      35200

The Levies being Settled this ℔sent year are found to Amount to 35200ᵇ. of Tobº. at 40ᵇ. ℔ Poll, it being Levied upon 880 Tithables —

[36]

Capt. Lyne & Docter Strachey are appointed Ch: Wardens and Capt Lyne Appointᵈ Collector for this Ensuing year —

Order'd that Mʳ. Thoˢ. Thorpe Account with the Ch: Wardens for yᵉ Tobº. Levied Last Vestry 7520ᵇ. at 14/℔ Cᵗ Deducting his own Accoᵗ. — And that yᵉ Ch: Wardens receive yᵉ Money & put it out on Interest —

Ordᵈ. that Den: MᶜKendree keep his wife the Ensuing year for 800ᵇ Tobº. to be Levied at Layᵍ Next Levˢ

Ordᵈ. that Grace Soward keep Eliz. Brown at yᵉ rate of 500ᵇ Tobº. ℔ Ann: till yᵉ. Ch: Wardens have opporʳ of Binding her out, to be Levied at Laying yᵉ Next Levies —

Ordᵈ. that yᵉ. Ch: Wardens Pay Docʳ: Strachey 40/. out of yᵉ. Fines ——

Ordᵈ. that Job Jackson keep Mary Joness Child John for 800ᵇ. Tobº. to be Levied at yᵉ. Layᵍ. of yᵉ. Next Levies

Ordᵈ. that Geo. Tureman have 500ᵇ. Tobº. Levied at yᵉ. Layᵍ. of yᵉ. Next Levies for yᵉ. Use of his Son John

Ord⁴. that Henry Brown keep Chaˢ: MᶜCarty for 800ˡᵇ. Tobᵒ. to be Levied at yᵉ. Layᵍ. of yᵉ. Next Levies

Ord⁴. that Capt. Lyne Pay Henry Brown 2/6 ⸺

Ord⁴. that yᵉ. Ch: Wardens Sell yᵉ. 6160ˡᵇ of Tobᵒ. & Cask at July or Augˢᵗ. Court, & out of yᵉ. Said Money Pay for wᵗ. repairs are done to yᵉ. Glebe ⸺

Ord⁴. that yᵉ. Ch: Wardens Pay Capt Taliaferro late Collecʳ 18/3 ⸺

Ord⁴. that yᵉ. Ch: Wardens Settle with Colᵒ. Corbin Mʳ. Shackelford & Colᵒ. Robinson

Teſt John Reade
Truely register'd ⅌ Fra. Gaines Clk

At a Vestry Held for Stratton Major Parish at the Lower Church on Thursday the 23ᵈ. Day of Febʸ. 1743

	Colᵒ. Corbin	Capt Gaines
Preſent	Capt. Dudley	Capt Taliaferro
	Mʳ. Anderson	Doctʳ. Strachey
	Colᵒ Robinson	Capt. Lyne
	Mʳ Livingston	Mʳ. Collier
	Majʳ. Rootes &	Mʳ. Thorpe

It is Order'd and agree'd on by this Vestry that The Reverᵈ. Meſsʳˢ. Bartholomew & Robert Yates do Officiate in this Parish on Wednesday in Each week till the Parish is Supplied or the Vestry shall Order to the Contrary, and that they be Paid at the rate *of of 16000ˡᵇ. Tobᵒ. ⅌ Ann. for each Sarmon — to begin at the Lower Church on the 1ˢᵗ. Wednesday in March ⸺

Teſt Gawin Corbin
Truely registred ⅌ Fra Gaines. Clk

---

*Erased in original but still legible.—C. G. C.

[37]
At a Vestry Held for Stratton Major Parish at the Upper Churc[ ] on Tuesday the 27th. March 1744 for Distributing the Fines

	Col°. Corbin	Doct^r. Strachey
Preſent	Capt. Dudley	Capt. Lyne
	Capt. Gaines	M^r. Collier
	Capt. Taliaferro	M^r. Thorpe

Order'd that Capt. Lyne Pay 14/. in Corn to John King for the Support of his family

Ord^d. that Capt. Lyne Pay 14/. in Corn to Mary Roff for D°.

Ord^d. that Capt. Lyne Pay 14/6 in Corn to Grace Birch for D°.

Ord^d. that Capt. Lyne Pay 14/. in Corn to John Walding for D°.

Ord^d. that Margret Bradger Molatto Bastard of Ann Bradger be bound to Stephen Haynes. According to Law. by the Church Wardens ——

Teſt. Gawin Corbin

Truely registered ⅌ Fra^s. Gaines Clk

At a Vestry held for Stratton Major Parish at the Uper Church on Fryday the 24th. August 1744.

	Col°. Corbin	Capt. Gaines	
	M^r. Anderson	Capt. Taliaferro	
Preſent	Col°. Robinson	M^r. Strachey	Veſtrymen
	M^r. Livingston	Capt. Lyne	
	Maj^r. Rootes	M^r. Thorpe	

Ordered that a Petition be Preſented to the Aſsembley to impower this Veſtry to sell the Preſent Glebe of this Parish —

Mʳ. John Shackelford &ᶜ. Proceſsioners return'd their Proceedings & it was ordᵈ: to be regiſtered

Capt. Gaines &ᶜ. Proceſsioners returned their Proceedings & it was ordᵈ. to be regiſtered —

Thoˢ. Dillard &ᶜ. Proceſsioners return'd their Proceedings & it was ordᵈ. to be regiſtered.

Robᵗ. Garrett. &ᶜ. Proceſsʳˢ. return'd their Proceedings &. it was ordᵈ. to be regiſtered.

Teſt. Gawin Corbin
Truely Regiſter'd ⅌ Franˢ. Gaines Clk.

[38]
At a Vestry held for Stratton Major Parish at the Lower Church on Wednesday the 10ᵗʰ. Day of Octobʳ. 1744

Preſᵗ. {Gawin Corbin, Robᵗ. Dudley, John Livingston, Robᵗ. Gaines} Veſtrymen {William Talliaferro, John Strachey, William Lyne, Charles Collier, Thomas Thorpe}

The Parish   Dʳ.

To the Reverᵈ. John Reade for 4 Months Service	5333
To the Reverᵈ. Barthˡ. & Robᵗ. Yates	9331
To Thoˢ. Lankford reader of the Lower Church	1200
To Anne Clear Sexton of Dᵒ.	750
To Henry Brown reader of the Upper Church & for Chaˢ. MᶜCarty	2000
To Grace Soward Sexton of Dᵒ. 750ˡᵇ & Keepᵍ. Elizᵗʰ. Brown 500ˡᵇ Tobᵒ.	1250
To Francis Gaines Clk of this Vestry	700
To Denis Mᶜkendree for keeping his Wife	800
To Job Jackson for keepᵍ. Mary Jones Child John Pᵗ. of the year	600

58   VESTRY BOOK OF STRATTON MAJOR PARISH

To George Tureman for the Use of his Son John	500
To Capt. Lyne for 4 Times Providing for the Comm. & 2 Delinq^{ts}.	320
To John Carter Acco^t. for a Horse block	150
To Docter Strachey for 4 Times Providing for the Comm.	240
To Thos. Lankford for Extraordinary Services Performed on y^e. weak Days	300
To Henry Brown for D°.	300
To Anne Clear Sexton for D°	150
To Grace Soward d°. for D°.	150
To Jn°: Atkins for keep^g. Jos. Moore 4 Months	429
	24503
To 4 ⅌ C^t. on D°. for Cask	980
	25483
To Capt R Tunstall for 2 Li∫ts Tiths	36
	25519
To 6 ⅌ C^t. on D°. for Collecting	1531
	27050

The Levies being Settled this ⅌sent Year are found to aMount to 27050^{lb} Tob°. being Levied upon 877 Tith's at 31^{lb}. Tob°. ⅌ Pole & there remains a fraction of 137^{lb}. Tob°. in the Collectors Hands ——

Col°. Jn°: Robinson & M^r. Jn°: Livingston are Appointed Churchwardens this ⅌sent Year & M^r. Jn°: Livingston is Appointed Collector ——

Ord^d. that Henry Brown Keep Ch^ws: McCarty the Ensuing Year for y^e. Sum of 800^{lb} Tob°. to levied at ye laying of the Next Levies ——

Ord⁴. that George Tureman Keep his Son John the Ensuing Year for yᵉ Sum of 500ˡᵇ. Tob°. to be Levied as above ——

Ord⁴. that Eliz^th. Ragan Keep Eliz^th. Brown the Ensuing Year for yᵉ Sum of 450ˡᵇ. Tob°. to be Levied as aforesaid ——

Ord⁴. that Eliz^th. Brown Daught^r. of Ann Brown be bound to Zach. Shackelford According to Law ——

Ord⁴. that Amey Devonport Mollatto Bastard of Ann Devonport be bound to Doct^r. Jn°: Strachey According to Law

Ord⁴. that the Late Ch: wardens Pay the ℔sent Ch. wardens the Money remaining in their Hands & that the Said Ch: wardens put Same out on Interest

      Teſt Gawin Corbin

   Truly Register'd ℔ Fraˢ. Gaines Clk

[39]

At a Vestry held for Stratton Major Parish at the Upper Church on Fryday the 16th. Day of November 1744 ——

	Gawin Corbin Esqr.	Robt Gaines
	Robt. Dudley	....
Preſ^t.	Rich⁴. Anderson	John Strachey
	John Robinson Esqr.	William Lyne
	Philip Rootes	Chaˢ: Collier
	John Livingston &	Thomas Thorpe

Gregory Smith Nich°. Dillard & John Foster Proſeſsioners, return'd their Proceedings & it is Order'd to be register'd —

William Hunt & Robt. Didlake Proceſsʳˢ. return'd their Proceedings & it's Ordered to be Registered —

Robᵗ. Ware, Thoᵒ. Cardwell, & Will: Ware Proceſsʳˢ: return'd their Proceedings & it's Order'd to be Registered —

The Gentlemen of this Vestry have agree'd to receive the Reverend William Robinson as Minister of this Parish —

Ordered that the Church Wardens Sell the Preſent Glebe in this Parish at Publick Sale —

Order'd that the Reveren'd Mʳ. Robinson be Paid 2000ˡᵇ. Tobᵒ. ℔ Annum untill there be a ſufficient Glebe Provided for him —

Order'd that the Church Wardens make Enquirey for a pᵉ: of Land to Purchase for a Glebe, & upon information thereof they make it known to this Vestry ——

         Teſt G Corbin

    Truly Register'd ℔ Franˢ. Gaines Clk

[40]

At a Vestry held for Stratton Major Parish at the Lower Church on Wednesday the 9ᵗʰ. Day of October 1745

	The Reverᵈ. William Robinson	
	Robᵗ. Dudley	John Strachey
	Richᵈ. Anderson	Willᵐ Lyne
Preſt.	John Robinson Esqr	Chaˢ: Collier Vestrymen
	John Livingston	Thoˢ. Thorpe
	Willᵐ. Taliaferro	

    The Parish   Dʳ

To the Reverᵈ. William Robinson	18000
To Thoˢ. Lankford readʳ. of the Lower Church	1200
To Anne Clear sexton of Dᵒ. & washing the surplice	750
To Henry Brown readʳ. of the Uppʳ. Church	1200
To Ditto for Keeping Charles Mᶜkarty	800

To Grace Soward Sexton of the Upp*. Church & Wash*. y* surplice	750
To Francis Gaines Clerk of the Vestry	700
To George Tureman for the Use of his son John	500
To Elizabeth Ragon for Keeping Eliza. Brown	450
To Geo. Bray ℔ Acco*. for a Horse block & a step at the Vestry House door	170
To Tho*. Shiptons Acco* for Work &*. done to the Upper Church	1504
To M*. Livingstons Acco* for D*. done to the Lower Church	550
To Augustine Bridges for 2 Levies over paid last year	62
To Capt. Tunstall for 2 Cop'ys List Tithables	36
To Will* Brushwood for Keeping Jane McKendree	800
To Col*. Robinson for Providing 4 Times for the Comm.	240
To Tob*. Levied for the Use of the Parish	10000
	37712
To 4 ℔ C*. on 37712*. Tob*. for Cask	1508
	39220
To 6 ℔ C*. on 39220*: for Collecting	2353
	41573

The Levies being settled this Present Year are found to amount to 41573ᴵᵇ. Tobᵒ. being Levied upon 872 Tithables at 47ᴵᵇ. of Tobᵒ. ℔ Poll, & there remains a Fraction of 589ᴵᵇ. Due to the Collector, and it is Ordered that the said fraction be Deducted. out. of the Tobᵒ. which is Levied for the Use of the Parish

Robᵗ. Dudley & Philip Rootes Gent: are Appointed Church Wardens and Robᵗ. Dudley is appointed Collector for this Present Year

Richard Corbin Gent. and Willᵐ. Hunt are appointed Vestrymen in the place of Gawin Corbin Esqʳ. & Robᵗ. Gaines decd.

Ordᵈ. that Thoˢ. Burnett John King, & James Robinson Barker be Exempted from Paying any more Parish Levies —

Ordᵈ. that William MᶜCarty Keep Chaˢ: MᶜCarty the Ensuing Year for the sum of 800ˡᵇ. of Tobº. & Cask to be Levied at the laying of the Next Levies —

[41]
Ordᵈ. that Elizabeth Ragon Keep Eliza. Brown the Ensuing Year for the sum of 500ˡᵇ. Tobº. & Cask to be Levied at the Laying of the Next Levies —

Ordᵈ. that Geo. Tureman Keep his son John the Ensuing Year for the sum of 800ˡᵇ. Tobº. & Cask to be Levied at the Laying of the Next Levies. —

Ordᵈ. that the Money in the Hands of the Late Church Wardens be paid to the Present Church Wardens ——

Ordᵈ. that John Robinson Esqʳ. & William Lyne Pay Doctor Strachey's Accoᵗ. being £4‖7‖6 out of the fines in their Hands —

Ordᵈ. that the Ball. of John Livingstons Accoᵗ. being 14/6. be paid to him out of the Next fines that is recd by the Collector —

    Test William Robinson Minʳ

   Truely Registered by Franˢ. Gaines. Clk

At a Vestry Held for Stratton Major Parish at the Upper Church on Monday the Second Day of Xber 1745

   The Rever⁴. William Robinson
   Robᵗ. Dudley William Taliaferro ⎫
   John Robinson Esqʳ. John Strachey ⎪
Preſᵗ. Philip Rootes William Lyne ⎬ Vestrymen
   John Livingston Charles Collier ⎪
   .... Thomas Thorpe ⎭

Richard Corbin and William Hunt took the Oaths and Subscribed to be conformable to the Church *of of England as by Law established and are added to this Vestry

It is Ordered by this Vestry that Richard Philips Underwood's Indentures to Thoˢ. Collins be Void, and the Church Wardens Sign other Indentures and bind the said Underwood to Franˢ. Gaines

      Teſt Wᵐ. Robinson, Minʳ.

  Truly Registered by Franˢ. Gaines Clk Vest.

[42]
At a Vestry Held for Stratton Major Parish at the lower Church on Monday the 3ᵈ Day of March 1745.

   The Rever⁴. Willᵐ Robinson   ⎫
   Robᵗ. Dudley John Strachey ⎪
Preſᵗ. Philip Rootes Willᵐ Lyne   ⎬
   John Livingston Chaˢ. Collier ⎪
   Willᵐ. Taliaferro Thomas Thorpe ⎭ Vestrymen

It is Ordered and agree'd that Mʳ. Taliaferro write to Mʳ Wᵐ Skipwith and acquaint him that this Vestry will buy his Land on the Terms he proposes to sell at, which is Seven Hundred Pounds, and that they will Pay him Two Hundred Pounds or there abouts at the time of his Ac-

---
*Scratched over in the original, but still legible.—C. G. C.

knowledging Deeds, and give their Bond for the remainder
to be Paid with Interest after he shall surender the Plantation, & also desire him the said Skipwith to Come and
Acknowledge his Deeds in June next

       Teſt Wᵐ. Robinson, Minʳ.
    Truly registered by
          Franˢ. Gaines Clk.

At a Vestry held for Stratton Major Parish at the Upper
Church on Monday the 13ᵗʰ. October 1746.

	The Reverend William Robinson		
	Robert Dudley	John Strachey	
	Richᵈ. Anderson	William Lyne	
Preſᵗ.	John Robinson Esqʳ.	Charles Collier	Vestrymen
	Philip Rootes	Thoˢ. Thorpe	
	John Livingston		
	Willᵐ. Taliaferro		

    The Parish   Dʳ

To The Reverᵈ. Mʳ. Robinson	18000
To Thomas Lankford readʳ. of the Lower Church	1200
To Anne Clear Sexton of dº. & Washing the Sur- plice	750
To Henry Brown readʳ. of the Upʳ: Church	1200
To Grace Soward Sexton of Dº. & Washing the Surplice	750
To Franˢ. Gaines Clk	700
To Willᵐ. MᶜCarty for Keeping Charles 1 year	800
To Eliza: Ragon for Keepᵍ: Eliza. Brown 1 year	500
To George Tureman for Keeping his son John 1 year	800
To Major Rootes for Providing for the Communion 4 times	240

To Sam¹. Shepards Acco⁴. for Benches at the Lower Church	100
To Mʳ Livingston Levied short Last Year	100
To George Piggs Acco⁴. £3‖3‖ Levied in Tob°. @ 12/6	504
To Mʳ. Thorpe for a Dial Poast for the Uppʳ: Church	60
	25704

[43]

Brought Up	25704
To Major Rootes Acco⁴. £6‖12‖5 Levied in Tob°. @ 12/6	1059
To Capt. Dudley for 4 Times Providing for the Comm:	240
To Capt. Willᵐ Lyne for his Acco⁴.	40
To John Shackelford for 1 Lev'y overcharged last year	47
To Moſes Shomack for the same	47
To Capt. Taliaferro for steps to the Lower Church	600
To Willᵐ Brushwood for Keeping Jane MᶜKendree 7 months	466
To Geo. Meddlicott for Schooling John Greens Children	134
To be sold for the Parish	10000
	38337
To 4 ℔ Cᵗ. on 38337ˡᵇ. Tob° for Cask	1533
	39870
To Major Richᵈ. Tunstalls Accoᵗ Clks fee's	207
	40077
To 6 ℔ Cᵗ. on 40077ˡᵇ. Tob°. for Collection	2404
	42481

The Levies being settled this Present year are found to amount to 42481ˡᵇ. Tobᵒ. being Levied upon 845 Tithables at 50ˡᵇ. Tobᵒ. ℔ Poll and there will remain a fraction of 231ˡᵇ. Tobᵒ. due to the Collector, and it's Order'd that the same be deducted out of the Tobᵒ. which is Levied to be sold for the Use of the Parish.

Richard Anderson, & Richard Corbin Genᵗ: is appointed Church Wardens for the Ensuing Year. & Richard Anderson is Appointed Collector

Order'd that Catherine Gaines be Excused from Paying any more Parish Levies for her Negro woman Philis.

Order'd that Wᵐ. MᶜCarty Keep his Broʳ. Charles the Ensuing year for the sum of Eight hundred Pounds of Tobᵒ. to be Levied at the Laying of the Next Levies

Order'd that Eliza: Ragon Keep Eliza: Brown the Ensuing year for the Sum of five hundred Pounds Tobᵒ. to be Levied at Laying the Next Levies.

Order'd that George Tureman Keep his son John the Ensuing year for the Sum of Eight Hundred Pounds Tobᵒ. to be Levied at Laying of the Next Levies

Order'd that the Churchwardens Pay Mʳ. Jaˢ: Power a Pistole his fee for Projsecuting a Suit against John Thach.

Order'd that the Church Wardens Pay John Robinson Esqʳ. One Pound Six shillˢ: for a fee Paid Mʳ. Jnᵒ Palmer for Drawing Deeds for the Use of this Parish.

Ordᵈ. That John Robinson Esq defend the Suit against the Church Wardens of Petsworth Parish in the General Court

Ordᵈ. that Colᵒ. Richard Corbin Present Church warden send to England for for two Surplices for the Use of this Parish.

Ord⁴. that a Kitchen be built on the Glebe with a Brick wall Twenty Six foot Long & Twenty foot wide, a Darey Sixteen foot Long & twelve foot wide, & a Meat house Twelve foot Square, & it is Also Ord⁴. That Capt. Dudley & Capt. Taliaferro agree with workmen to Build the above Mentioned Houses as soon as they Conveniently Can

       Teſt Wᵐ. Robinson
   Truely Register'd. Franˢ. Gaines Clk.

[44]
At a Vestry held for Stratton Major Parish at the Glebe on on Wednesday the 21ˢᵗ. Day of Janʳʸ. 1746.

Preſt.
Robᵗ. Dudley   John Strachey ⎫
Rich⁴. Anderson   Willᵐ. Lyne ⎬ Vestrymen
Jnᵒ. Livingston   Chaˢ: Collier ⎪
Willᵐ. Taliaferro & Wᵐ. Hunt ⎭

The Use of the Glebe Plantation for this Present year having been Put up to the Highest Bidder & Chaˢ: Collier Bidding Seventeen Hundred & fifty Pounds of Tobᵒ: Order'd that he have the Uſe of the said Plantation for the same till Christmas next, and that he take Care of the Orchards & leave the same in Tendable repair.

       Test Robᵗ Dudley
  Truely Registerd.
      Franˢ. Gaines Clk

At a Vestry held For Stratton Major Parish at the Uper Church on Monday the 17ᵗʰ. Day of August 1747.

Presᵗ.
The Revᵈ. William Robinson ⎫
Robᵗ Dudley   John Strachey ⎪
Rich⁴ Anderson   William Lyne ⎬ Vestrymen
John Robinson Esq   Rich⁴. Corbin ⎪
William Taliaferro   Willᵐ. Hunt ⎭

Ord⁴. that George Pigg, Jnº. Shackelford, & Thoˢ. Sowell do meet on the first Monday in Xber next and go in Proceſsion of & see all & Every Persons Land between Portopotank Creek & Matasip Swamp Plainly marked continuing their Proceedings in all Suitable Weather untill the whole Precinct be finished, and all the Inhabitants thereof are hereby required to attend the said Proceſsioners According to Law. and the said Proceſsioners are farther Ord⁴. to make & return to this Vestry at their next Sitting after the Last Day of March next a true Accoᵗ. of all the Lands they have Proceſsioned, of the Persons Present at the same, of what Lands they have not Proceſsioned, & the Particular Reason of such failure.

Ord⁴. that Samuel Shepard, William Berry & John Waller do meet on the first Wednesday in Xber next and go in Proceſsion of & see all and Every Persons Land between Mattaſip & Pepetico Swamps Plainly Marked Continuing their Proceedings in all Suitable Weather untill the whole Precinct be finished. and all the Inhabitants thereof are hereby required to attend the said Proceſsioners According to Law. and the said Proceſsioners are farther Ord⁴. to make & return to this Vestry at their next Sitting after the Last Day of March next a true Accoᵗ. of all the Lands they have Proceſsioned, of the Persons Present at the Same, of what Lands they have not Proceſsioned & the Particular Reason of such failure.

[45]
Ord⁴. that John Foster Nicholas Dillard & Henry Collier do meet on the first Fryday in Xber next and go in Proceſsion of & see all and Every Persons Land between Pepetico Swamp & the Southern branch of Arracaco Plainly marked Continuing their Proceedings in all Suitable Weather untill the whole Precinct be finished, and all the Inhabitants thereof are hereby required to attend the said

Proceſsioners According to Law. and the said Proceſsioners are farther Ord̃. to make & return to this Vestry at their next Sitting after the last Day of March next a true Acco.ᵗ of all the Lands they have Proceſsioned, of the Persons Present at the same, of what Lands they have not Proceſsioned and the Particular Reason of such failure.

Ord.ᵈ That Tho.ˢ Dillard, Thomas Lankford & Roger Field do meet on the Second Monday in Xber next and go in Proceſsion of & see all & Every Persons Land between the Southern & Western Branch of Arracaco Plainly marked Continuing their Proceedings in all Suitable weather untill the whole Precinct be finished and all the Inhabitants thereof are hereby required to Attend the said Proceſsioners According to Law. and the said Proceſsioners are farther Ord.ᵈ to make and return to this Vestry at their next Sitting after the Last Day of March next a true Acco.ᵗ of all the Lands they have Proceſsioned, of the Persons Present at the same, of what Lands they have not Proceſsioned, and the Particular Reason of Such failure.

Ord.ᵈ that Edward Trice, James Trice & George Bray do meet on the second Wednesday in Xber next and go in Proceſsion of & see all & Every Persons Land between Burgises swamp & the Monack Swamp to Morgan Myr'ys Corner thence A Straight Course to a Gum standing between Will.ᵐ Brushwood & Elizabeth Didlake, thence a Straight Course to Tarſatyan Swamp between Doct.ʳ Joyeux's & Mary Hollinger Plainly marked, Continuing their Proceedings in all Suitable weather untill the whole Precinct be finished, and all the Inhabitants thereof are hereby required to Attend the said Procſsioners according to Law. and the said Proceſsioners are farther Ord.ᵈ to make & return to this Vestry at their next Sitting after the last Day of March next a true Acco.ᵗ of all the Lands they have Proceſsioned, of the Persons Present at the same, of what Land they have Procefsioned, & the Perticular of such failure

Ord⁴. That William Hunt Robᵗ. Didlake & Edward Spencer do meet on the third Wednesday in Xber next & go in Procefsion of & see all & Every Persons Land between the Monack Swamp & the branch next above William Hunts Plainly marked Continuing their Proceedings in all Suitable weather till the whole Precinct be finished and all the Inhabitants thereof are hereby required to attend the said Procefsioners According to Law. and the said Procefsioners are farther Ordered to make & return to this Vestry at their next Sitting after the Last of March next a true Accoᵗ. of all the Lands they have Procefsioned, of the Persons Present at the same, of what Lands they have not Procefsioned, & the Particular Reason of Such failure

[46]
Ord⁴. that Robert Garrett Thomas Brown & Thomas Soward do meet on the Second Fryday in Xber next and go in Procefsion of and see all & Every Persons Land between Tarfatyan & Great Heartquake Swamps Plainly marked, Continuing their Proceedings in all Suitable weather untill the whole Precinct be finished and all the Inhabitants thereof are hereby required to Attend the said Procefsioners According to Law. and the said Procefsioners are farther Ord⁴. to make & return to this Vestry at their next Sitting after the Last of March next a true Accoᵗ. of all the Lands they have Procefsioned, of the Persons Present at the same, of what Lands they have not Procefsioned, and the Perticular Reason of such failure.

Ord⁴. that Robᵗ. Ware Thoˢ. Cardwell & William Ware do meet on the third Wednesday in in Xber next and go in Procefsion of & see all and Every Persons Land between the Branch next above William Hunts, and the Extent Upwards Plainly marked, Continuing their Proceedings in all

Suitable weather untill the whole Precinct be finished, and all the Inhabitants thereof are hereby required to Attend the said Proceſsioners According to Law. and the said Proceſsioners are farther Ord^d. to make and return to this Vestry at their next Sitting after the Last of March next a true Acco^t. of all the Lands they have Proceſsioned, of the Persons Present at the same, of what Lands they have not Proceſsioned, & the Perticular Reason of such failure

Ord^d. that William Lyne Richard Wyatt & Job Jackson do meet on the Third Fryday in Xber next and go in Proceſsion of & see all & Every Per Land between the Western branch of Arracaco, & Tarſsatyan Swamp Plainly marked, Continuing their Proceedings in all Suitable weather untill the whole Precinct be finished. and all the Inhabitants thereof are hereby required to Attend the said Proceſsioners according to Law. and the said Proceſsioners are farther Ord^d. to make & return to this Vestry at their next Sitting after the Last Day of March next, a true Acco^t. of all the Lands they have Proceſsioned, of the Persons present at the same of what Land they have not Proceſsioned, & the Perticular of such failure

       Teſt W^m. Robinson, M^r.
  Truly Regestered
       Fran^s. Gaines Clk

[47]
At a Vestry held for Stratton Major Parish at the Lower Church on Fryday the 9th. Day of October 1747.

	The Rev^d. William Robinson		
	Robt. Dudley	John Strachey	
Preſt.	Rich^d. Anderson	Willm. Lyne	Vestrymen
	John Livingston	Thos. Thorpe	
	Willm Taliaferro	Willm. Hunt	

72   VESTRY BOOK OF STRATTON MAJOR PARISH

The Parish	D`r`.
To the Rever`d`. W`m`. Robinson	18000
To Tho`s`. Lankford Read`r`. of the Lower Church	1200
To Henry Brown Read`r`. of the Uper Church	1200
To Ann Clear Sexton of the Lower Church & Wash`g`. the Surplice	750
To Grace Soward Sexton of the Uper Church & d°.	750
To Fran`s`. Gaines Clk	700
To W`m`. M`c`Carty for Keeping his Bro`r`. Charles	800
To Eliz`a`. Ragon for Keeping Eliz`a`. Brown	500
To George Tureman for Keeping his son John	800
To Rich`d`. Corbin Esq`r`. for four times Providing for the Comm	240
To Rich`d`. Anderson for the Same	240
To Rich`d`. Corbin Esq`r`. for his Acco`t`. against the Parish @ 12/6 ℔ C`t`.	468
To be Sold for the Use of the Parish	20000
	45648
To 4 ℔ C`t`. on 45648`lb` Tob°. for Cask	1826
	47474
To Rich`d`. Tunstall Clk of this County for two List Tithables	36
	47510
To 6 ℔ C`t`. on 47510`lb` Tob°. for the Collector	2850
	50360

The Parish	C`r`.	
By Charles Collier decd. Estate for Rent of the Glebe	1750`lb`.	
By Fran`s`. Gaines for Levies recd last year	372	
By Richard Anderson for the Same	300	
	2422	2422
		47938

The Levies being Settled this Present Year are found to amount to 47,938ᵇ. Tob°. being Levied upon 854 Tithables at 56ᵇ. Tob°. ℔ Poll, & there will remain a Fraction due to the Collector of 114ᵇ. Tob°. & it's Order'd that he reserve the same out of the Tob°. which is Levied to be sold for the Use of the Parish

William Taliaferro & William Hunt are Appointed Church Wardens and William Taliaferro is Appointed Collector for this Present Year.

John Shackelford is Chosen Vestryman in the Place of Charles Collier decd.

Ordᵈ. the Church Wardens make Indentures & Bind John Scuddy to Joseph Simco According to Law

[48]
Order'd that William Devonport Mollatto Baster'd of Ann Devonport be Bound by the Church Wardens to Doctor John Strachey According to Law.

Ordᵈ. that William MᶜCarty Keep his Brother Charles MᶜCarty the Ensuing year & that he have 800ᵇ. Tob°. Levied for the same at the Laying of the next Levies

Ordᵈ. that Elizᵃ. Ragon Keep Elizᵃ. Brown the Ensuing Year & that she have five Hundred Pounds Tob°. Levied for the same at Laying of the next Levies ——

Ordᵈ. that George Tureman Keep his son John the Ensuing year & that he have 800ᵇ. Tob°. Levied for the same at the Laying of the next Levies.

Ordᵈ. that the Church Wardens Bind John Gill Son of Patient Gill to Richᵈ. Kelley According to Law.

Ordᵈ. that Capt. Robᵗ. Dudley Pay the Money in his Hands for the Tob°. sold by him for the Use of this Parish, to Capt. William Taliaferro.

Ord^d. that Capt. Rich^d. Anderson Pay the Money for the Tob°. which he has in his Hands, to Capt. W^m. Taliaferro, when sold.

Teſt W^m. Robinson

Truely Registered. Fran^s. Gaines Clk.

At a Vestry held for Stratton Major Parrish at the Glebe on Monday the 4th. day of April 1748.

Preſ^t.
The Rev^d. William Robinson
Rich^d. Anderson
John Robinson Esq
John Livingston
Willm. Taliaferro
William Lyne
Thomas Thorpe
} Vestrymen

John Shackelford took the Oaths and Subscribed to be Conformable to the Church of England as by Law Established, and is added to this Vestry.

Ord^d. that there be a Poarch built to the Glebe House seven foot Square with a Rough set upon four Poasts, Seats on Each side, fourteen Inches broad a Floor of Good Pyne Plank, Steps to be made to the Poarch and to the back door of White Oak Scantling, to Shew fourteen Inches Broad & Six Inches Thick, Laid on Brick, likewise the Lower floor's of the House Plain'd over, the Doors, Windoors, &c. Painted with an Olive Colour on the inside, and the out side of the Doors & Windows Painted White. The Walls & Sealing Whitewashed, & the Windows Mended.

[49]
Ordered that the oven in the Glebe Kitchen be taken out and a Closet made in that End of the House as Large as the Jamm of the Chimney will allow, with a two & half foot door in the Middle, & two Dreſsers at Each End of the Closet to reach as far as the Door, and the inside

Lauthed & Plastered. and that a Brick Oven be built w{th}out in some Convenient Place.

Ord{d}. that there be a Neceſsesary House built Eight foot Long & Six foot Broad

Ord{d}. That the Church Wardens and John Shackelford or any two of them agree with workmen to do all the aforementioned work.

Teſt Will{m}. Robinson

Truly Registered   Fran⁸. Gaines Clk

At a Vestry Held for Stratton Major Parrish at the Uper Church on Thursday the 14{th}. Day of April 1748. To Distribute Fines to the Poor.

	The Rev{d}. William Robinson	
	Richard Anderson William Lyne	
Preſ{t}.	John Robinson Esq{r}. Thomas Thorpe	Veſtrymen
	Will{m}. Taliaferro William Hunt	
	John Strachey John Shackelford	

Ord{d}. That Capt. W{m}. Taliaferro Provide for
   Moſes Shomack 3 Barrills of Corn. for w{ch}.
   he is allowed at the rate of 10/ ℔ Bar. £ 1‖10‖—
3 Barrills of Corn for Isabell O Deer   1‖10‖—
2 Barrills of Corn for Mary Roffe   1‖—‖—
2 Barrills of Corn for Liddy Hill   1‖—‖—
1½ Barrills of Corn for Thomas Bowden   —‖15‖—
1 Rugg for Ann Simco of the Value   —‖17‖ 6

                                         £ 6‖12‖ 6

Ord{d}. That William Hunt Provide for Elizabeth M{c}Carty 3 Barrills Corn at the rate
   of 10/ ℔ Bar.   1‖10‖—
3 Barrills Corn for Jane Ransom   1‖10‖—
1 Barrill Corn for Elenor Morris & 10/. in Cash 1‖—‖—

For John King to be laid out in Bedding or Cloaths for his Children	1||10||—
2 Barrills Corn for Isabell Whitsides	1||—||—
1½ Barrills Corn for Michael Roane	—||15||—
£	13||17|| 6

[50]

George Pigg, John Shackelford & Thoˢ. Sowell Proceſsioners Return'd an Accoᵗ. of their Proceedings and it's Ordᵈ. that the same be Register'd

Samuel Shepard, William Berry & John Waller Proceſsioners Returnᵈ. an Accoᵗ. of their Proceedings which was Ordᵈ. to be Registered.

Thomas Dillard, Thoˢ. Lankford & Roger Field Proceſsioner Returnd an Acoᵗ. of their Proceedings, which is Ordᵈ. to be Registered.

John Foster, Nichᵒ: Dillard & Henry Collier. Proceſsioners Returnd an Accoᵗ. of their Proceedings Which is Ordᵈ. to be Register'd.

Richard Wyatt & Job Jackson Proceſsioners Return'd an Accoᵗ. of Proceedings Which is Ordᵈ. to be Register'd

Edward Trice, James Trice & George Bray Proceſsioners Return'd an Accoᵗ. of their Proceedings which is Ordᵈ. to be Registered.

Robert Garrett Thomas Soward & Thomas Bourn Proceſsioners Returᵈ. an Accoᵗ. of their Proceedings which was Ordᵈ. to be Registered.

William Hunt & Edward Spencer Proceſsioners Return'd an Accoᵗ. of their Proceedings & it was Ordᵈ. to be Registered.

Robert Ware, Thomas Cardwell & William Ware Proceſsioners Returnd an Accoᵗ. of their Proceedings Which is Ordᵈ. to be Registered.

Ordᵈ. that William Hunt Receive 40/ of Richᵈ. Corbin Esq. for the Ballance his Fathers Accoᵗ. due to this Parish.

Ordᵈ. that William Taliaferro Gent. Settle with the Exors of Capt Robᵗ. Dudley decd. for the Fine he Recd of John Bowles decd.

Ordᵈ. that the Present Collector demd. and Receive of Mʳ. Thoˢ. Thorpe Three Pounds four Shillings & Six pence which is due from him to the Parish

       Teſt Wᵐ. Robinson
   Truly Register'd Franˢ Gaines Clk.

[51]

At a Vestry held for Stratton Major Parish at the Upper Church on Monday the 10ᵗʰ. day of October 1748.

Present
- The Revᵈ. William Robinson
- Richᵈ. Anderson
- John Robinson Esq
- John Livingston
- Willᵐ. Taliaferro
- John Strachey
- William Lyne
- Richᵈ. Corbin
- Willᵐ Hunt
- John Shackelford

Vestrymen

The Parish   Dʳ.

To the Revᵈ. Mʳ. Wᵐ. Robinson	18000ᶫᵇ Tobˢ.
To Thomas Lankford Readʳ. of the Lower Church	1200
To Ann Clear Sexton of dᵒ. & for Washᵍ. the Surplice	750
To Henry Brown Readʳ. of the Uper Church	1200
To Grace Soward Sexton of dᵒ. & Washᵍ. the Surplice	750

To Francis Gaines Clerk V.	700
To William M°Carty for Keeping Charles M°Carty	800
To Elizabeth Ragon for Keeping Eliza. Brown	500
To George Tureman for Keeping his Son John	800
To Capt. W^m. Taliaferro for Providing for the Church four Times	300
To M^r. William Hunt for Providing for the Church four times	350
To d°. for one Lev'y over charged in the List of Tithes	56
To Jane M°kendree	400
To Richard Stones for burying Grace Stears	200
To be sold for the Use of the Parish	16000
	42006
To 4 ℔ C^t. on D°. for Cask	1680
	43686
To 6 ℔ C^t. on 43686^{lb}. Tob°. for Collecting	2621
	46307

The Levies being settled this Present year are found to amount to 46307^{lb}. Tob°. being Levied upon 857 Tithables at 54^{lb}. Tob°. ℔ Poll, & there remains a Fraction of 29^{lb}. Tob°. due to the Collector & it's Order'd that the same be deducted out of the Tob°. which is Levied to be Sold for the Use of the Parish.

Thomas Thorpe & John Shackelford are Appointed Churchwardens and Thomas Thorpe is Appointed Collector for this ℔sent Year

John Foster is Appointed Vestryman in the Place of Capt. Robt. Dudley decd.

Order'd the Collector Pay Catherine Gaines One Pound ten shillings out of the Money Ariſing for the Tob°. which is Levied to be sold.

[52]
Order'd that William M°Carty Keep his Broth'. Charles the Ensuing year, and that he have 800¹ᵇ. Tob°. Levied at the Laying of the Parish Lev'y for the same.

Order'd that Elizabeth Ragon Keep Eliza. Brown the ensuing year and that she have 500¹ᵇ. Tob°. Levied at Laying of the next Parish Lev'y

Order'd that George Tureman Keep his son John the Ensuing Year and that he have 800¹ᵇ. Tob°. Levied at Laying of the next Lev'y.

Order'd that Catherine Gaines keep Tho°. Whitsides the Ensuing Year and that she have 500¹ᵇ. Tob°. Levied at Laying of the next Lev'y.

Order'd that John Walding be exempted from Paying any more Parish Levies.

Order'd the Church-wardens Provide two Surplices for the Use of this Parish

Order'd that John Shackelford agree with a Workman to build a Brick Oven at the Glebe.

Order'd that the Collector Pay Capt Wᵐ. Taliaferro the Ballance due on his Acco'. being £4||15||4½ Curr'. Money out of the Money arrising for the Tob°. which is Levied to be sold for the Use of the Parish.

Order'd that the Collector Pay Capt Richᵈ. Anderson five shillings, for a Hatch made to the Poarch of the Lower Church.

Wᵐ. Robinson
Truely Register'd Franˢ. Gaines. Clk

80   VESTRY BOOK OF STRATTON MAJOR PARISH

At a Vestry held for Stratton Major Parish at the Lower Church on Fryday the 6ᵗʰ. Day of October 1749

Presᵗ.
| The Revᵈ. William Robinson |
| Richᵈ Anderson   William Lyne |
| John Robinson Esqʳ.   Thomas Thorpe | Vestrymen
| John Livingston   William Hunt |
| Willᵐ. Taliaferro   John Shackelford |
| John Strachey |

The Parish   Dʳ.

To the Revᵈ. Mʳ. Robinson   16000
To Thomas Lankford Readʳ. of the Lower Church   1200
To Ann Clear Sexton & for Washing the Surplice   750
To Henry Brown Readʳ. of the Uper Church   1200
To Grace Soward Sexton & for Washing the Sur-
   plice   750
To Francis Gaines Clk Vestry   700
                                                       —————
      Carrᵈ. up   20600
[53]
Dʳ. Brought up   20600
To William MᶜCarty for Keeping Chaˢ. MᶜCarty   800
To John Campbell for keeping Eliza. Brown   500
To George Tureman for keeping his son John   800
To Catherine Gaines for keeping Thoˢ. Whitesides   500
To Mʳ. Thomas Thorpe for Providing 4 Times for
   the Comm   350
To Mʳ. John Shackelford for the same   350
                                                       —————
                                                       23900
To 4 ℔ Cᵗ. on 23900ᵗᵇ Tobᵒ. for Cask   956
To John Lankford for his Accoᵗ. for keeping John
   Walding   657
To Mʳ. Thomas Thorpe his Accoᵗ. for Clothing the
   poor   915

To Francis Gaines for 2 Levies not recd Last Y'. Jn°. Walding & Jo. Adams	108
To the Clerk of this County for 2 lists Tithes	36
To Ditto for 2 Lists last year not Leved	36
To M'. John Shackelford for Ball. of his Acco'. against the Parish £2‖0‖6½ in Tob°. @ 12/6 ⅌ C'. is	324
To Stephen Haynes for a Horse block at the Uper Church	150
To Mary Hollinger for the Use of a Bedd for Isabel Whitsides	480
To Jane M°kendree	400
To Doctor Charles Leith for Sallavat⁵ Isabell Whitsides	800
To be Sold for the Use of the Parish	10000
	38762
To 6 ⅌ C'. for Collecting 38762ˡᵇ Tob°.	2326
	41088
To Henry Lyne for one Lev'y Paid last year	56
	41144

The Levies being settled this Present year are found to amount to the above Quantity of Tob°. being Levied upon 878 Tithables at 47ˡᵇ. Tob°. ⅌ Poll and there remains a Fraction due to the Parish of 122ˡᵇ. Tob°. in the hands of the Collector, and its Ordᵈ. that he Account for the same at laying of the next Parish Levies ——

John Strachey & William Lyne is appointed Church-wardens and John Strachey is appointed Collector for this Present year

Ordᵈ. That William M°Carty Keep his Broʳ. Charles the Ensuing Year, and that he have 800ˡᵇ. Tob°. levied for the same at laying the next Parish Levies.

Ord^d. that John Campbell keep Eliza. Brown the Ensuing year, and that he have 500^{lb}. Tob^o. levied for the same at laying the next Parish Levies ——

Ord^d. that George Tureman keep his son John the Ensuing Year, and that he have 800^{lb}. Tob^o. levied for the same at lay of the Parish Levies ——

Ord^d. That the Church-Wardens Put Thomas Whitsides out to some convenient Person to keep & Provide for the Ensuing year, & that they have 500^{lb}. Tob^o. levied for the same at laying of the next Parish Levies ——

Test. W^m. Robinson Min^r.

Truly Register'd Fran^s. Gaines Clk.

[54]
At a Vestry held for Stratton Major Parish at the Uper Church on Monday the 8th Day of October 1750.

	The Rev^d. William Robinson	
	Richard Anderson William Lyne	
Pres^t.	John Robinson Esq Thomas Thorpe	Vestrymen
	John Livingston John Shackelford	
	John Strachey	

The Parish   D^r.

To the Rever^d. William Robinson	16000
To Thomas Lankford read^r. of the Low^r. Ch:	1200
To Ann Clear Sexton of d^o. & for washing the Surplice	750
To Henry Brown read^r. of the Uper Church	1200
To Grace Soward Sexton of D^o. & Washing the Surplice	750
To Francis Gaines	700
To William McCarty for keeping Chas. McCarty	800
To John Campbell for keeping Eliza. Brown	500

To George Tureman for keeping his son John	800
To John Jones for keeping Thomas Whitsides'	500
To Doct'. John Strachey for 5 Times Provid⁵. for the Comm.	350
To Capt. William Lyne for the same	350
	23900
To 4 ℔ Cᵗ. on 23900¹ᵇ. Tob°. for Cask	956
To the Clk of this County for 2 lists of Tithes	36
	24892
To 6 ℔ Cᵗ. on 24892¹ᵇ. Tob°. for the Collectors Sallary	1494
	26386
To Jane Mᶜkendree 400¹ᵇ. Tob°. & Sallary for Collecting 24	424
	26810

The levies being settled this Present Year are found to amount to 26810¹ᵇ. Net Tob°. being levied upon 916 Tithables at 30¹ᵇ. Tob°. ℔ Poll, and there will remain a fraction of 670¹ᵇ. Tob°. in the Hands of the Collector and it's Ordered that he Account for the Same at laying of the next Parish Levies.

John Foster took the Oaths, and Subſcribed to be conformable to the Church of England as by Law Established & is added to this Vestry.

John Robobinson Esq & John Foster is appointed Churchwardens and John Robinson Esq is appointed Collector for this Present Year

Order'd that Doct^r. John Strachey late Collector Pay the Money in his Hands for Tob°. Sold for the Use of this Parish, to the Present Collector.

Ordered that the Present Collector Pay Daniel Guthrie five Shillings for Digging a grave for William Kattle

Order'd that the Collector Pay Sarah Gramshill One Pound two Shillings for taking Care of, & finding a burying Sheet for William Kattle .

[55]
Order'd that the Collector Pay M^r. Thomas Thorpe four Pounds One Shilling & Six pence for his Acco^t. for Cloaths for the poor.

Order'd that the Collector Pay M^r. William Skipwith the Ballance of his Acco^t. due from this Parish.

Order'd that William McCarty keep his Brother Charles the Ensuing year, & that he have 800^{lb}. Tob°. Levied for the same at laying of the next Levy.

Order'd that George Tureman Keep his son John the Ensuing Year & that he have 800^{lb}. Tob°. levied for the same at laying of the next Lev'y

Ordered that Capt William Lyne Pay the Ballance of his Account to the Pres^t. Collector.

Order'd that John Campbell Keep Elizabeth Brown the Ensuing Year & that he have 500^{lb}. Tob°. levied for the same at laying the next Lev'y

Order'd that William Ware Keep Ann Lewis wife of George Lewis the Ensuing year, & that he have 800^{lb}. Tob°. Levied for the same at laying of the next Lev'y.

Order'd that George Lewis be Exempted from Paying Parish Levies

This Vestry do consent and agree that the minister of this Parish shall not be liable to Delapedations or repairs.

     Test.
        W^m. Robinson Min^r.
  Truly Regist^d.
      Fran^s. Gaines. Clk.

[56]
At a Vestry held for Stratton Major Parish at the Lower Church on Monday the 22^d. Day of July 1751.

Pres^t.
The Rever^d. William Robinson
Richard Anderson   Thomas Thorpe
John Robinson Esqr.   William Hunt   Veſtrymen
John Livingston   John Shackelford
William Taliaferro   & John Foster
William Lyne

Pursuant to an Order of King & Queen County Court dated the 9th. Day of July 1751. That the Veſtrys of the Several Parishes in this County do divide their Parishes into so many Precincts as to them shall seem most convenient for Proceſsioning every Persons Land therein, and to appoint the particular Times for that purpose between the last Day of September and the last Day of March next ensuing. Pursuant to an Act of Aſsembly in that case made & Provided ———

Order'd that George Pigg John Shackelford & George Sowell or any two of them do meet on the first Monday in December next and goe in Proceſsion of & see all & every Persons Land between Poropotank Creek & Mattasip Swamp Pllainly Marked, Continuing their Proceedings in all Suitable Weather untill the whole Precinct be finished, and all the freeholders who are Inhabitants thereof are required to attend the said Proceſsioners according to Law. and the said Proceſsioners are farther Ordered to make and return to this Veſtry at their next Setting after the Last day of March next a true Acco^t. of all the Lands they have Proceſsioned, of the Persons Present at the same, of what Lands they have not Proceſsioned and the Perticular reason of Such failure.

Ord^d. that Samuel Shepard, William Richards & James Pryor or any two of them do meet on the first Wednesday in December next, and go in Proceſsion of and see all and every Persons Land between Mattasip and Pepetico swamps Plainly Marked, Continuing their proceedings in all Suitable Weather untill the whole Precinct be finished, and all the freeholders who are Inhabitants thereof are required to attend the said Proceſsioners according to Law. and and. the said Proceſsioners are farther Ordered to make and return to this Vestry at their next Setting after the Last day of March next a true Acco^t. of all the Lands they have Proceſsioned, of the Persons Present at the same, of what Lands they have not Proceſsioned and the Particular reason of such failure.

Ord^d. that John Foster Nicholas Dillard & Henry Collier or any two of them do meet on the first Fryday in December next and go in Proceſsion of & see all and every Persons Land between Pepetico Swamp & Arracaco Creek & the Eastern branch thereof Plainly Marked, Continuing their Proceedings in all Suitable Weather untill the whole Precinct be finished, and all the freeholders, who [57] who are Inhabitants thereof are required to attend the said Proceſsioners according to Law. and the said Proceſsioners are farther Ordered to make & return to this Veſtry at their next Setting after the Last Day of March next a true Acco^t. of all the Lands they have Proceſsioned, of the Persons Present at the same, of what Lands they have not Proceſsioned and the Particular reason of Such failure.

Ord^d. that Thomas Dillard Thomas Lankford & Roger Field or any two of them do meet on the Second Monday in December next & goe in Proceſsion of and see all and every Persons Land between the Eastern & Western branches of Arracaco Plainly Marked, Continuing their Proceedings in all Suitable Weather untill the whole Precinct be finished, and all the freeholders who are Inhabitants thereof are required to attend the said Proceſsioners according to Law. and the said Proceſsioners are farther Ordered to make and return to this Veſtry at their next Setting after the Last Day of March next, a true Acco^t. of all the Lands they have Proceſsioned, of the Persons Present at the same, of what lands they have not Proceſsioned, and the particular reason of Such failure.

Ord^d. that Edward Trice, James Trice & George Bray or any two of them do meet on the Second Wednesday in December next and goe in Proceſsion of & see all & every Persons Land between Burgises Swamp and the Monack Swamp, and from thence a strait Course between Mary Hollinger and Ann Joyeux's Lands to Tarsatyan Swamp Plainly Marked, Continuing their Proceedings in all Suitable weather untill the whole Precinct be finished, and the freeholders who are Inhabitants thereof are required to attend the said Proceſsioners according to Law. and the said Proceſsioners are farther Ordered to make and return to this Veſtry at their next Setting after the Last Day of March next, a true Acco^t. of all the Land they have Proceſsioned, of the Persons Present at the same, of what Land they have not Proceſsioned, & the Particular reason of Such failure.

Ord^d. that William Hunt, Robert Didlake & Edward Spencer or any two of them do meet on the Third Monday in December next and go in Proceſsion of and see all and every Persons Land between the Monack Swamp (& from thence on a strait Course to Tarsatyan swamp) and the branch next above William Hunts Plainly marked, Continuing their Proceedings in all Suitable weather untill the

whole Precinct be finished, and all the freeholders who are
inhabitants thereof are required to attend the said Proceſsioners According to Law, and the said Proceſsioners are
farther Ordered to make & return to this Veſtry at their
next Setting after the last Day of March next a true Acco^t.
of all the Land they have Proceſsioned, of the Persons
Present at the same, of what land they have not Proceſsioned, & the Particular reason of Such failure ——

[58]
Order'd that Robert Garrett John Leigh & Vincent Vaſs
or any two of them do meet on the Second Fryday in December next and go in Proceſsion of & see all and every
Persons Land between Tarsatyan and great Heartquake
swamps Plainly Marked, Continuing their Proceedings in
all Suitable weather untill the whole Precinct be finished,
and all the Freeholders who are Inhabitants thereof are required to attend the said Proceſsioners according to Law.
and the said Proceſsioners are farther Ordered to make
and return to this Veſtry at their next Setting after the
Last Day of March next a true Acco^t. of all the Land they
have Proceſsioned, of the Persons Present at the same, of
what Land they have not Proceſsioned, & the Particular
reason of Such failure.

Ord^d. That Robert Ware, William Ware, and Spencer
Boyd or any two of them do meet on the third Wednesday
in December next & goe in Proceſsion of & see all and
every Persons Land, between the Branch next above William Hunts and the Extent upwards Plainly marked, Continuing their Proceedings in all Suitable weather untill the
whole Precinct be finished. and all the Freeholders who
are Inhabitants thereof are required to attend the said Proceſsioners according to Law. and the said Proceſsioners are
farther Ordered to make & return to this Vestry at their
next Setting after the last Day of March next a true Acco^t.
of all Lands they have Proceſsioned, of the Persons Present

at the same, of what Land they have not Procefsioned, & the Particular reason of Such failure.

Ord⁴. that Richard Shackelford, John Smith & Richard Wyatt or any two of them do meet on the third Fryday in December next & goe in Procefsion of & see all and every Persons Land between the Western branch of Arracaco & Tarsatyan Swamp Plainly marked. Continuing their Proceedings in all Suitable weather untill the whole Precinct be finished. and all the Inhabitants thereof are required to attend the said Procefsioners according to Law. and the said Procefsioners are farther Ordered to make and return to this Veftry at their next Sitting after the last Day of March next, a true Accoᵗ. of all the Land they have Procefsioned, of the Persons Present at the same, of what Land they have not Procefsioned and the Particular reason of Such failure.

Ord⁴. that the Church wardens do agree with a workman to Build a Corn-House on the Glebe twenty four foot long & twelve foot wide, framed

Ord⁴. that the Collector Pay the Ball. of the Fraction which will remain in his Hands, of the last Parish Levy. to Capt William Taliaferro.

Teft. Wᵐ. Robinson Minʳ.

Truly Re⁴. Franᵉ. Gaines.

[59]

At a Vestry held for Stratton Major Parish at the Uper Church on Monday the 30ᵗʰ. Day of September 1751. to Lay the P. Lev'y

Prefent { The Reverᵈ. William Robinson
John Robinson Esqʳ. William Lyne
John Livingston   Thomas Thorpe
Philip Rootes   Richard Corbin Esqʳ.
William Taliaferro   William Hunt
John Strachey   John Shackelford
.... & John Foster } Vestrymen

The Parish   D^r. lb. Tob°.

To the Rev^d. M^r. William Robinson	16000
To Thomas Lankford Read^r. of the Lower Church	1200
To Ann Clear Sexton of d°. &^c.	750
To Grace Soward Sexton of the Uper Church &^c.	750
To Henry Brown decd. Estate late Read^r. of d°.	700
To Vincent Vaſs Present Read^r. of d°.	400
To Francis Gaines C. V.	700
To William McCarty for keeping his Bro. Charles	800
To John Campbell for keeping Eliza. Brown	500
To George Tureman for keeping his Son John	800
To William Ware for keep Ann Lewis	800
To Benjamin Soward for officiating as Clk two Sundays	100
To Griffith Elrington for the Same	100
To George Meddlicot for one Sunday	50
To John Robinson Esqr for Providing four Times for the Commu.	350
To M^r. John Foster for the Same	350
	24350
To 4 ℔ C^t. on 24350 ^{lb} Tob°. for Cask	974
To M^r. Thomas Thorpe for Goods dld for the Poor by Acco^t. £4‖18‖9¾	791
To M^r. John Foster for the Same ℔ Acco^t. £2‖1‖5 @ 12/6 ℔ C^t.	331
To Mary Brown's Acco^t. 3‖5	520
To Doctor John Strachey's d°. 4‖17‖7	781
To Arthur Pryor's d°. 1‖13‖4	267
To George Bowden for Making two Horse Blocks & Mending one	375
To Thomas Burnett	300
To Jane M^ckendree	400
To Solomon Damm his Acco^t. £1‖2	176

To Tob°. to be sold for the Use of the Parish	8000
To the Clk of this County for two Lists of Tithables	36
	37301
To 6 ⅌ Cᵗ. for Collecting 39600ᶫᵇ. Tob°.	2241
	39542
The Parish Cʳ. By 900 Tithables at 44ᶫᵇ. Tob°. ⅌ Poll	39600ᶫᵇ.

[60]
The Levies being Settled this Present Year are found to amount to 39542ᶫᵇ Tob°. being Levied upon 900 Tithables at 44ᶫᵇ. Tob°. ⅌ Poll & there will remain a fraction of 58ᶫᵇ. Tob°. in the Hands of the Collector.

Philip Rootes & John Livingston is Appointed Church Wardens, and Philip Rootes is Appointed Collector for this Present Year.

Ordᵈ. That William Mᶜ.Carty keep his Bro. Charles the Ensuing Year, and that he have 800ᶫᵇ. Tob°. Levied for the Same at Laying of the next Levies

Ordᵈ. that George Tureman keep his Son John the Ensuing Year, and that he have 800ᶫᵇ. Tob°. Levied for the Same at Laying the next Levies.

Ordᵈ. that Dorothy Wotherspon keep Eliza. Brown the Ensuing Year, and She have 500ᶫᵇ. Tob°. Levied for the same at Laying the next Levies.

Ordᵈ. that the Church-Warden's do agree with some Convenient Person to keep & take Care of Ann Lewis wife of George Lewis the Ensuing Year, & that he bring his Accoᵗ. of the Charge for the same to the Laying of the next Parish Levies

Ord⁴. that Doctor John Strachey Pay the fine in his Hands due to this Parish being 45/. to the Preſent Collector, & that he Accoᵗ. for the Same at Laying of next Levies.

Ord⁴. that Francis Gaines Pay the Money in his Hands which he recd for fines to the Collector, & that the said Collector Accoᵗ. for the same at Laying of the next Parish Levies.

     Test William Robinson Minʳ.

   Truely Register'd Franˢ. Gaines.

At a Vestry held for Stratton Major Paris

[61]

At a Vestry held for Stratton Major Parish at the Lower Church on Fryday the 17ᵗʰ. Day of November 1752 to lay the Parish Lev'y

The Reverᵈ. William Robinson	
Richard Anderson John Strachey	
Preſent John Robinson Esqʳ. William Hunt	Vestrymen
John Livingston & John Shackelford	
William Taliaferro	

  The Parish   Dʳ. Pounds Tobᵒ.

To the Reverend Mʳ. Robinson	16000
To 4 ℔ Cᵗ. on Ditto for Shrinkage	640
To Thomas Lankford Reader of the Lower Church	1200
To Ann Clear Sexton of Ditto & Washing the Surplice	750
To Vincent Vaſs Reader of the Uper Church	1200
To Grace Soward Sexton of Dᵒ. & Washᵍ. the Surplice	750
To Francis Gaines Clk	700
To William Mᶜ.Carty for keeping Charles	800

To George Tureman for keeping his Son John	800
To Dorothy Wotherspon for keeping Eliza. Brown	500
To William Tureman for keeping Ann Lewis	800
To Major Philip Rootes for Providing for the Com: 4 Times	350
To M^r. John Livingston for the Same	350
	24840
To 4 ℔ C^t. on Ditto for Cask	993
To M^r. Thomas Thorpe for Steps at the Uper Church Door	50
To Mary Brown for a Lev'y over Charged last Year	44
To M^r. John Livingston for a Dial Poast &^{c}.	100
To William Cardwell for keeping Ann Lewis 1 Month	67
To Jane Ransom to Buy Corn & meat	400
To Jane M^{c}kendree	400
To Major Richard Tunstall for 2 Lists of Tithables	36
To Thomas Tureman for Keeping Elenor Roney 2 Months	100
To Sarah Gramshill for keeping Mary Mansfield	400
To Tob°. Levied to be Sold for the Use of this Parish	9880
	37310
To 6 ℔ C^t. on 37310^{lb}. Tob°. for Collecting	2238
	39548
C^r. By 899 Tithables at 44^{lb}. Tob°. ℔ Poll	39556

The Levies being settled for this Present Year are found to amount to 39556^{lb}. Tob°. being Levied upon 899 Tithables at 44^lb. Tob°. ℔ Poll and there will be an overplus of 8^lb. Tob°. in the Hands of the Collector.

Richard Anderson & Richard Corbin Esqr. are Appointed Churchwardens and Richard Anderson is Appointed Collector for this Present Year

[62]
Ordered that William McCarty keep his Brother Charles the Ensuing Year, & that he have 800^lb. Tob°. Levied for the same at Laying of the next Levies

Ordered that Mary Brown keep Ann Lewis, wife of George Lewis the Ensuing Year, and that She have 800^lb. Tob°. Levied for the Same at Laying of the next Levies

Order^d. that M^r. John Livingston Pay the Money in his Hands being £1∥13.—for the Ball. of Ann Guthries fine to the Present Collector.

Ordered that the Collector Pay the Rev^d. M^r. Robinson One Pound Six Shillings for an Acco^t. Paid by him to Francis Low.

Ordered that the Collector Pay Doctor John Strachey 7/6 for his Acco^t. for means Admin^d: to the Poor

Order'd that Major Philip Rootes Pay Elizabeth Jackson One Pound two Shillings for her Acco^t. for burying Mollatto Hanah out of the Money in his Hands

Order'd that the Church Wardens Bind James Campbell Mollatto Basterd of Margret Campbell to Richard Guthrie According to Law.

Order'd that Susanna Brownen, be, and do the Office of Sexton of the Lower Church in this Parish.

Order'd the Collector dispose of the Tob°. that is Levied to be Sold, or any part thereof, for Cash at 15/ ℔ C^t. to any Person desirous to Purchase the same

Order'd that the Late Collector Settle an Acco‵. of the Money remaining in his Hands for the Tob°. Sold by him for the Use of this Parish, and that the same be put out, on Interest.

Test William Robinson Min⁣ʳ:

Truly Registered. Franˢ: Gaines Clk

[63]
At a Vestry held for Stratton Major Parish at the Uper Church on Fryday the 5ᵗʰ. Day of October 1753 to Lay the Parish Levy

Preſent
The Revᵈ William Robinson
Richard Anderson William Lyne
John Robinson Esqʳ. Thomas Thorpe
William Taliaferro Richard Corbin Esqʳ.
John Strachey & William Hunt
} Vestrymen

1753.

	Dʳ lb. Tob°.
The Parish	
To the Revᵈ. Mʳ. Robinson	16000
To ditto for Shrinkage of Notes to make Nett Tob°. 4 ℔ Cᵗ.	640
To Thomas Lankford Reader of the Lower Church	1200
To Vincent Vaſs Reader of the Uper Church	716
To Grace Soward Sexto of d°. & for Washing the Surplice	750
To Susanna Brownen Sexton of the Lower Church & the Same	750
To Francis Gaines Clk V.	700
To Griffith Elrington for Officiating as Clk in the absence of Vincent Vaſs from the 15ᵗʰ. April till the 9ᵗʰ. Day of 7ber 22 Sundays	484
To William MᶜCarty for keeping his Brother Charles	800
To William Cardwell for keeping Ann Lewis	800

To the Hon: Richard Corbin Esq'. for Providing for the Ch: 4 Times	350
To Richard Anderson for the Same	350
	23540
To 4 ℔ C'. on 23540ˡᵇ. Tobº. for Cask	941
To Mʳ. Thoˢ. Thorpes Accoᵗ. for Sundries dld for the Poor £4‖9‖6¾ @ 12/6	717
To Doctʳ. John Strachey for his Accoᵗ. for Medicines for Dº. 3‖19‖4 @ dº	635
To Jane Ransom to buy her Corn &ᶜ.	400
To Abraham Basket for keeping a Basterd Child 750 & Cask	780
To Dorothy Wotherspon for keeping Eliza. Brown	300
To ditto for a ℔ʳ Shoes & Stockins for Ditto	48
To Sarah Gramshill on Accoᵗ. of Mary Mansfield	250
To Richard Wyatts Accoᵗ. for Mending the Windows of the Lowʳ. Ch: £ 1‖	160
To Capt Wᵐ. Lyne's Accoᵗ. for Sundries to the poor & Glaſs for the Glebe W. 44/3	354
To Major Richard Tunstall for Copys 2 Lists Tithables	36
To Jane Mᶜkendree	400
To Tobº. to be Sold for the Use of this Parish	20000
	48561
To 6 ℔ C'. on 48561ˡᵇ. Tobº. for the Collector	2913
	51474

The Parish	Cʳ.
By 916 Tithables at 56ˡᵇ. Tobº. ℔ Poll	51296
By Ball. due to the Collector	178
	51474

[64]

The Levies being Settled this Present Year are found to amount to 51474^{lb}. Pounds of Tob°. being Levied upon 916 Tithables, at 56^{lb}. Tob°. Per Poll and there will remain a fraction due to the Collector of 178^{lb} which he is to retain out of the Tob°. Levied to be Sold for the Use of the Parish.

William Taliaferro & William Hunt are Appointed Church Wardens and William Taliaferro is Appointed Collector for this Present Year, whereupon William Hunt became his Security & they Acknowledged their Bond for the Same

Ord^d. that W^m. McCarty keep his Brother Charles the Ensuing Year, & that he have Eight hundred Pounds of Tob°. Levied for the same at Laying the next Levies

Ord^d. that Mary Brown Widow, keep Ann Lewis the Ensuing Year & that she have Eight hundred Pounds of Tob°. Levied for the same at Laying the next Parish Levies.

Ord^d. that the said Mary Brown Also keep Eliza. Jackson an Infant at the rate of 50^{lb}. Tob°. ℔ Month untill She is other ways Provided for

Ord^d. that Eliza Overstreet keep Eliza. Brown the Ensu.g year & that she have 300^{lb}. Tob°. Levied for the same at laying of the next Levies

Ord^d. the Collector dispose of the Tob°. which is Levied to be sold for the Use of the Parish or any Part thereof for Cash at 13/. ℔ C^t

Ord^d. that the Late Collector Pay the Money remaining in his Hands for the Tob°. sold by him for the Use of this Parish to the Present Collector

Ord^d. that the Collector Pay the Rev^d. M^r. Robinson £20. out of the Money which he is to receive of the Late Collector. to Pay for the building a Corn House on the Glebe

Test W^m. Robinson Min^r.

Registered ⅌ Fran^s. Gaines Clk.

At a Vestry held for Stratton Major Parish at the Lower Church on Fryday the 1st. Day of February 1754.

Preſent
The Rev^d. William Robinson	
Richard Anderson	William Lyne
John Robinson Esqr.	Thomas Thorpe
John Livingston	The Hon: Rich^d. Corbin Esqr.
Philip Rootes	William Hunt
William Taliaferro	John Shackelford
John Strachey	& John Foster

} Vestrymen

It is Ordered and Appointed by this Vestry that Joseph Addams do the Office of Sexton at this Church, in the Place of Susanna Brownen

Test
W^m. Robinson Min^r.

Registerd by
Fran^s. Gaines

[65]

At a Vestry held for Stratton Major Parish at the Uper Church on Monday the 7th. Day of October 1754. to lay the Parish Lev'y

Preſent
The Rev^d. William Robinson	
Richard Anderson	William Lyne
John Robinson Esqr.	Thomas Thorpe
John Livingston	William Hunt
Philip Rootes	John Shackelford
William Taliaferro &	John Foster
John Strachey	....

} Vestrymen

The Parish	Dr. lb. Tobo.
To the Revd. William Robinson	16000
To do. for Shrinkage of Notes 4 ℔ Ct.	640
To Thomas Lankfordr Readr. of the Lower Church	1200
To Vincent Vaſs Reader of the Uper Church	1200
To Grace Soward Sexton of Ditto & for Washing the Surplice	750
To Joseph Adams Sexton of the Lower Church & the same 2/3 of a Year	500
To Susanna Brownen for being Sexton of do. 1/3 of the Year	250
To Francis Gaines C V.	700
To William M.cCarty for Keeping his Brother Charles	800
To Mary Brown for keeping Ann Lewis 5 Months at 67lb.	330
To ditto for keeping Elizabeth Jackson 12 Months at 50lb.	600
To Elizabeth Overstreet for keeping Elizabeth Brown	300
To Capt. William Taliaferro for Providing four Times for the Commu:	350
To William Hunt for the Same	350
	23970
To 4 ℔ Ct. on Ditto for Cask	959
To Smith South for removing Ann Lewis to Mary Browns.	50
To Major Richard Tunstall for Copys of the Lists Tithables	36
To George Pigg for a Horse block at the Lower Church	150
To George Collier for keeping two Children of Jno. Guthrie jurs:	875
To William Brushwood for keeping Jane Mdkendree	400

To Capt. William Lyne for his Acco'. of Sundrey Goods dld. to the Poor of this Parish £ 8‖1‖1 Levied in Tob°. at 12/6. ℔ C'.	1289
To Doctor John Strachey for Medicines Administer'd to Ann Lewis & Jane Bradshaw £2‖2‖8, as above	341
To William Hunts Acco'. for Corn to the Widow Stevens and Cording the Church Windows £1‖6‖	208
To Thomas Shipton for Work done to the Glebe House £2‖3‖6	348
To Mary Brown for a Sheet &c. to Bury Ann Lewis 11/6	92
To Capt William Taliaferro for Paid a Woman for Attending Jane Bradshaw 9/.	72
To William M°Carty 1 ℔' Shoes found his Brother Charles 5/.	40
To Tob°. Levied for the Use of this Parish to be Sold by the Collector	10000
	38830
To 6 ℔ C'. on Ditto for the Collector	2330
	41160
C'. By 921. Tithables at 45¹ᵇ. Tob°. ℔ Poll	41445

[66]
The Levies being settled for this Present Year are found to amount to 41445¹ᵇ. of Tob°. being Levied upon 921. Tithables at 45¹ᵇ. of Tob°. ℔ Poll and there will be an Overplus of 285¹ᵇ. Tob°. remaining in the Collectors Hands, which is Ordered to be Sold for the Use of the Parish.

Thomas Thorpe & John Shackelford are Appointed Church-Wardens, and Tho'. Thorpe is Appointed Collector for this Present Year, whereupon John Shackelford became

Security & they have Acknowlidged their Bond for the Same

Order'd that William M.ᶜCarty keep his Brother Charles the Ensuing Year and that he have Eight hundred Pounds of Tob°. Levied for the same at laying of the next Parish Levies.

Order'd that Elizabeth Overstreet Keep Elizabeth Brown the Ensuing Year and that she have four hundred Pounds of Tob°. Levied for the same at laying of the next Parish Levies.

Order'd that William Brushwood keep Jane Mᶜkendree the Ensuing Year and that he have Eight hundred Pounds of Tob°. Levied for the same at laying of the next Parish Levies.

Order'd that Mary Brown keep Elizabeth Jackson the Ensuing Year & that she have Six hundred Pounds of Tob°. levied for the same at laying of the next Parish Levies.

Order'd that the Church Wardens agree with some Peron to take Care of Barbary Stevens a Widow in this Parish.

Order'd that the late Collector Pay the Money remaining in his Hands for the Tob°. Sold for the Use of this Parish to the Present Collector.

Order'd that the Collector dispose of the Tob°. that is Levied to be sold for the Use of this Parish, or any Part thereof for Cash at 12/6. ℔ hundred.

     Test Wᵐ. Robinson
    Franˢ. Gaines

[67]

At a Vestry held for Stratton Major Parish at the Glebe on Thursday the 10ᵗʰ. Day of July 1755. To Appoint Proceſsioners

The Rever__d__. William Robinson

Preſent William Taliaferro ⎫   Thomas Thorpe ⎫
       John Strachey   ⎬   William Hunt   ⎬ Vestrymen
       William Lyne   ⎭   & John Shackelford ⎭

Pursuant to an Order of King & Queen County Court Dated the 12th. Day of June 1755. That the Vestrys of the Several Parishes within this County do divide their Parishes into so many Precincts as to them shall seem most convenient, for Proceſsioning Every Persons Land therein, and to Appoint the Particular Times for that Purpose between the last Day of September and the last Day of March next ensuing. Pursuant to an Act of Aſsembly in that Case made and Provided.

Ordered that George Pigg John Shackelford and George Sowell or any two of them do meet on the first Monday in December next & go in Proceſsion of and see all the Lands between Portopotank Creek and Matasip Swamp plainly marked, Continuing their Proceedings in all Suitable weather till the whole Precinct be finished, and all the Freeholders who are inhabitants thereof are required to Attend the said Proceſsioners according to Law. And the said Proceſsioners are further Ordered to make and return to this Vestry at their next Sitting after the last Day of March next, a true Acco^{t}. of all Lands they have Proceſsioned, of the Persons Present at the same, of what Land they have not Proceſsioned, and the Particular reason of such failure.

Order'd that James Pryor, William Collier & Christopher Pryor or any two of them do meet on the first Wednesday in December next, and go in Proceſsion of and see all the Lands between Matasip swamp & Pepetico swamp Plainly Marked. &^{c}.

Order'd that Nicholas Dillard, Henry Collier & James Collier or any two of them do meet on the first Fryday in

December next and go in Procefsion of & see all the Lands between Pepetico swamp & Arracaco Creek & the Eastern branch thereof Plainly Marked. &ᶜ.

Order'd that Thomas Dillard James Didlake & Robert Garland or any two of them do meet on the Second Monday in December next and go in Procefsion of & see all the Lands between the Eastern & Western branches of Arracaco Creek Plainly Marked Continuing their Proceedings &ᶜ. ——

[68]
Order'd that Richard Shackelford John Smith & Richard Wiattt or any two of them do meet on the third Fryday in December next & go in Procefsion of & see all the Lands between the Western branch for Arracaco Creek & Tarsatyan Swamp Plainly Marked &ᶜ.

Order'd that Edward Trice James Trice & George Bray or any two of them do meet on the Second Wednesday in December next and go in Procefsion of & see all the Lands between Burgefes Swamp & the Monack Swamp, and from thence a strait Course between Mary Hollinger & Doctor John Joyeaux decd, to Tarsatyan Swamp Plainly Marked &ᶜ. ——

Order'd that William Hunt Edward Spencer & Richard Garrett or any two of them do meet on the third Monday in December Next and go in Procefsion of & see all the Lands between the Monack Swamp and on a Strait Course to Tarsatyan Swamp as before Mentioned, and the branch next above William Hunts Plainly Marked Continuing their Proceedings &ᶜ. ——

Order'd that Spencer Boyd Arthur Ware & John Cardwell or any two of them do meet on the third Wednesday in December Next & go in Procefsion of & see all the Lands between the Branch next above William Hunts & the Extent upwards of this Parish Plainly Marked Continuing their Proceedings &ᶜ. ──

Order'd that Robert Garrett John Leigh & Richard Garrett or any two of them do meet on the Second Fryday in December next and go in Proceſsion of & see all the Lands between Tarsatyan Swamp & great Heartquake Swamp Plainly Marked, Continuing their Proceedings in all Suitable Weather till the Whole Precinct be finished, and all the Freeholders who are inhabitants thereof are required to attend the said Proceſsioners according to Law. And the Said Proceſsioners are further Order'd to Make and return to this Vestry at their next Sitting after the last Day of March next, a True Accoᵗ. of all the Lands they have Proceſsioned of the Persons Present at the same, of what Lands they have not Proceſsioned and the Particular reason of such failure

       Test.
         Wᵐ. Robinson
  Truely Registered.
         Franˢ. Gaines

*At a Vestry held for Stratton Major Parish at the Glebe on Satturday the 26ᵗʰ. Day of July 1755.

Present
 The Revᵈ. William Robinson
 John Robinson Esqʳ. Thomas Thorpe
 Willᵐ. Taliaferro William Hunt ⎫Vestrymen
 John Strachey & John Shackelford
 William Lyne

[69]
At a Vestry held for Stratton Major Parish at the Upper Church on Fryday the 26ᵗʰ. Day of September 1755.

---

*This whole entry, down through the last name in the list of vestrymen, has been scratched through with a pen, but is still plainly legible. —C. G. C.

The Rev{make}^d^. William Robinson
Richard Anderson   John Strachey
John Robinson Esqr.   William Lyne
Present John Livingston   Thomas Thorpe   }Vestrymen
                          The Honble. Rich^d^.
Philip Rotes   Corbin Esqr.
William Taliaferro & John Shackelford

The Parish	D^r^. lb. Tob^o^
To the Rev^d^. William Robinson	16000
To Ditto for Shrinkage of Notes 4 ℔ C^t^.	640
To Thomas Lankford reader of the Lower Church	1200
To Vincent Vaſs late reader of the Uper Church Eight Months & half	850
To Griffith Elrington Present reader of the same three Mo: & a half	350
To Grace Soward Sexton of the Uper Church & for Washing the Surplice	750
To Joseph Adams Sexton of the Lower Church & the same	750
To Francis Gaines Clerk of the Vestry	1000
To William M^c^.Carty for keeping his brother Charles	800
To Elizabeth Overstreet for keeping Elizabeth Brown	400
To William Brushwood for keeping Jane M^c^kendree	800
To Mary Brown for keeping Elizabeth Jackson	600
To Thomas Thorpe for Providing for the Church four times	350
To John Shackelford for the Same	350
To Abram Basket for keeping a B. Child	750
To George Collier for keeping Jno. Guthrie j^rs^. two Children	1500
	27090

To 4 ℔ Cᵗ. on Ditto for Cask	1084
To the Clerk of this County for 2 Lists Tithables	36
	28210
To Salary for Collecting 30208ᵗᵇ. Tobᵒ. at 6 ℔ Cᵗ.	1812
	30022
Cʳ. By 944 Tithables at 32ᵗᵇ. Tobᵒ. ℔ Poll	30208

The Levies being Settled for this Present Year are found to amount to 30208ᵗᵇ. Tobᵒ. being levied upon 944 Tithables at 32ᵗᵇ. Tobᵒ. ℔ Poll, and there will remain a fraction of 186ᵗᵇ. Tobᵒ. in the Hands of the Collector, and it is Ordered that he Account for the Same at Laying of the next Parish Levies.

John Strachey & William Lyne are appointed Church Wardens, *and for the Ensuing Year, and William Lyne is appointed Collector for this Present Year, whereupon John Strachey became his Security and they Acknowledged their Bond for the Same

Order'd that the Collector Pay Capt Wᵐ. Lyne £1‖6‖7¾ for his Accoᵗ. for Goods delivered for the Poor.

[70]
Order'd that the Collector pay Thomas Lankford £2‖ for Corn dld Mary Roff

Order'd that the Collector Receive Five Shillings of Mʳ. John Shackelford for a Ball. of Ann Loes fine due from him to the Parish —

On the Petition of Richard Wiatt it is agreed by this Vestry that a Negro Woman Named Venus beloning to

---

*This word scratched through in the MS. but still legible.—C. G. C.

the said Wiatt, being blind may be Exempted from Paying any more Parish Levies

Order'd that William M͏ᶜCarty keep his Brother Charles the Ensuing Year & that he have Eight hundred Pounds of Tobᵒ. Levied for the same at the laying of the Next Parish Levies. ——

Order'd that Elizabeth Overstreet keep Elizabeth Brown the Ensuing year & that she have four hundred Pounds of Tobᵒ. levied for the same at laying of the Next Parish Levies ——

Order'd that the Church Wardens do agree with some Convenient Person to take Care of and Provide for Jane M͏ᶜkendree the Ensuing Year, & that an Accoᵗ. for the same be brought to the laying of the Next Parish Levies —

Order'd that the Collector Pay Mary Brown Thirty Shillings Value in Goods for to Cloath Elizabeth Jackson

Order'd that Abram Basket keep the Child which he now has in Care the Ensuing Year and that he have Five hundred Pounds of Tobᵒ. Levied for the same at laying of the next Parish Levies —

Order'd that the Church Wardens agree with a Person to keep the two Children of John Guthrie juʳˢ. (which are now in the Care of George Collier) the Ensuing Year, and that an Accoᵗ. for the same be brought to the laying of the Next Parish Levies ——

Order'd the Collector Pay Doctor Strachey £2‖9‖9 for Sundry Medicines for Job Jackson &ᶜ.

Order'd that a Poarch be built to the Glebe House nine feet Square, Sett on Brick Pillows, and to be Compleated According to the Directions of the Church wardens a Window up Stairs to be made new, all the Plastering that is Wanting to be Mended, & the House Whitewashed.

Order'd that a Garden be Built at the Glebe in the same Place and of the same Size of the Garden formerly built, with good Poasts Hewed out of White Oak or Chesnut, the Rails to be hewed out of the Heart of Pine, with Pails Rived out of Pine & Drawn five & half feet long, and three Quarters of an Inch thick Nailed on with 10^d & 8^d Nails and the Rails Nailed on the Poasts with 20^d Nails, & the said Work be let as soon as Conveniently may, by the Church Wardens —

Order'd that the Quarter at the Glebe be Covered, & the Cover Nailed on with 20^d Nails

Order'd that the late Collectors Pay the Money in their Respective Hands due to this Parish to the Present Collectors, & that he receive the same and Dispose of it to any Person on Interest with Bond & Security.

Test W^m. Robinson Min^r.

Register'd by.
Fran^s. Gaines

[71]
At a Vestry held for Stratton Major Parish at the Lower Church on Tuesday the 24th. Day of August 1756.

Present
The Rev^d. William Robinson
John Livingston   William Hunt
William Taliaferro   John Shackelford
William Lyne   &   John Foster
} Vestrymen

George Pigg, John Shackelford & George Sowell Proceſsioners return'd a report of their Proceedings in Writing which is Order'd to be Recorded. ——

James Pryor Christopher Pryor & William Collier Proceſsioners return'd a report of their Proceedings in Writing which is Order'd to be recorded

Nicholas Dillard Henry Collier & James Collier Proceſsioners return'd a report of their Proceedings in Writing which is Order'd to be recorded ——

Thomas Dillard James Didlake & Robert Garland Proceſsioners return'd a report of their Proceedings which is Order'd to be recorded ——

Richard Shackelford, John Smith & Richard Wyatt Proceſsioners return'd a report of their Proceedings in Writing which is Order'd to be recorded

Edward Trice James Trice & George Bray Proceſsioners return'd a report of their Proceedings in Writing which is Order'd to be Recorded

William Hunt & Edward Spencer Proceſsioners return'd a report of their Proceedings in Writing which is Order'd to be recorded

Spencer Boyd Arthur Ware & John Cardwell Proceſsioners return'd a report of their Proceedings in Writing which is Order'd to be recorded

Robert Garrett & Richard Garrett Proceſsioners return'd a report of their Proceedings in Writing which is Order'd to be recorded

     Test W^m. Robinson Min^r.
   Registered by
     Fran^s. Gaines

[72]

At a Vestry held for Stratton Major Parish at the Upper Church on Fryday the 19th. Day of November 1756—

Preſent
- The Rev^d. William Robinson
- John Robinson Esqr.
- Thomas Thorpe
- The Hon: Richd Corbin Esqr.
- John Livingston
- William Taliaferro & John Foster
- William Lyne

} Vestrymen

The Parish is	Dr. lbs. Tobo.
To the Reverend William Robinson	16000
To do. for Shrinkage of Notes 4 ℔ Ct.	640
To Thomas Lankford reader of the Lower Church	1200
To Griffith Ellrington reader. of the Uper Church	1200
To Grace Soward Sexton of Do. & for Washing the Surplice	750
To Joseph Adams Sexton of the Lower Church & for the same	750
To Francis Gaines Clk of the Vestry	700
To William Mc.Carty for keeping his Brother Charles	800
To Elizabeth Overstreet for keeping Elizabeth Brown	400
To William Brushwood for keeping Jane Mckendree	1000
To Abram Basket for keeping a B. Child	500
⎰ To William Walding for keeping Major the Son of John Guthrie jr.	550
*⎱ To Mary Gardner for keeping Ann Daughter of the sd. Guthrie	550
To Sarah Gramshill for keeping Chrisn. Grindleys B. Child to this Day	183
To John Osburn for keeping Mary Cannons B. Child 4. Months	183
To Ditto for a Coffin & burying the said Child	50
To Ditto for keeping Chris. Grindleys B. Child 3 Months	125
To John Stracheys Exors for Providing for the Com: 3 Times	263
To William Lyne for the Same 5 Times	437
	26281

*Note!—On the left hand margin of the page opposite the two bracketed entries occur these words: "Both W. Walding."—C. G. C.

To 4 ℔ C⁺. on D°. for Cask	1051
To the Clk of this County for Cop'y two Lists Tithables	36
To John Livingston for a horse Block at the Lower Church	100
To Spencer Boyd for 2 Levies over paid in the year 1750	60
To William Brushwood for keeping Jane Mᶜkendree 1 Mo: & 9 Days	100
	27628
To Salary for Collecting 29326¹ᵇ. Tob°. at 6 ℔ C⁺.	1759
	29387

The Parish	Cʳ.	
By 946 Tithables at 31¹ᵇ. Tob°. ℔ Pole		29326
By Ball. due from William Lyne late Collector		26
		29352
Due to the Collector		35
		29387

[73]
The Levy being Settled for this Present Year are found to amount to 29387¹ᵇ Tob°. being Levied upon 946 Tithables at 31¹ᵇ. of Tob°. ℔ Poll, & there will remain a fraction due to the Collector of 35¹ᵇ. Tob°. which is to be Accounted for at Laying of the Next Parish Levy

John Robinson Esqʳ. & John Foster is Appointed Church Wardens for the Ensuing year & John Foster is Appointed Collector for this Present year, Whereupon John Robinson Esqʳ. became his Security & they have Acknowledged their Bond for the same.

Order'd that the Collector Pay M.ʳ John Livingston Six Pounds for his Account for Steps at the Lower Church, out of the Money to be received by him of the late Collectors.

Order'd that the Collector Pay Solomon Damm One Pound for his Account for Burying Job Jackson out of the said Money to be received of the Late Collectors ———

Order'd that the Collector Pay Richard Wiatt Seven Pounds for his Account for Work done at the Glebe

Order'd that the Collector Pay Hugh Livingston Fifteen Shillings for his Account for Work done at the Glebe

Order'd that the Collector Pay William Lyne Nine Pounds Ten shillings 8½ᵈ for Ballance of his Account for Corn & Cloathing delivered for the poor.

Order'd that William M.ᶜCarty keep his Brother Charles the Ensuing Year & that he have 800ˡᵇ. Tob°. Levied for the same at Laying the Next Parish Levies.

Order'd that Abram Basket keep the Child he now has in his Care the Ensuing Year, & that he have 550ˡᵇ Tob°. Levied for the same at Laying the Next Parish Lev'y

Order'd that Elizabeth Didlake keep Major Guthrie the Child Which she now has in Care the Ensuing Year & that she have Five hundred & fifty Pounds of Tob°. Levied for the same at Laying the next Parish Lev'ys ———

Order'd that Mary Gardner keep Ann Guthrie the Child she now has in Care the Ensuing Year, & that she have five hundred & fifty Pounds of Tob°. Levied for the same at Laying the Next Parish Lev'ys ———

Order'd that the Church wardens agree with some Convenient Person to keep and take Care of Jane Mᶜkendree and Elizabeth Brown the Ensuing Year and that an Acco.ᵗ for the same be brought to the Laying of the Next Parish Lev'y

It is agree'd that Application be made to the Aſsembly by this Vestry that a Bill may be paſsed for Selling the Glebe Land in this Parish

Richard Shackelford is Appointed a Vestryman in the Place of Rich^d. Anderson decd.

Philip Rootes is Appointed a Vestryman in the Place of Philip Rootes decd.

William Collior is Appointed a Vestryman in the Place of Jn°. Strachey decd.

[74]
By the Petition of Robert Dudley, It is agree'd by this Vestry that Sambo a Negro fellow belonging to the Orphans of Robert Dudley decd. be Exempted from Paying any more Levies in this Parish

W^m. Robinson Min^r.

Register'd by Fran^s. Gaines

At a Vestry held for Stratton Major Parish at the Upper Church on Fryday the 4th Day of March 1757.

The Rev^d. William Robinson
John Robinson Esqr. ....
Present John Livingston   Thomas Thorpe   Vestrymen
     William Taliaferro   The Hon^{le}. Rich^d.
                           Corbin Esqr.
     William Lyne   &   John Foster

The Petition to the Aſsembly for the Paſsing an Act for Selling the Glebe Land in this Parish was Presented to this Vestry & read, Agree'd to & Signed by the Minister and Vestrymen Present, And it is Order'd the same be delivered to the Burgeſses of this County in Order to be presented to the next Aſsembly.

W^m. Robinson Rector

Register'd by Fran^s. Gaines

At a Vestry held for Stratton Major Parish at the Upper Church on Fryday the 8th. Day of July 1757.

The Rev^d. William Robinson

Preſent John Robinson Esqr. The Hon^{le}. Richard Corbin Esqr.
John Livingston   William Hunt
William Taliaferro   Richard Shackelford   } Vestrymen
William Lyne   &   William Collier

In Pursuance of an Act Obtained the last Seſsion of Aſsembly the Vestry have Come to the following Agreement with the Reverend M^r. Robinson about the Purchase of the Glebe, that is, that the Vestry Shall Convey the said Glebe to the Said William Robinson & his Heirs, and in Consideration thereof, that the Said William Robinson Shall Pay the Sum of Four hundred & thirty Pounds Curr^t. Money and Covenant with the said Vestry that he shall make no Demand of a Glebe, nor of any Satisfaction in Lieu thereof so long as he shall Continue Minister of this Parish, and Accordingly the Vestrymen here Present have Executed a Deed of Bargain & Sale for the said Glebe, with the Appurtenances to the said William Robinson, Who with Frances Gaines his Security Enter'd into Bond for the Payment of the Said Sum of Four hundred & Thirty Pounds to the said Vestry.

W^m. Robinson Min^r.

Registerd, by Fran^s. Gaines

[75]
At a Vestry held for Stratton Major Parish at the Lower Church on Wednesday the 16th. Day of November 1757.

Present
The Revd. William Robinson
John Livingston   Thomas Thorpe
William Taliaferro   William Hunt   } Vestrymen
William Lyne   &   John Foster

The Parish is   Dr. lb. Tobo

To the Revd. William Robinson	16000
To do. for shrinkage of Notes	640
To Griffith Elrington Reader of the Uper Church	1200
To Grace Soward Sexton of Do. & Washing the Surplice	750
To Christopher Pryor Reader of the Lower Church	1200
To Joseph Adams Sexton of do. & Washing the Surplice	750
To Francis Gaines Clk of the Vestry	700
To William Macarty for keeping his Brother Chas. Mc.Carty	800
To Abram Basket for keeping a Bastd. Child Thos. Barram	550
To Elizabeth Didlake for keeping Major Guthrie	550
To Mary Gardner for keeping Ann Guthrie	550
To Sarah Gramshill for keeping Chris. Grindleys B. Child	550
To Elizabeth Overstreet for keeping Jane Mckendree Wife of D. Mckendree	1000
To Mary Hollinger for keeping Elizabeth Brown	400
To John Robinson Esqr. for Providing 4 Times for the Com:	350
To John Foster for the same	350
	26340

To 4℘ C^{t}. for Cask on 26340^{lb}. Tob^{o}.	1053
To Col^{o}. Richard Tunstall for Cop'ys 2 Lists Tithables	36
To John Foster late Collector for a Fraction to make up the last y^{r}. Levy	35
To d^{o}. for 3 Levies not recd. of People who are Moved &c.	93
To Robert Minion for keeping Elizabeth Burnet one Month	83
To Mary Gardner for Keeping Ann Guthrie one Month Omitted	46
To Jane Didlake for Major Guthrie the same	46
	27732
To Salary for Collecting 30304^{lb}. Tob^{o}. at 6 ℘ C^{t}.	1818
To Ballance due to the Parish to be Accounted for by the Collector	754
	30304

The Parish C^{r}.	
By 947 Tithables at 32^{lb}. Tob^{o}. ℘ Pol amount to	30304

[76]

The Levies being settled this Present Year are found to amount to 30304^{lb}. of Tob^{o}. being Levied upon 947 Tithables at 32^{lb}. Tob^{o}. ℘ Pole which is order'd to be received of Every Tithable Person within the List for this Present year, & there will remain an Overplus due to the Parish 754^{lb}. Tob^{o}. to be Accounted for by the Collector at Laying the Next Parish Levy.

We Richard Shackelford & William Collier do declare that we & each of us do agree to be Conformable to the

Doctrine & decipline of the Church of England as by Law Established.

Rich^d. Shackelford
W^m. Collier

Richard Sackelford & William Collier having the Oaths appointed by Act of Parliment & Subscribed to the above Declaration are Admitted as Vestrymen for this Parish. Present Richd Shackelford & W^m. Collier Vest.

Richard Shackelford & William Collier are Appointed Churchwardens for the Ensuing Year. & Richard Shackelford is Appointed Collector for this Present year. Whereupon William Collier became his Security, & they have enter'd into & Acknowledged their Bond for the Same.

Order'd that the Collector Pay Robt. Garrett his Acco^t. for Corn & meet for Martha Coats	£ 3‖4‖—
Order'd that the Collector Pay William Lyne his Acco^t. for Sundrey Goods delivered for the Poor of the Parish	£ 14‖4‖ 4
Order'd that the Collector Pay John Metcalfe his Acco^t. for Sundrey Goods delivered for James Brook's	1‖7‖11
Order'd that the Collector Pay Jane Didlake for 2 yds Virg^a. Cloth Used for Maj^r. Guthrie a Child she has the Care of	‖4‖—
Ord^d. that the Collector Pay Ben. Williams for Making a Wescoat & Breches for Charles M^c.Carty	‖6‖—
Ord^d. That the Collector Pay Mary Hollinger for her Acco^t. for Shoes & Stockings for Elizabeth Brown	‖5‖—

Order'd that the Collector Pay Abram Basket
for Shoes & Stockings found for Tho⁸. Barram
a Child in his Care ‖4‖—

Ordᵈ. that the Collectʳ. Pay Chaˢ. Roane for
getting wood for Mary Roffe ‖6‖—

Ordᵈ. that the Collectʳ. Pay Wᵐ. MᶜCarty for
1 ℔ʳ. Shoes for his Bro: Charles ‖5‖—

Ordᵈ. that the Collectʳ. Pay Elias Wells for
one Barrell Corn for Elizᵃ. Burnett ‖6‖—

Ordᵈ. that William Mᶜ.Carty keep his Brother Charles the Ensuing Year, & that he have 800ˡᵇ. Tobᵒ. Levied for the Same at laying the next Parish Levy

Ordᵈ. that Abram Basket keep Thomas Barram the Ensuing Year, & that he the said Abram be Paid Forty Shillings for the same at laying the next Parish Lev'y, and on his giving Bond & Security to the Churchwardens, to keep the said Thomas Barram free from being any Expence to this Parish, it's Order'd that the Said Churchwardens Make Indentures & Bind him to the said Abram Basket According to Law

[77]
Ordered that Thomas Brushwood Keep Jane Mᶜkendree the Ensuing year & that he have One Thousand Pounds of Tobᵒ. Levied for the same at laying the Next Lev'y.

Ordᵈ. that Mary Hollinger keep Elizabeth Brown the Ensuing Year & that she have 400ˡᵇ. Tobᵒ. Levied for the same at laying the Next Lev'y

Order'd that Richard Guthrie keep Major Guthrie & ann Guthrie Children of John Guthrie jʳ. the Ensuing year, & that he have 1000ˡᵇ. Tobᵒ. Levied at Laying the Next Parish Levies, and on the said Guthries giving Bond & Security to the Churchwardens to keep the said Children free from being any more Expence to this Parish, its Order'd that the Churchwardens Make Indentures & Bind the Said Major & Ann Guthrie unto the Said Richard Guthrie According Law.

Ord^d. that Richard Eubank Keep John Green the Ensuing Year & that he have 600^{lb}. Tob^o. Levied for the same at laying the Next Lev'y

Order'd that Amey Adams be Sexton at the Lower Church, & that she Keep Ann Morrise Daughter of John Morrise decd. the Ensuing Year & that she have 750^{lb}. Tob^o. Levied for the same at laying the Next Lev'y

Ord^d. that Susanna Brownen keep Elizabeth Burnet the Ensuing Year & that She have 1000^{lb}. Tob^o. Levied for the same at laying the Next Lev'y

Ord^d. that the Church wardens of this Parish make Indentures & Bind George Davenport a Mulatto Baster'd of Ann Davenport unto Mary Strachey as Guardian to her son Henry Strachey According to Law.

Ord^d. that the said Church wardens make Indentures & bind Thomas Davenport Mulatto Basterd of Ann Davenport unto Thomas Metcalfe According to Law. ———

Ord^d. that the Church wardens agree with some Person to take Sally Morrise Daughter of John Morrise decd. and on the said Person's giving Bond & Security to keep the said Sally Morrise off this Parish, its Ordered that the said Church wardens make Indentures & Bind the said Sally Morrise to any such person According to Law. & are hereby impowered to Allow them 1000^{lb}. Tob^o. to be Levied at Laying the next Parish Lev'y

It is agreed by this Vestry that Joseph Simco be Exempted from paying any more Levies in this Parish.

Ord⁴. that Sarah Gramshill keep the Child of Chris. Grindleys which she now hath in Care the Ensuing year & that she have 550ˡᵇ. Tob°. Levied for the same at Laying the Next Parish Lev'y.

Wᵐ. Robinson Rector

Truly Register'd.
Franˢ. Gaines Clk

[78]
At a Vestry held for Stratton Major Parish at the Upper Church on Tuesday the 21ˢᵗ. Day of November 1758.

Present Vestrymen:
The Revᵈ. William Robinson
John Robinson Esqʳ.
William Taliaferro
William Lyne
Thomas Thorpe
The Honᵇˡᵉ. Richᵈ. Corbin Esqʳ.
William Hunt
John Foster
Richard Shackelford
William Collier

The Parish is	Dʳ. lbs Tob°.
To the Revᵈ. William Robinson	16000
To ditto for Shrinkage	640
To Griffith Elrington readʳ. of the Uper Church	1200
To Christopher Pryor readʳ. of the Lower Church	1200
To Grace Soward Sexton of the Uper Church &c.	750
To Amey Adams Sexton of the Lower Church &c.	750
To Francis Gaines Clk. V.	700
To the Adminʳˣ. of Wᵐ. M°Carty decd for keeping Chaˢ: M°Carty	800
To Thomas Brushwood for Keeping Jane M°kendree	1000
To Mary Hollinger for keeping Elizabeth Brown	400
To Richard Guthrie for keeping Major & Ann Guthrie	1000

To Richard Eubank for keeping John Green	600
To Amey Adams for keeping Ann Morrise	750
To Susanna Brownen for keeping Elizᵃ: Burnett	83
To William Richards for keeping Sally Morrise &ᶜ.	1000
To Richard Shackelford for finding for the Church 4 Times	360
To William Collier for the Same	360
To Sarah Gramshill for keeping Chris. Grindleys Child	550
To Walter Rhymer for keeping Said Grindleys youngʳ. Child	625
	28768
To 4 ⅌ Cᵗ. on Ditto for Cask	1150
To Richard Shackelford Ball. of Accoᵗ. for Delinquents	128
To the Clerk of this County for Cop'y 2 Lists Tithables	36
To 6 ⅌ Cᵗ. on 30082ˡᵇ. Tobᵒ. for Collecting	1805
	31887

The Parish   Cʳ.

By an Overplus Recd last year & now due from Richard Shackelford late Collector	754
By Cash in the former Collectors Haṅds £150. to be Accounted for as Tobᵒ. at 2ᵈ ⅌ Pound amounts to	18000
By 950 Tithables at 14ˡᵇ. Tobᵒ. ⅌ Pol	13300
	32054

The Levies being Settled for this Present Year are found to amount to 31887 Pounds of Tobᵒ. 18000ˡᵇ. part of the same to be discharged by Payment of £150 Cash in the several late Collectors Hands, & the Remainder 13887 is to be discharged by 950 Tithables at 14¹ᵇ. Tob°. ℔ Poll & the last years Fraction, on which there will be an Overplus in the Collectors Hands of 167¹ᵇ. Tob°. to be by him Accounted for at laying the next Levies ———

[79]
Philip Rootes having taken the Oaths Appointed by Act of Parliament & Subscribed to be Conformable to the Church of England as by Law Established is Added to this Vestry.
Present Philip Rootes Vestryman

John Livingston & Philip Rootes are Appointed Church wardens for the Ensuing Year

Lyne Shackelford is Appointed Collector of the Parish Levy for this Present year, Whereupon William Lyne & Richard Shackelford became his Security & they have enter'd into & Acknowledged their Bond for the Same

Order'd that the Collector Receive & take in all the Moneys due to this Parish from the Several late Collectors & other Gentlemen both by Bond & Accoᵗ. and Apply the same According to the Orders of this Vestry.

Ordᵈ. that the Collector Pay William Lyne his Accoᵗ for Goods deliver'd for the Use of the Poor of this Parish   £ 11||13|| 7

Ordᵈ. that the Collector Pay Robᵗ. Garrett for necefsarys found Patty Coats   4|| 3|| 1

Ordᵈ. that the Collector Pay John Collier ||10||—

Ordᵈ. that the Collector Pay Ben: Moore part of his Accoᵗ.   1|| 5||—

Ordᵈ. that the Collector Pay Amey Mᶜ.Carty her Accoᵗ. || 5||—

Ordᵈ. that the Collector Pay James Guthrie his Accoᵗ. || 6||—

Ord⁴. that the Collector Pay Mary Hollinger
her Acco*. || 6||—

Ord⁴. that the Collector Pay Susan Brownen
for Burying Eliz^th. Burnet ||14||—

Ord⁴. that Amey Mᶜ.Carty keep Chaˢ. MᶜCarty the Ensuing year & that she have 600^lb. Tob°. Levied for the same at laying the Next Levies.

Ord⁴. that Thomas Brushwood keep Jane Mᶜ.kendree the Ensuing year & that he have 1000^lb. Tob°. Levied for the Same at laying the Next Levies.

Ord⁴. that Mary Hollinger keep Elizabeth Brown the Ensuing year, & that she have 400^lb. Tob°. Levied for the same at Laying the Next Levies —

Ord⁴. that Amey Adams Keep Ann Morrise the Ensuing year & that she have 750^lb. Tob°. Levied for the same at laying the Next Levies —

Ord⁴. that Sarah Gramshill keep the Child of Chris. Grindleys which she now hath, & that she have 400^lb. Tob°. Levied for the same at laying the Next Lev'ys

Ord⁴. that Walter Rhymer keep Christ°. Gringleys youngˢᵗ. Child which he now hath with him & that he have 750^lb. Tob°. Levied for the same at laying of the Next Levies —

John Whiting is Appointed Vestryman in the Place of Jn°. Shackelford decd.

Ord⁴. that John Mᶜ.Carty keep his Brother Natha. Macarty the Ensuing Year & that he have 400^lb. Tob°. Levied for the same at laying the Next Levies —

Ord⁴. that the Collector Pay Catherine Nettles £6|| Cash to be laid out in Corn & meat for the Support of her & her Children ——

Ord^d. that the Collector Pay Unity Ellis £5|| Cash to be laid out in Corn & meat for the Support of her & her Children ——

       Test John Robinson
  Truly Register'd.
       Fran^s. Gaines Clk Vestry

[80]

At a Vestry held for Stratton Major Parish at the Lower Church on Fryday the 27th. Day of July 1759.

Present
 The Reverend William Robinson
 John Livingston William Hunt
 William Taliaferro John Foster Vestrymen
 William Lyne & William Collier

  Pursuant to an Order of King & Queen County Court Dated the 12th. Day of June 1759. That the Vestrys of the Several Parishes within this County do divide their Parishes into so many Precincts as to them shall seem most convenient, for Processioning every Persons Land therein, and to Appoint the Particular Times for that Purpose between the last Day of September and the last Day of March next ensuing, Pursuant to an Act of Assembly in that case made & Provided.

  Order'd That John Foster, John Abbot & Rich^d. Crittenden or any two of them do meet on the first Monday in December Next & go in Procession of & see all the Lands between Portopotank Creek & Matasip Swamp Plainly Marked

  Ord^d. that William Collier James Pryor & Christopher Pryor or any two of them do meet on the first Wednesday next & go in Procession of & See all the Lands between Matasip Swamp & Pepetico Swamp Plainly Marked.

  Ord^d. that Nicholas Dillard James Collier & Jno. Collier j^r. or any two of them do meet on the first Fryday in December next & go in Procefsion of & see all the Lands between Pepetico Swamp & Arracaco Creek Plainly Marked

Ord^d. that James Didlake George Dillard & William Bland or any two of them do meet on the second Monday in December next & go in Procefsion of & see all the Lands between the Eastern & Western branch's of Arracaco Creek Plainly Marked

Ord^d. That William Lyne John Smith & Richard Wyatt or any two of them do meet on the second Fryday in December next & go in Procefsion of & see all the Lands between the Western branch of Arracaco Creek & Tarsatyan Swamp Plainly marked

Ord^d. that Edward Trice James & George Bray or any two of them do meet on the second Wednesday in December next & go in Procefsion of & see all the Lands between Burgefses Swamp & the Monack Swamp, & from thence a Strait Course between Mary Hollinger & Doctor Joyeux decd. to Tarsatyan Swamp Plainly Marked

Ord^d. that Edward Spencer Christopher Ware & Rich^d. Garrett or any two of them do meet on the third Monday in December next, & go in Procefsion of & See all the Land, between the Monack Swamp & on a Strait Course to Tarsatyan Swamp, & the branch next above William Hunts Plainly Marked

[81]
Ord^d. that Spencer Boyd Arthur Ware & John Cardwell or any two of them do meet on the third Wednesday in December next & go in Procefsion of & see all the Lands between the branch next above Willm. Hunts & the extent upwards of this Parish plainly Marked.

Ord^d. that Robert Garrett James Boyd & Rich^d. Garrett or any two of them do meet on the third Fryday in December next & go in Procefsion of & See all the Lands between Tarsatyan Swamp, & Great heartquake Swamp Plainly Marked, Continuing their Proceedings in all Suitable wether untill the whole precinct be finished, and all the Freeholders who are inhabitants thereof are hereby required to Attend the said Procefsioners According to Law. And the Said Procefsioners are further Ordered to make & return to this Vestry at their next meeting after the last Day of March Next, a True Acco^t. of all the Lands they have Procefsion'd of the Persons Present at the same, of what Lands they have not Procefsioned, & the Particular Reason of such Failure

Test. W^m. Robinson

Truly Recorded by Fran^s. Gaines ――

At a Vestry held for Stratton Major Parish at the Uper Church on Wednesday the 8th. Day of August 1759.

John Robinson Esqr.	John Foster	
W^m. Taliaferro	Rich^d. Shackelford	
Present William Lyne		
The Hon. Rich^d.	William Collier	Vestrymen
Corbin Esqr &	Philip Rootes	
William Hunt	……………………	

A Letter from the Reverend M^r. Robinson was delivered to this Vestry & is as follow's
    Gent.

       Sicknefs has prevented my Attendance at Vestry. The Reason of my calling you together is to acquaint you, we have recd. a Letter from our Agent in England, whose Advise to us is, not to Acquiesce in the least degree under the two penny Act. He has ordered his Attorney here to bring Suit immediately for his Tob^o.
  If it is agreeable to you Gent. I am willing to receive the Money in the Collectors Hands as part of my Salary, and

to be determined by M'. Camms Suit for the Remainder, Your Answer by the Bearer will Oblige
    Gent.
        Your most humble Servant.
                      W^m. Robinson
Augst. 8th. 1759.

[82]
Upon the Receipt of the foregoing Letter It is agree'd by this Vestry that the Collector Pay the Rever^d. M^r. W^m. Robinson the Sum of One hundred & forty four Pounds four Shillings & two pence Currant Money, which is the amount of his Salary at Two pence ℔er Pound, And if on the determination of a Suit to be brought by the Rev^d. M^r. Camm against the Vestry of the Parish of York Hampton in York County it shall be adjudged that he recover a further Sum for his Salary then the said Vestry do further agree to lev'y for the said M^r. Robinson as much as will make the above Sum Equal to the Sum recovered by the said M^r. Camm for his Salary
                      John Robinson
    Truly Recorded. by
            Fran^s. Gaines.

At a Vestry held for Stratton Major Parrish at the Lower Church on Fryday the 30th. Day of November 1759.

Present
The Rev^d. William Robinson
John Robinson Esqr.
John Livingston
William Taliaferro
William Lyne &
William Hunt
John Foster
Rich^d. Shackelford
William Collier
Philip Rootes
} Vestry Men

The Parish	D⁻.
To the Revᵈ. Wᵐ. Robinson	16000
To dº. for Shrinkage of Notes	640
To Griffith Elrington Readʳ. of the Uper Church	1200
To Christº. Pryor Reader of the Lower Church	1200
To Grace Soward Sexton of the uper Church & Washing the Surplice	750
To Amey Adams Sexton of the Lower Church & for the Same	750
To Francis Gaines Clk Vestry	1000
To Jnº. Livingston for Providing for the Commu: 4 Times	360
To Philip Rootes for the same	360
To Amey Mᶜ.Carty for Keeping Charles Mᶜ.Carty	600
To Tho. Brushwood for Keeping Jane MᶜKendree	1000
To Mary Hollinger for keeping Elizabeth Brown	400
To Amy Adams for keeping Ann Morrise 1 Month	62
To Sarah Gramshill for keeping Chris. Grindleys Bas. Child	400
To Walter Rhymer for keeping the sᵈ. Grindleys Youngest Child	750
To John Mᶜ.Carty for Keeping his Brother Nathaniel Mᶜ.Carty	400
To Robᵗ. Minion for keeping Mary Barret	400
	26272
To 4 ℔ Cᵗ. on Dº. for Cask	1051
To Richᵈ. Eubank for keeping Jnº. Green 1200 & Cask	1248
To dº. for his Accoᵗ. £2∥4.2 to be pᵈ. in Tobº. at 15/ ℔ Cᵗ.	294
	28865

Mr. Benj:n Needler is appointed a Vestryman in the room of Mr. Roy dec'd.

Test John Skaife Rector

Truly Registered ℗ John Pigg Cl: V:

At a Vestry held for Stratton Major parish at the upper Church on the 18th of October 1730.

The Revd Mr. John Skaife

Present:
Mr. Valent. Ware   Mr. Tho. Foster
Coll. Gawin Corbin   Mr. Rich'd Anderson
Cap.t Henry Hickman
Mr. Edward Ware

The Parish   is   Dr.

	£ s d
To Mr. Skaife	16000
To John Pigg Clerke of ye Vestry	700
To Tho. Lanhford reader of ye lower Church	12
To Gab.l Mitchell reader of the upper Church	1200
To Anne Clear Sexton of the lower Church	600
To Grace Saward Sexton of the upper Church	600
To Maj.r Johnson in part toward the Gleb worke	2000 0
To Mr. Valent. Ware Church Warden by Acco.t	472
To Mr. Foster by acc.t	240
To Mr. John Elliss by acc.t	
To James Muire for worke done at the Glebe	7 0 3 ¼
To Mr. Shiplon for the Pedestile for the ffont	2 0 0 0
To Maj.r Johnson for lead glass & soder for ye Glebe	1 1 19 10
To Charles Collier for keeping Susana ffoy one year	600
To Anne Clear for four times washing the Surplis	200
To John Graneil for keeping Rich'd Sholson 4 weeks	240
To Tob.o levied to defray the above money doble	700 0
To Cask & Sale of 29061 lb Tob.o at 18 ℔ C.t	52
	34280

The levy being Settled for this present year is found to amount

Order'd that Tho.ᵉ Brushwood keep Jane M⁽ᶜ⁾ardex y.ᵉ Ensuing Year, & that he have 1500 T⁰t. Leved for ther same at laying the next Parish Levie —

Order'd that Walter Rymer keep Mary Grindley the Ensuing Year, & that he have 750 T⁰t. Leved for ther same at laying the next Parish Levy —

Order'd that Chr.ˢ M⁽ᶜ⁾Gehy keep his Brother Nathaniel the Ensuing Year, & that he have 750 T⁰t. Leved for ther same at laying the next Levy —

It is agreed by this Vestry that 600 T⁰t. be Leved for Rob.ᵗ Garrett at laying the next Levy for the Boarding of Martha Cook the Ensuing Year —

Order'd that the Church Wardens Bind Ann Grindley Daughter of Chris.ᵗⁿ Grindley to Sarah Grameshill according to Law —

Will.ᵐ Robinson Rect.ʳ

Truly Recorded Fran.ˢ Gaines Cl.k V.

At a Vestry held for Stratton Major Parish the 27.ᵗʰ Day of Feb.ʸ 1766.   The Rev.ᵈ William Robinson

Present John Robinson Esq.ʳ   Will.ᵐ Hunt
        Will.ᵐ Taliaferro   Rich.ᵈ Shackelford } Vestrymen
        Will.ᵐ Lyne   Philip Rooter
        The Hon.ᵇˡᵉ Rich.ᵈ Corbin Esq.ʳ & Will.ᵐ Collier

It was farther agreed that a Church should be Built on some part of the Old field belonging to y.ᵉ Hon.ᵇˡᵉ Rich.ᵈ Corbin Esq.ʳ Wall'd Gibichs, 80 feet long and 30 feet wide in the Clear, the Foundation to be begun 3 Bricks Thick, & so continue to the Surface of the Earth, from thence 2½ Bricks thick to the water Table which is to be 4 feet above the top of the Earth, thence 1½ Bricks thick to 27 feet Pitch from the Surface of the Earth, the Piles to be laid with the same kind of Stone of that in the present Church, a Door in the North and South sides; Twelve foot high & 6 foot wide from outs; one Door in the West End 16 foot high & 8 foot wide; 5 Compas Windows in each side and two at the East 13 foot high & 6 foot wide to be Glazed with the Best London Crown Glass, to contain 32 lights in the Square Part, 2 Windows in the West End Convenient for the Gallery; The flooring of the Church to be laid with well seasoned quarterd Pine Plank 1½ ofp of Plank on good plank Oak Sleepers, the Wainscot for Pews to be of well seaond Pine or Cypress Plank raised on one Side; Five Pillars of Cypress on each side, for the Support of the Roof, the Colomns to be 16 Inches Diameter at the bottom of the Shaft, to be Fluked & the Capitols of the Doric Order, a Gallery at the West End 10 foot wide to be Divided into tiers of Pews with Stairs to go up on each side; the Roof to be raised on Brick gable ends to be carried up 2 Bricks thick from the main Body, to be well fram'd with Poplar or Cypress Timber, the Girders to be 12 Inches Square, the Summers 12 Inches Square, the Joists to be 12 by 3 the Principal Rafters to be

10 Inches by 8, the Studines to be 10 by 8, & the small Rafters to be 10 by 4 Inches, the Roof to be covered with [Scantling] Cypherd and [Lapp]t 1 1/2 Inches &, then covered with Shingles of good Cypress 20 Inches long 3/4 of an Inch thick, & not to shew more than 6 Inches, the Church to have the Seats, Modillion Cornice on the inside of each End, the Pews to be the same height of them in the present Church to be floored with white [Lard] & to be Painted with a Wainscot Colour, and all the outside of the Doors and Windows & Cornish to be Stoned or Plaistered three times over with white Lead, also a Compleated Altar Piece with Black Walnut hand Rails, & Banisters, a Neat Pulpit and Desks, and all the outside Mortar to be made up 2/3 Lime & 1/3 Sand, & the inside Mortar to be of Lime, & 1/2 Sand. The Church to be compleatly Finish'd by the first of August 1762. Four Hundred Pounds to be paid to the Undertaker on the 10 Day of August next, Three Hundred Pounds on the 10 Day of August 1761, if the Bricks are then made & the Foundation laid, or otherwise when the Foundation is laid, if it is not laid at that time, one half of the remaining [Sum] to be paid in August 1762, if the Church is then cover'd in, otherwise when the Covering in is finish'd, & the Residue at the finishing of the same. Will'm Taliaferro, Will'm Lyne, & Rich'd Shackelford are Appointed to see that the said Work is forwarded & Faithfully done with good Materials.

It was agreed by this Vestry that Will'm Taliaferro & Rich'd Corbin Esq'r Church Wardens shall prepare Articles & underwrite with Harry Gaines Gent'n for Building the before mentioned Church According to the Plan herewith, & that he shall be paid Thirteen hundred Pounds Current Money in the manner above Mentioned.

Truly Recorded Fran'ce Gaines Clk V.

At a Vestry held for St Stratton Major Parish at the Upper Church on Monday the 24th Day of November 1760.

The Rev'd William Robinson

Present: John Robinson Esq'r .... Rich'd Shackelford
John Livingston .... William Collier
The Hon'ble Rich'd Corbin Esq'r ....
Will'm Hunt ...... & Philip Rootes
John Foster
} Vestry Men

Thomas Reade Rootes having taken the Oaths appointed by Act of Parliament & Subscribed to be Conformable to the Church of England as by Law Establish'd is added to this Vestry

Present Tho: Reade Rootes

New Church

W:^m Robinson Rector

1767 Decr 11 Pews Allotted to Families &c in the New Church Viz^t

North side

N° 11
The Honble Richd Corbin Esqr
and his Family

N° 10
Mr William Meredith
and his Family

N° 9
Messrs Thos Metcalfe
Saml Metcalfe
Richd Anderson
Hansford Anderson
Andrew Crawford
Cornelius Livingston
Hen^y Wedderburn
John Dyne
John Smith
Henry Strachey
John Shackelford
Ben: Shackelford
Philip Taliaferro

N° 9
Messrs Thos Metcalfe's Wife
Saml Metcalfe's Wife
Richd Anderson's Wife
Mrs Mary Anderson Wid^w
Mrs Mary Ann Tibbs Wid^w
Mrs Ann Collier Wid^w
Mrs Nich Smith Wid^w
Mrs Fra^s Collier Wid^w
Mrs Wedderburn's Wife

Southside

N° 11
The Lady & Family of
John Robinson Esqr dec^d

N° 10
Col^o Philip Rootes & Family
Maj^r Richd Shackelford & Family
Mr John Waller & Family
Mr Wm Saliafore & Family

N° 9
Messrs William Hurst
Francis Gaines
Thos Dillard
William Shackelford
Lyne Shackelford
William Hare
Thos Dudley
Gregory Smith
John Pendleton

} Vestry men

N° 8
Miss Wm Hurst's Wife & Daughters
Fra^s Gaines Wife & Daughters
Thos Dillard Wife
Lyne Shackelford's Wife
Wm Hare's Wife
Mrs Fra^s Shackelford Wid^w
Cornelius Livingston's Wife
Thos Dudley's Wife
John Pendleton's Wife

N° 7 The Wives of
James Collier &
John Collier Junr
Thos Drummond's Wife
Richd Coffendaw's Wife
James Dudley's Wife
John Dudley's Wife
William Dudley's Wife
Robt B. Dudley's Wife
John Townley's Wife
Spencer Boyd's Wife
James Boyd's Wife
Mr Collins Daughters
George Dillard's Wife

N° 6
George Livingston's Wife
Wm Dudley's Wife
Edwd Waldrin's Wife
Joyeuse Collins Wife
Jach? Shackelford's Wife
Henry Collins Wife
Nich^s Dillard's Wife
George Standard's Wife

N° 7
James Collier
John Collier
George Pegg
Richard Coffendaw
James Dudley
John Dudley
Nicholas Dillard
John Townley
Robt B. Dudley
Thos Drummond
George Dillard S^r

N° 6
George Livingston
Wm Dudley
Edwd Waldrin
Joyeuse Collins
Jach? Shackelford
Henry Collins
George Standard
John Carr

N° 7
Nich^s Mickell
Chas Collier
Edwd Spencer
James Trice
Jno: Ware
John Abbott
Spencer Boyd
James Boyd
Robt Dudley
Wm Dudley
Robt Smith
Thos Dudley
Jach? Shackelford
Fra^l Gaines

N° 6
Arthur Ware
Thos Warren
George Dillard
John Ware
James Ware
Richd Bray
Humphrey Garrett

N° 7
Pulpit &c

N° 6
The Revd Mr Commissary
Robinson's Family

N° 5
Mrs Rachel Garrett Wid^w
Mrs Jane Trice Wife
James Trice Wife
Arist^l Warren Wife
Thos Warren's Wife
Cath^y Collins Wid^w
George Brays Wife
Mrs Abells Daughters
George Dillard's Wife
Richd Brays Wife
Humphrey Garrett's Wife

[83]

Dr. Brought up	28865lb.
To Robert Minion for his Acct. 9/9 in Tobo. at 15/ ℔ Ct.	62
To Capt. William Lyne for his Acct. Sundries dld for Parish Pr.	1274
To Robt. Garrett for Neceſsaries found Martha Coats	475
To Thoˢ. Shipton for a Horse Block & Benches at the upper Church	166
To Mary Hollinger for Shoes &c for Elizᵃ Brown	40
To Amey Mᶜ:Carty for ℔r. Shoes found Charles Mᶜ:Carty	34
To Richd: Garrett for 1 ℔r. do. found Ditto	34
To John Waller for 1 Levy overpaid last Year	14
To Hugh Livingston for his Acct: for work done to the lower Church	770
To Majr. Rootes for 250lb. Pork found Martha Coats	250
To Coll: Cary for 3 Levies overpaid last Year	42
To the Clerk of this County for 2 Lists of Tithables	36
To Catharine Nettles for to support her Children with Corn & Meat £6	300
To Mary Brown to buy her Corn & Meat	300
To Charles Roan for his acct: Neceſsaries found Mary Roffe	230
To Mary Roffe for to buy her Corn and Meat	400
To John Collier for removing Richd. Haynes to Richmond County	100
To Isabel ODear to buy her Corn and Meat	400
To Benjᵃ Williams for Taylors Work	68
To Tobo. to be Sold & the Money Ariseing therefrom to be apply'd toward Building the New Church	10619
To Salary for Collecting at 6 ℔ Ct.	2688
	47667

Cr
By 950 Titheables at 50lb Tobº. ℔ Poll   47500
By Lyne Shackelford Late Collector for the last
  years Fraction   167

                                               47667

The Levies being Settled for this present Year are found to Amount to 47667lb. Tobº: to be Levied on 950. Titheables at 50lb of Tobº ℔ Poll which is Order'd to be Collected for every Titheable Person within the List for this said Year, & if there is any Overplus to be accounted for by the Collector at the Laying of the next Levies

William Taliaferro, & the Hon: Richd: Corbin is appointed Church Wardens for the Ensuing Year, & William Taliaferro is Appointed is appointed Collector for this Present Year, Whereupon Francis Gaines became Security & they have Acknowledg'd their Bond for the same ——

Thoº: Reade Rootes is appointed a Vestryman in the Place of Thomas Thorpe Decd.

It is Agreed by this Vestry that the Church Wardens do give Publick Notice that a New Church is to be Built in this Parish, & that a Vestry is appointed to Meet at the Upper Church on the last Wednesday in February next if fair if not the next fair Day in Order to receive Planns from Undertakers & agree for Building of the same

Order'd that Rebeckah Didlake of St. Stephens Parish Keep Charles Mc:Carty the Ensuing Year & that she have 600lb Tobº: Levied for the same at laying the next Parish Levy

[84]

Order'd that Thos: Brushwood keep Jane M^c.andree & Eliz^a Brown the Ensuing Year & that he have 1500^{lb} Tob^o levied for the same at laying the next Parish Levies ———

Order'd that Walter Rymer keep Mary Grindley the Ensuing Year & that he have 750^{lb} Tob^o: Levied for the same at laying the next Parish Levy ———

Order'd that John M^c:Carty keep his brother Nathaniel the Ensuing Year & that he have 400^{lb} Tob^o: Levied for the same at laying the next Levy

It is agreed by this Vestry that 600^{lb} Tob^o be Levied for Robt: Garrett at laying the next Levy for the Boarding of Martha Coats the Ensuing Year ———

Order'd that the Church Wardens Bind Ann Grindley Daughter of Christ^s: Grindley to Sarah Gramshill according to Law —

        Willm: Robinson Rector
   Truly Recorded.
     Fran^s. Gaines. Clk V.

At a Vestry held for Stratton Major Parish the 27th. Day of Feby. 1760.

Present
  The Rev^d. William Robinson
  John Robinson Esqr. Willm: Hunt
  Willm. Taliaferro Rich^d. Shackelford
  Willm. Lyne
  The Hon: Rich^d. Philip Rootes
  Corbin Esqr. & Willm. Collier
} Vestrymen

It was farther agreed that a Church should be Built on some part of the Old field belonging to the Honble. Richd Corbin Esqr: Call'd Goliahs, 80 foot long and 50 foot wide in the Clear, the Foundation to be began 5 Bricks thick

& so continue to the Surface of the Earth, from thence 4½ Bricks thick to the water Table which is to be 4 foot above the top of the Earth, thence 4 Bricks thick to 27 foot Pitch from the Surface of the Earth, the Isles to be laid with the same kind of Stone of that in the Present Church A Door in the North and South sides, Twel've foot high, & six foot wide from outs, one Door in the West End 16 foot high & 8 foot wide, 5 Compaſs Windows in each side and two at the East 13 foot high & 5 foot wide to be Glazed with the Best London Crown Glaſs, to contain 32 lights in the Square Part, 2 Windows in the West End Convenient for the Gallery, The flooring of the Pews &c to be laid with well season'd quarter'd Pine Plank clear of Sap on good white Oak Sleepers, the Wainscot for Pews to be of well season'd Pine or Cypreſs Plank raised on one Side, Five Pillars of Cypreſs on each side for the support of the Roof, the Columns to be 15 Inches Diameter at the bottom of the Shaft, to be Fluted & the Capitols of the Dorick Order, a Gallery at the West End 13 foot wide to be Divided into sets of Pews with Stairs to go up on each side the Roof to be rais'd on Brick Gable Ends to be carried up 2 Bricks thick from the main Body, to be well fram'd with Poplar or Cypreſs Timber, the Girders to be 12 Inches Square the Summers 12 Inches Square, the Jists to be 12 by 3 the Principal Rafters to be [85] 10 Inches by 8 the Purlines to be 10 by 8 & the small Rafters to be 10 by 4 Inches, the Roof to be Cover'd with Plank Cypher'd and Lapp'd 1½ Inches & then Cover'd with Shingles of good Cypreſs 20 Inches long ¾ of an Inch thick, & not to shew more then 6 Inches, the Church to have a Neat, Modilion Cornish on the sides & each End, the Pews to be the same height of them in the present Church to be prim'd with white Lead & to be painted with a Wainscot Colour, and all the outside of the Doors and Windows & Cornish to be prim'd or painted three times over with white Lead, also a Compleat Altar Piece with Black Walnut hand Rails &

Banisters, a Neat Pulpit and Desks, and all the outside Mortar to be made up 2/3 Lime & 1/3 Sand, & the inside Mortar to be ½ Lime & ½ Sand. The Church to be Compleatly Finish'd by the last of August 1763 Four Hundred Pounds to be paid to the Undertaker on the 10 Day of August next, Three Hundred pounds on the 10 Day of August 1761, If the Bricks are then made & the Foundation laid, or otherwise when the Foundation is laid if it is not laid at that time, one half of the remaining Part to be paid in August 1762, if the Church is then Cover'd in, otherwise when the Covering in is finish'd, & the Residue at the finishing of the same Willm: Taliaferro Willm: Lyne & Rich^d. Shackelford are Appointed to see that the said Work is forwarded & Faithfully done with good Materials

It was agreed by this Vestry that Willm Taliaferro & Rich^d. Corbin Esqr Church Wardens shall prepare Articles & underwrite with Harry Gaines Gent: for Building the before mentioned Church According to the Plan herewith and that he shall be paid Thirteen hundred pounds Current Money in the manner above Mentioned.
  Truly Recorded.
    Fran^s. Gaines Clk V.

At a Vestry held for Stratton Major Parish at the Upper Church on Monday the 24th Day of November 1760

   The Rev^d. William Robinson
Present John Robinson Esqr. Rich^d. Shackel-⎫
  John Livingston   ford   ⎪
  The Honble: Rich^d. William Collier ⎪
   Corbin Esqr.   ⎬ Vestry Men
  Willm Hunt   & Philip Rootes ⎪
  John Foster   ⎭

Thomas Reade Rootes having taken the Oaths appointed by Act of Parliament, & Subscribed to be Conformable to the Church of England as by Law Establish'd, is added to this Vestry

Present Tho*: Reade Rootes

[86]

The Parish	D^r
To the Rev^d: W^m: Robinson	16000
To d°: for Shrinkage of Notes	640
To Griffith Elrington Reader of the Upper Church	1200
To Christ^r. Pryor reader of the lower Church	1200
To Grace Soward Sexton of the Upper Church & Wash^g: the Surplice	750
To Amey Adams Sexton of the lower Church & d°	750
To Fran: Gaines Clk Vestry	700
To the Honble: Rich^d: Corbin for providing for the Church	360
To William Taliaferro's Ex^{rs}: for the same	360
To Rebeckah Didlakes Estate for keeping Charles M^c.Carthy	600
To Thos: Brushwood for Jane M^c.andree & Eliz^a Brown	776
To Walter Rymer for Mary Grindley	750
To John M^c.Carty for his Brother Nathaniel	400
To Robt. Garrett for Boarding Martha Coats	600
	25086
To 4 ℔ C^t. on D°. for Cask	1003
To the Clerk for Copy of the List of Titheables	36
To Edward Ware jun^r: for keeping Rachel Stratton in her Sickneſs	330
To John Collier for his Acco^t: moving a woman	50
To John Foster for his Acco^t.	56
To Thos. Brushwood his Acco^t.	180
To Benj^a Williams ℔ his Acco^t.	100
To John Didlake for 1 ℔^{r}: Shoes for Charles McCartey	30

To Edward Spencer for Corn deliver'd Betty Soward	100
To John Mᶜ:Carty for his accᵗ. burying Nat: Mᶜ:Carty and Sundry Neceſsaries found	250
To Grace Soward to buy her Corn &c	250
To Charles Roane for getting Firewood for Mary Roffe	50
To Sarah Bird to buy her Corn & Meat &c	500
To Mary Brown for dᵒ.	300
To Isabel ODear for the same	300
To Catharine Nettles to support her Children	600
To Richᵈ Eubank for burying John Green	150
To Tobᵒ: to be sold to Raise Money for the second payment towards the New Church	36000
To the Collectors Salary at 6 ℔ Cᵗ	3922
	69293

The Levy being Settled for this present Year are found to amount to 69293ˡᵇˢ Tobᵒ which is Levied upon 970 Titheables at 72ˡᵇ Tobᵒ. ℔ poll 40ˡᵇ of which is to be paid as the Owners of the Titheables Chooses, that is to say at 2ᵈ ℔ lb Cash or in Tobᵒ: & there will remain a Ballance due to the Parish of 547ˡᵇ Tobᵒ: to be accounted for at laying the next Parish Levies

William Hunt & Thoˢ: Reade Rootes is appointed Church Wardens for this Ensuing Year & Lyne Shackelford is appointed Collector of the Parish Levy for this present Year. Whereupon James Collier & Edward Spencer Enter'd into Bond with the said Lyne Shackelford as security and have acknowledged the same

[87]

It is agreed by this Vestry that the Honᵇˡᵉ: Richᵈ: Corbin Esqʳ: & Philip Rootes see Over the Building of the Church instead of William Taliaferro & William Lyne Dec.d

Order'd that William Bland keep & find Necefsaries for Mary Roffe the Ensuing Year & that he have 800ᵇ Tob°: Levied for the same at laying the next Levies

Order'd that Richᵈ: Groom keep Charles Mᶜ.Carty the Ensuing Year & that he have 600ᵇ Tob° Levied for the same at laying the next Levy

Order'd that the Church Wardens bind Mary Grindley to Walter Rymer & Margaret his Wife according to Law

Francis Gaines is appointed Vestry man in the place of William Lyne Decd. & Thoˢ: Dillard is appointed in the place of William Taliaferro Decd

Order'd that Jane Didlake keep Elizᵃ Brown the Ensuing Year & that she have 400ᵇ Tob°. Levied at laying the next Levy

Willᵐ: Robinson Rector

At a Vestry held for Stratton Major Parish at the Upper Church on Monday the 22ᵈ Day of February 1762

John Robinson Esqʳ.	Philip Rootes	
The Honᵇˡᵉ: Richᵈ:		
Corbin Esqʳ:	Thoˢ: R e a d e	Vestry Men
Present Willᵐ: Hunt	Rootes	
John Foster		
Richᵈ. Shackelford		

John Whitinge & Francis Gaines having taken the Oaths appointed by Act of Parliament & Subscrib'd to be Conformable to the Church of England as by Law Establish'd is Added to this Vestry

Present John Whitinge & Francis Gaines

The Parish	Dʳ
To the Revᵈ: William Robinson	16000
To Shrinkage of Notes for d°.	640

To Griffith Elrington Reader of the Upper Church	1200
To James Pryor ditto of the lower Church	1200
To Grace Soward Sexton &c of the upper Church	750
To Amey Adams dº: Lower Church	750
To Franˢ. Gaines Clk of the Vestry	700
To William Hunt for Providing for the Church	360
To Thoˢ: Reade Roots for the same	360
Carried Over	21960

[88]

Brought Over	21960
To William Bland for keeping and finding for Mary Roffe	800
To Richᵈ. Groom's Exʳˢ. for keeping Charles Mᶜ:Carty	600
To Jane Didlake for keeping Elizᵃ Brown	400
To Robᵗ: Garrett for Boarding Martha Coats	600
	24360
To 4 ℔ Cᵗ. on dº. for Cask	974
To the Clk of this County for Lists Titheables	36
To Thoˢ. Reade Rootes for his Accoᵗ. for Sundry Goods delivered for the use of the poor Settled in Tobº. at 2ᵈ ℔ lb £9‖ 1‖10½	1091
To William Leigh for dº. 2‖12‖10	317
To William Lyne's Exʳˢ. 4‖10‖ 2	541
To William Edmond Waller for his accoᵗ. neceſsaries found Ann Newton	298
To Thoˢ: Brushwood for his accoᵗ: Burying Matthew Burgeſs	100
To dº. for moving Mary Dance to Catharine Nettles 5/	30
To Ann Brushwood for keeping Mary Dance 4 Weeks	180

138   VESTRY BOOK OF STRATTON MAJOR PARISH

To Barbary Groom for finding Charles Mᶜ.Carty 1 ℔ʳ Shoes. & 1 ℔ʳ Stockings 9/	54
To Thoˢ: Shipton for a Coffin & carrying Jane Mᵒ:Andree to the Grave 15/	90
To Edward Walden for a Coffin & carrying Mary Dance to the Grave	90
To William Hunt for Steps at the Upper Church Door	100
To Catharine Nettles for keeping Mary Dance 4 Weeks, finding a Sheet & burying her £2‖11‖	306
To Grace Soward to buy her Corn &c	250
To Thoˢ. Bird for the support of his Mother	600
To Mary Brown to Buy Corn	300
To Isabel ODear for her Support	400
To Tobᵒ: to be sold to Raise money for the third payment for the New Church	24000
To Salary for Collecting at 6 ℔ Cᵗ.	3247
	57364

Cʳ

By 961 Ttheables at 60¹ᵇ ℔ Poll	57660
By Ballance in the Late Collectors hands	43
	57703

The Levy being this Day Settled for the Year 1761 and is found to Amount to 57703¹ᵇ. of Tobᵒ. being Levied upon 961 Titheables, at 60¹ᵇ. Tobᵒ. ℔ Poll & there will be an Overplus in the Hands of the Collector of 339¹ᵇ Tobᵒ: to be accounted for at the Laying the next Parish Levy

John Whitinge & Francis Gaines is appointed Churchwardens for this present Year and Lyne Shackelford is appointed Collector of the Parish Levy for the year 1761.

John Lyne became his security & they have Acknowledged their Bond for the same

Order'd that the Collector receive Cash of all Persons desirous to pay in money at 2^d ℔ lb for 24^{lb} Tob° ℔ Poll in Part of the Parish Levy

[89]
Order'd that the Collector Pay William Hunt & Thos: Reade Rootes Each 90^{lb} Tob° more then is already Levied for them for finding for the Church a fifth time

William Taliaferro & James Collier are Appointed Vestrymen in the place of John Livingston & William Collier Decd

Orderd that the Collector pay the money now in his hands for the Tob°. Collected last Year amounting to £300 to John Robinson Esqr: which he agrees to allow Interest for untill it is Order'd to be Paid to the Undertaker for the second Payment towards the New Church

Order'd that William Bland keep & provide for Mary Roffe this Present Year, & that he be allow'd 800^{lb}. Tob° Levied for the same, at Laying the next Parish Levy

Order'd that Barbary Groom Keep Charles M^c:Carty this Present Year, & that she have 600^{lb} Tob° Levied for the same at Laying the next Levy

Order'd that Jane Didlake keep Eliz^a Brown this Present Year & that she be allow'd 400^{lb} Tob° at laying the next Parish Levy

Order'd that Robt: Garrett have 600^{lb} Tob° Levied at Laying the next Parish Levy for Boarding Martha Coats this Year. —

John Robinson

At a Vestry held for Stratton Major Parish at the upper Church on Fryday the 24th Day of Sept': 1762. to lay the Parish Levy

Present
The Rev?: William Robinson Commi∫sary
John Robinson Esq'
The Hon: Rich?: Corbin Esq'
William Hunt
John Foster
Philip Rootes
Fran⁸: Gaines

William Taliaferro having taken the Oaths appointed by act of Parliament, & Subscribed to be conformable to the Church of England as by Law Established, is added to this Vestry.

Present   William Taliaferro

The Parish	D'. lb Tob°
To the Rev? William Robinson	16000
To D°. for Shrinkage of Notes	640
To Griffith Elrington Reader of the upper Church	1200
To James Pryor Reader of the lower Church	1200
To Grace Soward Sexton	750
To Amey Adams Sexton	750
To Fran⁸: Gaines Clk of the Vestry	700
To d°: for finding the Church 2 times	180
To John Whiting for the same	180
	21600

[90]

Brought Over	21600
To William Bland for keeping & providing for Mary Roffe	800
To Barbary Groom for keeping Charles M°Carty	600
To Jane Didlake for keeping Eliz⁸ Brown	400
To Rob'. Garrett for Boarding Martha Coats	600
	24000

To 4 ℔ Cᵗ: for Cask	960
To the Clerk of this County for Copy's List Tithes	36
To David Kerr for his accoᵗ: for drawing Articles of agreement with Harry Gaines for the Building of the Church	167
To Thoˢ: Read Rootes, accoᵗ: sundry Goods dld for Alice Newton & Charles Mᶜкнярty £2‖19‖8½	332
To Jane Didlake by her accoᵗ: Shoes &c for Elizᵃ Brown 9/	50
To Richᵈ: Waldens accoᵗ: mending a Horse Block &c 8/	44
To Wᵐ: Ed: Waller for finding & taking care of Alice Newton	600
To Lyne Shackelford for Balˢ: his accoᵗ	81
To Thoˢ: Soward for the Subsistance of his Wife	400
To Thoˢ: Bird for the support of his Mother	600
To Grace Soward to Buy her Corn	250
To Mary Brown to Buy her Corn &c	400
	27920
To John Whiting for finding for the Church a third time	93
To Francis Gaines for the same	93
	28106
Tobᵒ. to be sold to raise money for the fourth & last Payment for the Building the new Church and a Vestry house at the same place	30000
	58106
To 6 ℔ Cᵗ: Collectors Salary	3486
	61592

The Levy being settled for this present year is found to amount to 61592 Pounds Tob°: being Levied on 980 Titheables at 63 lb. Tob°. ℔ Pole & there will remain an Overplus in the Collectors hands of 148 Tob°. to be accounted for at the laying the next Parish Levy

John Robinson Esq' & Tho': Dillard is appointed Church Wardens & John Robinson Esq'. is appointed Collector of the Parish Levy for this present year Harry Gaines became his Security & they acknowledged their Bond for the same

It is agreed by this Vestry that Harry Gaines Build a Vestry House at the New Church. twenty foot long & Sixteen foot wide in the clear, of Brick Wall ten foot Pitch with a Chimney inside one Pannell'd Door & two Sash windows Eighteen lights each. to be cover'd with Shingles the Wall to be 2 Bricks thick as high as the water Table & 1 & ½ Bricks thick above to be compleatly Finished in a workmanlike manner. for which it is also agreed by this Vestry that he be paid seventy Pounds Current money with the last Payment for the Church

Order'd that the Churchwardens Bind Turner Moore Son of Mary Moore Dec^d to Christopher Stedman according to Law ——

[91]
Order'd that William Bland keep & provide for Mary Roffe the Ensuing year & that he have 800 lb': of Tob°: Levied for the same at laying the next Parish Levy

Order'd that Barbary Groom keep Charles McCarty the Ensuing year & that she have 600 lb' Tob° Levied for the same at laying the next Levy

Order'd that John Bowen keep Eliz^a Brown the Ensuing year, & that he have 400^{lb} Tob° Levied for the same at laying the next Parish Levy

John Robinson

At a Vestry held for Stratton Major Parish at the Upper Church on Tuesday the 8th: Day of November 1763

The Rev^d: M^r: Willm: Robinson Commiſsary

Present
William Hunt Thos. R Rootes
John Foster Fra^s: Gaines
Rich^d: Shackelford Willm: Taliaferro
Philip Rootes

Pursuant to an Order of King & Queen County Court Dated the   Day   1763 That the Vestry's of the several Parishes within this County do Divide their Parishes into so many Precincts as to them shall seem most convenient, for Proceſsioning Every Persons Land therein, and to appoint the Particular times for that Purpose between the last Day of September & the last Day of March next Ensuing. Pursuant to an Act of Aſsembly in that Case made and Provided

Order'd that Lyne Shackelford, Rich^d. Crittenden and Alexander Wedderburn, or any two of them do meet on the first Monday in December next & go in Proceſsion of & see all and Every Persons Land between Portopotank Creek & Matasip Swamp plainly Marked. Continuing &c

Order'd that James Pryor, Richard Anderson, & James Muir or any two of them do meet on the first Wednesday in December next & go in Proceſsion of & see all the Lands between Mataſsip Swamp & Pepetico Swamp plainly Marked.

Order'd that Nicholas Dillard, James Collier & John Collier jun^r: or any two of them, do meet on the first Friday in December, next & go in Proceſsion, of & see all the Lands between Pepetico Swamp & Arracaco Creek & the Eastern branch thereof plainly Marked.

Order'd that James Didlake, George Dillard, & William Bland or any two of them do meet on the second Monday in December next, & go in Proceſsion of & see all the Lands between the Eastern & Western Branch of Arracaco Creek Plainly Marked.

[92]
Order'd that Richard Wyatt, William Shackelford & John Smith, or any two of them do meet on the second Friday in December next & go in Proceſsion of and see all the Lands between the Western branch of Arracaco Creek & Tarsatyan Swamp Plainly Marked.

Order'd that James Trice, Thoˢ: Brushwood & George Dillard, or any two of them do meet on the second Wednesday in December next & go in Proceſsion of & see all the Lands between Burgeſses Swamp & the Monack Swamps, & from thence a Strait Course between Mary Hollinger & Doct͏ʳ. Joyeux decᵈ: to Tarsatyan Swamp plainly Marked.

Order'd that Edwᵈ: Spencer, Richᵈ: Garrett Junʳ: & Robᵗ: Garrett Junʳ: to meet on the third Monday in December next & go in Proceſsion of & see all the Lands between the Monack Swamp & on a strait Course to Tarsatyan Swamp & the Branch next above William Hunt's Plainly Marked.

Order'd that Spencer Boyd, Arthur Ware & John Cardwell or any two of them do meet on the third Wednesday in December next & go in Proceſsion of & see all the Lands between the Branch Next above William Hunts & the Extent upward plainly Marked.

Order'd that Richard Garrett, Chris: Ware & John Nichols or any two of them do meet on the third Friday in December next & go in Proceſsion of & see all the Lands between Tarsatyan Swamp & Great Heart:quake Plainly Marked. Continuing their Proceedings in all suitable

Weather untill the whole Precinct be finish'd, And all the freeholders who are Inhabitants thereof are hereby requir'd to Attend the said Proceſsioners According to Law. And the said Proceſsioners are farther Order'd to Make & return to this Vestry at their next meeting after the Last Day of March Next, a true Acco^t: of what Lands they have Proceſsion'd, of the Persons present at the same, of what Lands they have not Poſseſsion'd and the Particular reason of such failure.

The Parish is	D^r. lb^s, Tob^o:
To the Rev^d: Mr Commiſsary Robinson	16000
To ditto for Shrinkage of Notes	640
To Griffith Elrington Reader of the Upper Church	1200
To James Pryor Reader of the Lower Church	1200
To Grace Soward Sexton & Wash^r: the Surplice	750
To Amey Adams d^o	750
To Francis Gaines Clk. of the Vestry	1000
To John Robinson Esqr: for Finding for the Comm:	360
To Thos: Dillard for the same	360
To William Bland for keeping & providing for Mary Roffe	800
To Barbary Groom for keeping Charles M^c:Carty	600
To Mary Hollinger for keeping Eliz^a Brown	400
To Robert Garrett for Boarding Martha Coats	600
	24660
To 4 ℔ C^t: on ditto in Cask	986
To the Clerk for Copy's List of Tithes	36
To John Kidd for keeping Mildred Evans 15 Months	1000
To Robt: Garrett ℔ his Acco^t: £3	360
To Thos: Dillard ℔ d^o. £1‖3‖9	144
To Chr: Stedman ℔ d^o: 7^s‖6^d	45

To Doct^r. Fercharson ℔ d°: £1‖1‖6	129
To Rich^d: Garrett d°.	63
	27423

[93]
D^r: Brought up   lb^s Tob°
                                                                27423

To Francis Gaines ℔ Acco^t.	293
To d°. ℔ d° £1‖0‖6	123
To William Leigh's Acco^t Sundry's £5‖19‖3¾	665
To Dennis Brenin ℔ Acco^t £1‖10	180
To Chris^r: Stedman for a Levy Overpaid in 1759	50
To Thos Bird for keeping his Mother	700
To Major Rich^d: Shackelford for Meat found Thos Soward	324
To Mary Brown to buy her Corn & Meat	400
To William Edward Waller for keeping Alice Newton	800
To Frances Raines for her Support	600
To Unity Ellis for the Support of her Children	600
	32158
To Salary for Collecting 6 ℔ C^t.	1929
	34087

The Levies being settled for this Present Year are found to amount to 34087^{lb} of Tob°. being Levied upon 985 Titheables at 35 lb Tob°: ℔ Poll & there will be an Overplus in the Collectors hands amounting to 88^{lb} Tob°: to be accounted for at Laying the next Levies

Rich^d: Shackelford & William Taliaferro are appointed Church Wardens, & Richard Shackelford is appointed Collector of the Parish Levy, for this Present Year Whereupon

William Taliaferro became his Security & they acknowledged their Bond for the Same

Order'd that William Bland keep & provide for Mary Roffe the Ensuing Year & that he have 800^lb Tob°. Levy'd for the same at laying the next Parish Levies.

Order'd that John Burton keep Eliz^a Brown the Ensuing Year & that he have 400^lb Tob° Levy'd for the same at Laying the next Parish Levies

Order'd that Willm: Ed^d: Waller keep & provide for Alice Newton the Ensuing Year & that he have 800^lb Tob°: Levy'd for the same at Laying the next Parish Levies

Order'd that Barbary Groom keep Charles M^c.Carty the Ensuing Year & that she have 700^lb Tob°: levy'd for the same at laying the next Parish Levies

It is agreed by this Vestry that Ann Soward be Sexton of this Upper Church

Order'd that Thos: Bird keep his Mother the Ensuing Year & that he have 700^lb Tob° Levy'd for the same at Laying the next Parish Levies

        Willm: Hunt

[94]

At a Vestry held for Stratton Major Parish at the New Church on Monday the 24th Day of September 1764

    The Rev^d: M^r: Commiſsary Robinson

Present
John Robinson Esqr	Philip Rootes	
The Hon: Rich^d:	Thos. Reade	
Corbin Esqr	Rootes	Vestry men
William Hunt	John Whitinge	
Rich^d: Shackelford &	Francis Gaines	

The Parish	Dr lbs: Tobo.
To the Revd. Mr. Commiſsary Robinson	16000
To do: for Shrinkage of Notes	640
To Griffith Elrington Reader of the Upper Church	1200
To Ann Soward Sexton of Ditto	750
To James Pryor Reader of the Lower Church	1200
To Amey Adams Sexton of ditto	750
To Francis Gaines Clk of the Vestry	700
To Richard Shackelford for Providing for the Comm	360
To William Taliaferro for the same	360
To William Bland for keeping Mary Roffe &c	800
To John Burton for keeping Eliza Brown } To Robt: Brown & Richd: Falkner for Ditto	400
To Willm: Edmd: Waller for keeping Alice Newton three Months	200
To Barbary Groom for keeping Charles Mc:Carty	700
To Thos. Bird for keeping his Mother Sarah Bird	700
To Ann Soward for the support of Martha Coats	600
	25360
To 4 ℔ Ct. on ditto for Cask	1014
To the Clerk for 2 Lists Tithes	36
To Edwd Wallers Acco t: for Burying Alice Newton £1‖5‖6	204
To Frances Raines for her Support	600
To Unity Ellis for the same with her Children	600
To Mary Brown to buy her Corn &c	400
To Richard Shackelford by his Accot. Delinqts	52
To do. for Meat & Corn found Thos: Soward £5‖6‖3	850
To Alexr: Wedderburns Accot. £1‖12‖8	261
To Willm: Shackelford's Store Accot: £2‖13‖4	427
To Thos. Reade Rootes ℔ 19½ Barrels Corn for Thos: Sowards	150

To Fran⁸. Gaines ℔ Acco ᵗ £1‖14	272
To Will ᵐ: Taliaferro ℔ d°. 8/6	68
To Geo: Standard ℔ d° 15/	120
To Lyne Shackelford for Corn dld Jn°. Atkins	160
	30574
To 6 ℔ Cᵗ. for Collecting	1834
	32408
The Parish Cʳ	
By 997 Titheables at 33ˡᵇ Tob°: ℔ Poll	32901

The Levy's being settled for this Present Year is found to Amount to 32901ˡᵇ ˢ Tob°: being Levy'd upon 997 Titheables at 33ˡᵇ Tob° ℔ Poll & there will be an Overplus in the hands of the Collectors of 493ˡᵇ Tob° to be Accounted for at the Laying the next Levies

Philip Rootes & John Whitinge are appointed Church Wardens, for the Ensuing Year, & Philip Rootes is appointed Collector of the Parish Levies for the Present Year. And John Whitinge has Enter'd into Bond with him as security for Performance thereof & Acknowledg'd the same

[95]
Order'd that William Bland Keep Mary Roffe the Ensuing Year & that he be allow'd 800ˡᵇ Tob°: for the same at laying the next Levies

Order'd that Barbary Groom keep Charles Mᶜ:Carty the Ensuing year & that she shall be allow'd 700ˡᵇ Tob°: Levied for the same at laying the next Levies

Order'd that Tho⁸: Bird keep his Mother Sarah Bird the Ensuing Year & that he be allow'd 700ˡᵇ Tob°: to be levy'd at the laying the next Levies

150   VESTRY BOOK OF STRATTON MAJOR PARISH

Order'd that the Church Wardens Provide a place & Necefsaries for the support of Thoˢ: Soward his Wife & Eliz* Brown, the Ensuing Year & that they bring in their Accoᵗ for the same at the laying of the Next Parish Levies.

It is Agreed by this Vestry that the Honᵇˡᵉ: Richᵈ: Corbin Esqʳ: send home to England for a Communion Table Cloth a Pulpit Cloth, a Cloth of the Desk, & 2 Surplices for the use of the New Church

It being the Opinion of this Vestry that the Pillars mention'd in the Agreement for Building the Church with Harry Gaines will be of but little service, they do hereby agree that the same may be left out, without his making any Abatement in the Sum to be paid for the said Building.

The several Procefsioners having return'd reports of their Proceedings in Procefsioning the Lands in this Parish the same are receiv'd & Order'd to be Recorded

Wᵐ: Robinson Rector

At a, Vestr held for stratto

[96]

At a Vestry held for Stratton Major Parish at the New Church on Friday the 4ᵗʰ Day of October 1765 to lay the Parish Levy.

John Robinson Esqʳ: Thoˢ: Reade Rootes
William Hunt   John Whiting   }Vestrymen
Present Richᵈ Shackelford   Franˢ: Gaines
Philip Rootes   & Wᵐ: Taliaferro

The Parish is   Dʳ. lbˢ Tob°
To the Revᵈ. Mʳ. Willᵐ: Robinson Comifsary   16000
To ditto for Shrinkage of Notes   640
To Griffith Elrington Reader   1200

To James Pryor d°	1200
To Ann Soward Sexton	750
To Amey Adams d°	750
To Francis Gains Clk. Vestry	700
To d°. for finding for the Communion	360
To John Whiting for the same	360
To William Bland for keeping Mary Roffe	800
To Barbary Groom for keeping Charles M°.Cartey	700
To Tho˙. Bird for keeping Sarah Bird	700
To ditto for keeping Tho˙: Soward	900
To ditto for keeping Mary Soward 6 Months	400
To Mary Hollinger for keeping Elizabeth Brown	500
To Mary Smith for keeping Mary Soward 6 Months	400
	26360
To 4 ℔ Cᵗ: on the above for Cask	1054
To the Clerk of this County for Copy Lists of Tithes	36
To Franˢ. Rain's to buy her Corn and Meat	600
To Unity Ellis for the support of her Children	600
To Mary Brown to buy her Corn &c	400
To Ann Soward for Martha Coats Support	600
To Jane Peacock to buy her Corn and Meat	400
To Mʳ. Robᵗ. Reid's Accoᵗ. for Store Goods dld for the use of the several poor of this Parish £15∥1∥7 @ 15/	2009
To Capᵗ. Wᵐ: Shackelford for d°. £4∥ 10 @ 15/	600
To Robᵗ. Brown's Accoᵗ: for a Coffin for Elizˢ Jones &c 20/	133
To Tho˙. Warren's Accoᵗ: for a sheet &c for d° 13/10	92
To Francis Gaines's Accoᵗ for the Poor Ballˢ £2∥17∥4½	383
To Benjˢ Williams's Accoᵗ: Taylors work 7/	46

To Zachⁿ: Groom for 1 ℔ʳ Shoes for Charles Mᶜ:Carty	33
To John Kidd for keeping and finding for Mildred Evans to this time	1500
To Thoˢ. Bird for his Wife's Accoᵗ: makᵍ: Cloth for Sarah Bird	63
To Benjᵃ Williams for his Taylors Accoᵗ. 7/6	50
To Majʳ. Richᵈ. Shackelford for Edwards & Peacock's Levy 63	140
	35099
To 6 ℔ Cᵗ: for Collection	2106
	37205

The Levies being Settled for this Present Year are found to amount to 37205ˡᵇˢ Tob°. which is Levied upon 990 Titheables at 38 lb Tob°: ℔ Poll and there will be an Overplus in the Hands of the Collector of 415ˡᵇ Tob°: to be accounted for at the laying of the next Parish Levies

[97]
The Honᵇˡᵉ: Richard Corbin & William Hunt are appointed Church Wardens for the Ensuing Year & William Hunt is appointed Collector for this Present Year Whereupon the said William Hunt has Enter'd into Bond with Wᵐ: Shackelford his Security & have Acknowledged the same

Order'd that the Collector Pay Sarah Edwards the abovemention'd Fraction of 415ˡᵇ Tob°: for the Support of her Children

Order'd that Barbary Groom keep Charles Mᶜ:Carty the Ensuing Year & that she have Seven Hundred Pounds

Tob°: Levied for the same at the Laying the next Parish Levies ——

Order'd that Thomas Bird keep Tho°: Soward the Ensuing Year & that he have Nine hundred Pounds Tob°: Levied for the same, at laying the next Parish Levies. Also that the said Bird keep his Mother the Ensuing Year & that he have Seven hundred Pounds Tob°. Levied for the same

Order'd that Charles Roane keep Mary Roffe the Ensuing Year & that he have 800[lb] Tob°: Levied for the same at Laying of the next Parish Levies

Order'd that John Kidd keep Mildred Evans the Evans the Ensuing Year & that he have 600[lb] Tob° Levied for the same at laying the next Parish Levies

Order'd that Mary Smith keep Mary Soward the Ensuing Year & that she have 800[lb] Tob°: Levied at the Laying the Next Levies ——

Order'd that the Church Wardens Provide a place for Elizabeth Brown, & that the Acco[t]. for the same be brought to the laying of the next Levies ——

William Shackelford is Appointed Vestryman in the Place & stead of John Foster who is removed out of this Parish

John Robinson

[98]

At a Vestry held for Stratton Major Parish at the New Church on Monday the 25 Day of August 1766

Present
The Rev[d]: M[r]. Commiſsary Robinson
The Hon Richard Corbin Esq[r]
William Hunt — John Whiting
Rich[d]: Shackelford — Francis Gaines
Philip Rootes — Tho°: Dillard

William Shackelford having taken the Oaths appointed by Act of Parliament & Subscribes to be Conformable to the Church of England as by Law Establish'd and is Added to this Vestry

Present William Shackelford

William Meredith is Appointed a Vestry man in the Place of John Robinson Esqr dec^d: & Samuel Metcalfe is appointed a Vestry man in the place of Thomas Reade Rootes dec^d:

W^m: Robinson Rector

At a Vestry held for Stratton Major Parish at the New Church on Monday the 29th Day of September 1766. to lay the Parish Levy

	The Rev^d: M^r. Commiſsary Robinson	
	The Hon Richard Corbin Esqr.	
Present	William Hunt Fra^s. Gaines	Vestrymen
	Rich^d: Shackelford Thos Dillard	
	Philip Rootes W^m: Taliaferro	
	John Whiting & W^m: Shackelford	

The Parish	D^r. lb^s Tob^o
To the Rev^d: M^r. Commiſsary Robinson	16000
To ditto for Shrinkage of Notes	640
To Griffith Elrington reader of the Upper Church	1200
To James Pryor ditto of the Lower	1200
To Ann Soward Sexton & for Washing the Surplice	750
To Amey Addams d^o: & d^o:	750
To Francis Gaines for being Clk of the Vestry	700
To the Hon Richard Corbin Esqr. & William Hunt for finding for the Communion Each 360 lb^s	720
	21960

To Barbary Groom for keeping Chaˢ: Mᶜ.Carty	700
To Charles Roan for keeping Mary Roffe	800
To Thoˢ. Bird for keeping his Mother Sarah Bird	700
	24160

[99]

Brought up	24160ˡᵇˢ
To ditto for keeping Thomas Soward 8 Months @ 900 lbˢ ℔ Annum	600
To John Kidd for keeping Mildred Evans	600
To Mary Smith for keeping Elizᵃ Brown	800
To Dennis Brenin for keeping Mary Soward	800
	26960
To 4 ℔ Cᵗ: on ditto for Cask	1078
To the Clerk of this County for 2 Lists Tithes Nʳ	36
To Frances Raines to buy her Corn and Meat	600
To Unity Ellis for the same	500
To Mary Brown to buy her Corn and Meat	400
To Ann Soward for Martha Coats	600
To Jane Peacock to buy her Corn and Meat	400
To Sarah Edwards to buy her Corn &c	400
To Elizabeth Guthrie to buy her Corn &c	400
To Ann Bowers to buy her Corn &c	400
To John Hooker for his Support	300
To William Shackelford's Accoᵗ for Sundry Goods dld for the Poor £6‖13‖7 @ 20/ ℔ Cᵗ	670
To Robert Reid & Cᵒ: for dᵒ: £3‖3‖8	320
To Alexʳ Roane for making 1 ℔ˣ Breeches for Charles MᶜCarty	18
To William Hunt for his Accoᵗ: for Steps and Benches	450
To dᵒ: for his Accoᵗ: of his Collection delinquents &c	304

To Tho⁸ Bird's Acco⁽: for Sundry's & Burying Thomas Soward	165
To Nicholas Burch for a Coffin for ditto	75
To William Drapers Wife to buy her Corn and Meat	400
	34476
To Salary for Collecting @ 6 ⅌ C^t 37222^{lb} Tob°	2107
	36583

The Levies being settled for this Present year are found to amount to 36583 lb⁸ of Tob° being levied upon 1006 Tithables at 37^{lb} Tob° ⅌ Poll and there will be an Overplus of 639^{lb} Tob°. in the Hands of the Collector to be accounted for at Laying the next Parish Levy.

Francis Gaines & William Shackelford are Appointed Church Wardens for the Ensuing Year, & William Shackelford is Appointed Collector of the Parish Levy for this Present Year, Francis Gaines became his Security & they have Acknowledged their Bond for the same

Order'd that Barbary Groom keep Cha⁸: M°Carty the Ensuing Year and that she have 700^{lbs} Tob°: levied for the same at Laying the Next Parish the next Parish Levies.

Order'd that Tho⁸: Bird keep his Mother Sarah Bird the Ensuing Year & that he have 700^{lb} Tob°: Levied for the same at Laying the next Parish Levies.

Order'd that Charles Roane keep Mary Roffe the ensuing Year & that he have 800^{lb} Tob° Levied for the same at laying the next Parish Levies.

[100]
Order'd that John Kidd keep Mildred Evans the Ensuing Year & that he have 600^{lb} Tob° Levied for him at Laying the next Parish Levies.

Order'd that Jane Didlake keep Eliz^a Brown the Ensuing Year & that She have 600^{lb} Tob°: Levied for the same at Laying the next Parish Levies

Order'd that Dennis Brenin keep Mary Soward the Ensuing Year & that he have 600^{lb} Tob°: Levied for the same at Laying the next Parish Levies.

Whereas James Collier having been for several Years Appointed to succeed his Brother William Collier as Vestryman in this Parish and having failed to Qualifie himself for that Purpose, it is agreed by this Vestry that Lyne Shackelford be Appointed a Vestryman instead of the said James Collier.

Order'd that the Collector demand and receive of the Administrators of John Robinson Esqr dec^d: the Sum of Two Hundred & Seventy Pounds Curr^t. Money which remains in his Hands for Tob°: Levied on this Parish and Collected and sold by him for the last Payment Allowed for Building the New Church in said Parish.

Order'd that William Hunt and William Shackelford make enquiry for a Convenient Piece of Land to Build a House on to keep and Entertain the Poor People of this Parish in and make information to this Vestry of their Proceedings.

W^m: Robinson Rector

At a Vestry held for Stratton Major Parish at the New Church on Tuesday the 21st: Day of April 1767.

Present
{ The Rev^d: M^r: Commiſsary Robinson
William Hunt Thos. Dillard
Richard Shackelford W^m: Taliaferro
John Whiting & W^m: Shackelford
Francis Gaines } Vestry men

I Lyne Shackelford do hereby Promise & agree to be Conformable to the Rules & Discipline of the Church of England, as by Law Established
       Lyne Shackelford

Lyne Shackelford having taken the Oaths Appointed by Act of Parliament & Subscribed to be Conformable to the Church of England as by Law Established is Added to this Vestry
     Present Lyne Shackelford

[101]

It is agreed & Order'd by this Vestry that the Church wardens Apply to Capt. John Pendleton, and know of him whether he will undertake in Behalf of the Administrators of John Robinson Esqr: dec^d to finish the Present Building of the above mention'd New Church in this Parish as it appears to the said Vestry that the said Administrators are Answerable to this Parish for the Sum of Two hundred & seventy Pounds Curr^t. Money which was Levied by the said Vestry on the Titheables in said Parish for the last Payment for Building the said Church & Vestry House, & Collected by him the said John Robinson Esqr: dec^d:
      W^m: Robinson Rector

At a Vestry held for Stratton Major Parish at the New Church on Wednesday the third day of June 1767

Present
{ The Rev^d: M^r. Commiſsary Robinson
The Hon. Rich^d: Corbin Esqr
William Hunt W^m. Taliaferro
Francis Gaines W^m. Shackelford
Thos: Dillard & Lyne Shackelford } Vestrymen

Whereas William Hunt & William Shackelford, Pursuant to a former Order of the Vestry of this Parish, have Reported that the Honble: Rich^d. Corbin Esqr: has Promised to make them a Title to Fifty Acres of Land Convenient to Build a House to Contain & accommodate the Poor People of this Parish in, It is thereupon agreed by a Majority of this Vestry that a House be Built thereon Thirty six foot long, sixteen foot wide, nine foot Pitch, with a Brick Chimney in the Middle, with two good fire places, to be fram'd of good Oak Timber Underpinn'd with Stone or Brick and cover'd with Cyprefs or Chestnut Shingles, 18 Inches long to shew six inches, a Shedd on one side, Ten foot wide with two Petitions & convenient Doors thereto, William Hunt with the Church Wardens are hereby impower'd & Order'd to prepare Articles of Agreement & employ a Workman to undertake Building the same, soon as Convenient.

I William Meredith do Promise and agree to be conformable to the Rules and Discipline of the Church of England as by Law Established
William Meredith

William Meredith having taken the Oaths appointed by Act of Parliament & Subscribed to be Conformable to the Rules Discipline of the Church of England as by Law Established and is Added to this Vestry
Present William Meredith

Order'd that the Church wardens agree with an undertaker to build a Corn House convenient to the before mentioned House for the use of the Poor, twelve foot long eight foot wide, & Six foot deep of good Oak Loggs or Chesnut Cover'd with Cyprefs Boards & set upon Stone.
W^m: Robinson

[102]

At a Vestry held for Stratton Major Parish at the New Church on Thursday the 3^d Day of December 1767

The Rev.ᵈ: Mʳ. Commiſsary Robinson
The Hon: Richard Corbin Esqʳ:
William Hunt   Thoˢ Dillard
Richᵈ. Shackelford   Wᵐ: Meredith
Francis Gaines   Lyne Shackelford

Pursuant to an Order of King & Queen County Court Dated the 11ᵗʰ Day of August 1767 That the Vestry of the several Parishes within this County Do Divide their Parishes into so many Precincts as to them shall seem most Convenient for Proceſsioning Every Persons Land therein, and to appoint Particular times for that purpose between the last Day of September and the last Day of March next Ensuing. Pursuant to an Act of Aſsembly in that Case made and Provided.

Order'd that Lyne Shackelford, Richard Crittenden, & Alexʳ Wedderburn, or any two of them do meet on the first Monday in January next, & go in Proceſsion of & see all & Every Persons land between Portopotank Creek & Mattasip Swamp plainly Marked. Continuing their Proceedings in all suitable Weather, untill the whole Precinct be finished. And all the Freeholders who are Inhabitants thereof are hereby required to attend the Proceſsioners According to Law. and the said Proceſsioners are farther Order'd to make & return to this Vestry at their next Meeting after the last Day of March Next a true Accoᵗ: of what Lands they have Proceſsioned, of the Persons Present at the same, of what Lands they have not Proceſsioned, and the Particular reason of such failure.

Order'd that Richᵈ. Anderson, William Taliaferro & George Standard, or any two of them do meet on the first Wednesday in January Next & go in Proceſsion of & see all & every Persons Land between Matasip & Pepetico Swamps Plainly Marked Continuing their Proceedings According to Law &c.

Order'd that Nicholas Dillard, James Collier, & John Collier Jun[r]: or any two of them do meet on the first Friday in January next & go in Proceſsion of & see all & Every persons Land Between Pepetico Swamp & Aracaco Creek & the Western Branch thereof plainly Marked. Continuing their Proceedings According to Law &c

Ordered that James Didlake, George Dillard, & William Bland, or any two of them do meet on the second Monday in January Next and go in Proceſsion of & see all & Every Persons Land between the Eastern & Western Branch, of Aracaco Creek Plainly Marked &c

Order'd that W[m]: Shackelford, Rich[d]: Wyatt & John Smith or any two of them do meet on the second Fryday in January next, & go in Proceſsion of & see all the Lands between the Western Branch & Aracaco Creek plainly Marked &c.

Order'd that James Trice, Tho[s]: Brushwood & George Dillard or any two of them do meet on the second Wednesday in January next, & go in Proceſsion of & see all the Lands between Burgeſses swamp & the Monack swamp, & from thence a strait Course between Mary Hollinger & Doctor Joyuex dec[d]: to Tarsatyan Swamp plainly Marked &c

[103]
Order'd that Edward Spencer Richard Garrett j[r]. & Tho[s]: Spencer or any two of them do meet on the third Monday in January next & go in Proceſsion of & see all the Lands between the Monack Swamp & on a strait Course therefrom to Tarsatyan Swamp, & the Branch next above William Hunts Plainly Marked &c

Ordered that Spencer Boyd, Arthur Ware, & Edward Ware, or any two of them do meet on the third Wednesday in January next & go in Proceſsion of and see all the Lands between the Branch next above William Hunts & the Extent upwards Plainly Marked &c

Order'd that Richard Garrett Christopher Ware & Humphrey Garrett jʳ: or any two of them do meet on the third Friday in January next and go in Proceſsion of & see all the Lands between Tarsatyan Swamp & great Heartquake, plainly Marked, Continuing their Proceedings in all suitable Weather untill the whole Precinct be finished, and all the Freeholders who are Inhabitants thereof are hereby required to Attend the said Proceſsioners According to Law and the said Proceſsioners are further Ordered to make & return to this Vestry at their next meeting after the last Day of March Next, a true Accoᵗ: of all the Lands they have Proceſsion'd, of the Persons present at the same, of what Lands they have not Proceſsion'd, and the particular reason of such failure.

	Dʳ lbˢ Tobº
The Parish	
To the Revᵈ: Mʳ. Commiſsary Robinson's Salary	16000
To allowance of Shrinkage of Notes 4 ℔ Cᵗ	640
To Griffith Elrington reader at Upper Church	1200
To Ann Soward Sexton at dº. &c	750
To James Pryor's Exors for his part of the Year Clk of Lower Church	300
To Willis Wills for the remaining part of the Year dº	900
To Amey Addams Sexton a dº. &c	750
To Francis Gaines for being CLK of the Vestry	1000
To ditto for finding for the Communion 4 times	360
To ditto for his Accoᵗ. Neceſsaries for the Poor &c £1∥12	160
To Barbary Groom for keeping Chaˢ. MᶜCarty	700
To Chaˢ. Roane for keeping Mary Roffe &c	800
To Thoˢ. Bird for keeping his Mother	700
To John Kidd for keeping Mildred Evans	600

To Jane Didlake for keeping Elizabeth Brown	600
To Dennis Brenin for keeping Mary Soward 6 Months	300
To Mary Hollinger for keeping d°: 6 Months @ 600ˡᵇ ℔ Ann	300
To William Shackelford for finding for the Communion	360
	26420
To 4 ℔ Cᵗ. on ditto for Cask	1057
To the Clerk of the Court Copy List of Tithes	36
To Wᵐ. Shackelfords Accoᵗ. Goods dld for the Poor £6‖12‖3 in Tobº: @ 20/ ℔ Cᵗ	662
To Robᵗ. Reid & Cº: for ditto £5‖7‖10½	540
To Robert Brown's Accoᵗ: mending Church Windows	100
To Alexʳ Roane's Accoᵗ. Taylors Work 7/6	38
To Thoˢ: Dillard's Accoᵗ: Neceſsaries found Jaˢ. Webb	106
To Frances Raines to buy her Corn & Meat	600
To Unity Ellis for the same	500
To Mary Brown for the same	400
To Martha Coats for the same	500
To Jane Peacock for the same	400
	31359

[104]

Dʳ. Brought up	31359ˡᵇˢ
To Elizabeth Guthrie to buy her Corn & Meat	400
To Ann Bowers for the same	400
To John Hooker for the same	300
To William Drapiers Wife to buy her Corn & Meat	400
To John Ireson for keeping Wᵐ. Draper 1 Month	50

To W{m}: Edw{d}: Waller for the Support of his Family	300
	33209
To David for the Support of his Daughter Eliz{a}	300
	33509
To Salary for Collecting 6 ⅌ C{t}	2010
	35519
C{r}. By 973 Titheables at 37{lb} Tob° ⅌ Poll	36001

The Levies being settled for this Present Year are found to Amount to 35519. lb{s} Tob° which is Levied upon 973 the Titheables of this Parish at 37{lbs} Tob°. ⅌ Poll, and there will be an Overplus in the Hands of the Collector of 482{lbs}: to be accounted for at the Laying of the next Parish Levies.

William Meredith, and Lyne Shackelford, is Appointed Church wardens for the Ensuing Year And Lyne Shackelford is Appointed Collector of the Parish Levies for this Present Year and it is agreed by this Vestry that Francis Gaines take his Bond with Security for the due Performance of the same.

Order'd that Barbary Groom keep Cha{s}. M{c}.Carty the Ensuing Year & that she be allowed 700{lb} Tob°: at the Laying of the next Parish Levies

Order'd that Cha{s}: Roane keep Mary Roffe and that he be allowed 800{lb} Tob°: at Laying the next Levies.

Order'd that Tho{s}: Bird keep his Mother the Ensuing Year and that he be allowed 700{lb} Tob°: at the Laying of the next Parish Levies.

Order'd that Margarett Campbell keep Elizabeth Brown the Ensuing Year & that she be allowed 600^{lb} Tob°: at laying the next Parish Levies.

Order'd that Dennis Brenin keep Mary Soward the Ensuing Year. & that he be allowed 600^{lb} Tob°. at the laying the next Parish Levies.

Order'd that John Kidd keep Mildred Evans the Ensuing Year & that he be allowed 400^{lb} Tob° at laying the next Parish Levies.

Order'd that Mary Smith keep Clayton Jones Wilburn, the Ensuing Year & that she be allowed 400^{lb} Tob° at laying the next Levies.

William Hare is Appointed Vestry man instead of Samuel Metcalf who refuses to Qualifie himself for that Purpose.

Amey Addams is continued Sexton, and it is Order'd that she be allowed 1000^{lb} Tob°: & Cask at the Laying of next Levies, and that she Perform that Office according to direction of the Vestry.

Order'd that the Church Wardens, Rich^d. Shackelford, William Hunt, and Francis Gaines or any Three or more of them, Allot the several Parishioners their Seats in the [105] New Church

Willm: Robinson Rector

1767
Dec.r 11th Pews Allotted to Families &c in the New Church Viz.t

North side
N.º 11
The Hon Rich.d: Corbin Esq.r
and his Family

N.º 10
M.r William Meredith
and his Family

South side
N.º 11
The Lady & Family of
John Robinson Esq.r. Dec.d

N.º 10
Col.º Philip Rootes & Family
Maj.r Rich.d: Shackelford & Family
M.r John Whiting & Family
M.r. W.m. Taliaferro & Family

N° 9

Mef.rs: Tho.s: Metcalfe
Sam.l Metcalfe
Rich.d. Anderson
Hansford Anderson
Andrew Crawford
Cornelius Livingston
Alex.r. Wedderburn
John Lyne
John Smith
Henry Strachey
John Shackelford
Ben: Shackelford
Philip Taliaferro

N° 8

Mef.rs: Tho.s: Metcalfes Wife
Sam.l: Metcafes Wife
Rich.d Anderson's Wife
M.rs. Mary Anderson Wid.o:
M.rs. Mary Ann Tibbs Wid.o
M.rs. Ann Collier Wid.o
M.rs. Cath.n Smith Wid.o
M.rs. Fra.s: Collier Wid.o
Allex.r: Wedderburn's Wife

N° 9

Mef.rs. William Hunt   ⎫
Francis Gaines   ⎪
Tho.s Dillard   ⎪
William Shackelford   ⎬ Vestrymen
Lyne Shackelford   ⎪
William Hare   ⎪
Tho.s. Dudley   ⎭
Gregory Smith
John Pendleton

N° 8

Mef.rs W.m: Hunts Wife & Daughters
Fra.s. Gaines Wife & Daughters
Tho.s Dillards Wife
Lyne Shackelford's Wife
W.m: Hare's Wife
M.rs. Fran.s. Shackelford Wid.o
Cornelius Livingston's Wife
Tho.m. Dudleys Wife
John Pendletons Wife

Nº 7 The Wives of	Nº 7		Nº 7	Nº 7
James Collier &	James Collier		Nichs: Mitchell	Pulpit &c
John Collier junº	John Collier		Chas. Collier	
Thos Drummonds Wife	George Pigg		Edw. Spencer	
Richd Crittendens Wife	Richard Crittenden		James Trice	
James Didlakes Wife	James Didlake		Chr. Ware	Nº 6
John Didlakes Wife	John Didlake		John Abbott	The Revd Mr Commissary
William Dudleys Wife	Nicholas Dillard		Spencer Boyd	Robinsons Family
Robt. B. Dudleys Wife	John Townley		James Boyd	
John Townleys Wife	Robt B. Dudley		Robt. Dudley	
Spencer Boyds Wife	Thos Drummond		Wm. Dudley	Nº 5
James Boyds Wife	George Dillard Drª		Robt. Smith	Mrs Rachel Garrett Widº
Mrs. Colliers Daughters			Thos. Dudley jr	Mr Jane Trice Widº
George Dillard Drª Wife			Zachy Shackelford jr	James Trices Wife
Geo Piggs Wife			Fras. Gaines jr	Christ. Wares Wife
				Thos Warrens Wife
Nº 6			Nº 6:	Cathª Collins Widº
George Livingstons Wife	George Livingston		Arthur Ware	George Brays Wife
Wm. Dudleys Wife	Wm Dudley		Thos Warren	Mr. Abbotts Daughters
Edw: Waldens Wife	Edward Walden		George Dillard	George Dillards Wife
Joyeux Collins Wife	Joyeux Collins		John Ware	Richd Brays Wife
Zachy Shackelfords Wife	Zachy Shackelford		Spencer Ware	Humphrey Garretts Wife

KING AND QUEEN COUNTY, VIRGINIA, 1729-1783

Henry Colliers	Wife	Henry Collier		Rich[d]: Bray	
Nich[s]: Dillards	Wife	George Standard		Humphrey Garrett j[r]	
George Standards	Wife	John Corr			

[106]

N° 6		**N° 6**		**N° 4**	
John Corr's	Wife	Willis Wills	Edw[d] Trice	Marg[t]. Campbell	
Willis Wills	Wife	Charles Roane	Ja[s]. Trice j[r]	Tho[s] Spencer's	Wife
John Robinsons	Wife	Jn°. Robinson	Rich[d] Wyatt	Jn° Ware's	Wife
Tho[s] Drummond j[r]	Wife	Tho[s] Drummond j[r]	Jn° Mitchell	W[m] Garretts	Wife
Widow Pryor		Jn° Drummond	Jacob Falkner	Edward Trices	Wife
			Tho[s] Spencer	James Trice j[r]	Wife
N° 5		**N° 5**	George Bray	Rich[d] Garrett j[r]	Wife
John Wallers	Wife	Cha[s]. Edwards		Jane Didlake	
W[m]. Blands	Wife	Jn°. Waller	**N° 5**	Rich[d]. Falkners	Wife
W[m] Bowdens	Wife	W[m]. Bland	Rich[d]. Falkner	Frances Didlake	
Jrem°. Majors	Wife	W[m]. Bowden	Rich[d]. Garrett j[r]	Jn° Mitchells Wife & Sister	
Widow Major		Jn° Muir	W[m]. Garrett	Chr[rs].: Stedmans	Wives
W[m]. Muirs	Wife	Jrem°. Major	W[m]. Muir		
Jn°. Muir's	Wife	Croxton Pryor	Chr: Stedman	**N° 3**	
Ja[s] Guthries	Wife	James Guthrie	Chr: Stedman j[r].	Tho[s] Brushwoods	Wife
Sam[l] Flemmings	Wife	W[m]. Wright	George Collins	Mary Hollinger	Wid°.

N° 5—Continued		N° 5—Continued	N° 5—Continued	N° 3—Continued	
Jn° Colliers	Wife	Wᵐ. Webley	Thoˢ Mitchell	James Milbeys	Wife
		Samˡ. Flemming	Danˡ. Shackelford	Humphrey Garretts	Wife
N° 4		John Collier Cobˢ:	Rich⁴. Walden	Rich⁴. Garretts	Wife
Rich⁴: Wyatts	Wife	Robᵗ. Groom		Fraˢ. Ware	Wid°
Solomon Damms	Wife		**N° 4**	Jn° Ware Drˢ.	Wife
Wᵐ: Bakers	Wife	**N° 4**	Gabriel Overstreet	Robᵗ. Garretts	Wife
Wᵐ. Bland jʳ.	Wife	Rich⁴. Guthrie	Robᵗ Brown	George Collins	Wife
Samˡ. Browns	Wife	Solomon Damm	Humphrey Garrett	Robᵗ. Browns	Wife
Willᵐ: Webleys	Wife	Wᵐ. Baker	Rich⁴. Garrett	Thoˢ Mitchells	Wife
John Kidds	Wife	Wᵐ. Bland jʳ	Robert Garrett	Daniel Shackelfords	Wife
Thoˢ Corr's	Wife	Samˡ. Brown	Thoˢ: Brushwood	Rich⁴ Waldens	Wife
Wᵐ. Corr's	Wife	John Kidd	Edw⁴: Ware		
Zachʸ Grooms	Wife	Thoˢ. Corr	John Ware Dragⁿ	**N° 2**	
John Newcombs	Wife	Wᵐ. Corr	James Milbey	Ben: Moores	Wife
Thoˢ Wyatts	Wife	Zachʸ Groom	Rich⁴ Burk	John Holderby's	Wife
		John Newcomb	Nichˢ. Burch	Thoˢ Cookes	Wife
N° 3		Thoˢ. Wyatt	Robᵗ. Green	Thoˢ Sowards	Wife
Sarah Gramshill		David Pearce	Lewis Walden	Ben: Soward's	Wife
Jaˢ Emmons	Wife			Elizⁿ Tureman	Wid°

KING AND QUEEN COUNTY, VIRGINIA, 1729-1783   171

	Nº 3		Nº 3	
Anne James			John Holderby	Jnº Morris's — Wife
Jnº Guthrie's — Wife	John Briggs		Thoˢ Bird	Jnº Holderby's — Wife
Jnº Ireson's — Wife	James Emmons		Ben: Moore	Nichˢ Burches — Wife
Wᵐ. Sykes — Wife	Jnº Evans		John Holderby Jr	Barbara Groom — Widº
	John Gramshill		Thoˢ Cooke	
	John James		Thoˢ Soward	
	John Osborn		Ben: Soward	
	John Guthrie		Ben: Tureman	
	Jnº Ireson		Jnº. Morris	
	Willᵐ: Sykes		Wᵐ. Mansfield	
			Jnº. Mᶜ.Carty	

	Nº 2	Nº 2
	John Hooker	Dennis Brenin
	Wᵐ. Hooker	Jnº. Banks
		Thoˢ. Gill
		Jos: MᶜCarty

[107]
At a Vestry held for Stratton Major Parish on Friday the 4th Day of March 1768

Present
The Honble: Rich^d: Corbin Esqr.	
William Hunt	Thos: Dillard
Rich^d: Shackelford	William Taliaferro
Philip Rootes	William Shackelford
Francis Gaines	Lyne Shackelford

Vestry men

I William Hare do Promise and agree to be Conformable to the Doctrine & Discipline of the Church of England as by Law Establish'd

W Hare

William Hare having taken the Oaths appointed by Act of Parliament and Subscribed to be conformable to the Doctrine and Discipline of the Church of England as by Law Established is added to this Vestry

Richd Corbin

At a Vestry held for Stratton Major Parish on Monday the 4 Day of April 1768

Present
The Honble. Richard Corbin Esqr	
William Hunt	Willm. Taliaferro
Philip Rootes	Willm. Shackelford
Willm Meredith	Francis Gaines
Lyne Shackelford	Thos: Dillard
William Hare	

Vestry men

Order'd that the Church Wardens give Publick Notice that the Vestry will meet on the 10th Day of May next, to receive Proposals of all Persons inclineable to supply this

Parish with a piece of Land suitable and agreeable for a Glebe.

It is Agreed by this Vestry that the Church Wardens Certifie the Administrators of John Robinson Esqr: dec^d: that the said Vestry have Received the Church which was built by Major Harry Gaines dec^d: and finished by William Muir according to their Directions, and that it will be agreeable to the said Vestry for the said Muir to be paid the Money agreed with him for, by Capt. John Pendleton, being Two hundred & fifty Pounds Curr^t. Money.

It is also agreed by a Majority of this Vestry to receive the Rev^d: William Donlap as Minister of this Parish

R^d: Corbin

[108]

At a Vestry held for Stratton Major Parish the 10th Day of May 1768.

The Honble: Rich^d. Corbin Esqr.		
William Hunt.	William Taliaferro	
Present Rich^d: Shackelford.	Willm. Shackelford	Vestry men
Philip Rootes.	Lyne Shackelford	
Francis Gaines.	William Hare	

Rich^d. Anderson, W^m: Taliaferro, & George Standard Proceſsioners return'd a Report of their Proceedings which is Order'd to be register'd

James Didlake, George Dillard, & William Bland Proceſsioners return'd a Report of their Proceedings which is Ord^d: to be Register'd

Lyne Shackelord, & Alexander Wedderburn Proceſsioners return'd a Report of their Proceedings which is Ord^d: to be Register'd

John Smith, & Richard Wyatt Procefsioners, return'd a Report of their Proceedings which is Ord⁴: to be Register'd

Nicholas Dillard & James Collier, Procefsioners return'd a Report of their Proceedings which is Order'd to be Register'd

Edward Spencer, & Thoˢ. Spencer Procefsioners return'd a report of their Proceedings which is Order'd to be Register'd

The Vestry have agreed to purchase the Houses and Land belonging to Col: Philip Rootes lying on the Main Road, containing 300 Acres or thereabouts, for a Glebe for the Use of the Minister of this Parish, and do agree to pay the said Rootes, Six hundred Pounds Current Money for the same, on or before, the first Day of January next, or whatever part of that Sum remains unpaid at that Day to carry Interest untill it shall be paid a Good and sufficient Conveyance of the said Tract of Land & Houses being first made thereto.

          Richᵈ: Corbin

[109]

At a Vestry held for Stratton Major Parish at the House Purchased of Colˡ: Philip Rootes for a Glebe the 3 Day of October 1768.

Present

The Revᵈ: William Dunlap
The Hon: Richᵈ: Corbin Esqʳ:
William Hunt
Philip Rootes
Francis Gaines
Thomas Dillard &
William Taliaferro
William Shackelford
William Meredith
Lyne Shackelford
William Hare

} Vestry men

Order'd that the Church Wardens agree with Workmen to find Materials & do what repairs are by this Vestry found neceſsary to be done to the Glebe House and the out Houses belonging thereto. and it is agree'd that Tobacco be Levied for the Payment thereof at the Laying of the Parish Levy for this Present Year

Whereas the Rev^d M^r. Dunlap hath agreed with Thomas Lambeth to Finish and fit up the Out house at the Glebe, formerly made use of as a Wash-house, for a Study, for the Sum of Seventeen Pounds, it is agreed by this Vestry that Tob^o. be Levied on the Parish at laying the Levies for this present Year, to raise that Sum of Money to pay the said Lambeth Provided he finish the same according to agreement

Rich^d: Corbin

Absent the Hon: Rich^d: Corbin Esqr:

Order'd that the Church Wardens do agree with some Workman to Studd & Board up the Windows at the upper Church & secure the Doors, Also that they turn W^m: Broadway & his Family out of the Vestry House, and dispose of it to any well dispos'd Person on the best terms they can, for the benefit of the Poor of this Parish

W^m: Hunt

[110]

At a Vestry held for Stratton Major Parish the 8th: Day of November 1768 To lay the Parish Levies

The Rev^d: William Dunlap

The Hon Rich^d: Corbin Esqr.	William Taliaferro	
William Hunt	William Shackelford	
Present Philip Rootes	William Meredith	Vestry men
Francis Gaines	Lyne Shackelford	
Thomas Dillard	William Hare	

	Dr. lbˢ Tobᵒ
The Parish	
To the Revᵈ. Mʳ. Commiſsary Robinson for 3 months	4000
To dᵒ: for Shrinkage of Notes 4 ⅌ Cᵗ.	160
To the Revᵈ: Wᵐ. Dunlap. for 6 Months	8000
To dᵒ: for Shrinkage of Notes 4 ⅌ Cᵗ.	320
To Griffith Elrington Reader	1200
To Willis Wills Reader of the Lower Church 3 Months	300
To Ann Soward Sexton of the upper Church 3 Months	188
To Amey Adams Sexton ⅌ Agreement	1000
To Francis Gaines for performing the Office of Clk Vestry	700
To Barbary Groom for keeping Charles Mᶜ:Carty	700
To Charles Roane for keeping Mary Roffe &c	800
To Thomas Bird for keeping his Mother	700
To Margaret Campbel for keeping Elizᵃ Brown	600
To Dennis Brenin for keeping Mary Soward	600
To John Kidd for keeping Mildred Evans	400
To Mary Smith for keeping Clayton Jones Wilburne	400
	20068
To 4 ⅌ Cᵗ. on Ditto for Cask	803
	20871
To William Shackelford for providing for the Communion ⅌ Agreement	1000
To the Clerk of this County Court for 2 Copies List of Tithes	36
To Frances Raines for her Support	600
To Unity Ellis for the same	500
To Mary Brown for the same	400
To Martha Coats for the same	500

To Jane Peacock for the same	400
To Elizᵃ Guthrie for the same	400
To Ann Bowers for the Support of her Children	400
To the Hon. Richᵈ: Corbin Esqʳ for his accoᵗ £19‖—‖— @ 20 ℔ Cᵗ	1900
To David Ker for drawing deeds for the Glebe Land £2‖10	250
	27257
To John Lyne's Store Accoᵗ: Sundries for the Poor £4‖16‖4½	482
To William Shackelford for D°. £9‖14‖2½	971
To William Muir for his Accoᵗ £3‖	300
To Philip Rootes for mendᵍ: the Plastering & whitewashing the Glebe House	300
To David Pearce for the Support of his Daughter	500
To Alexʳ. Roane ℔ his accoᵗ. 7/6	38
To Mary Bowdric for her support to be laid out by the Church Wardens	400
To Mary Smith for keeping Clayton Jones Wilburne 1766 & 7	600
To Elizᵃ Jones to be laid out in Necefsaries by the Church Wardens	200
	31048
To Edward Walden his Accoᵗ £2	200
To Tob°. To be sold by the Collector for raising Money towards Paying for the Glebe and the repairs on the Same	15000
	46248
To 6 ℔ Cᵗ for Collecting 46248ˡᵇ Tob°	2775
	49023

[111]

	lbs Tob°
C^r By 980 Tithables @ 50^lb Tob° ℔ Poll	49000
By Ball^s of Lyne Shackelfords Acco^t ℔ last years Collection	205
	49205

Absent the Rev^d: M^r. Dunlap

The Levies being Settled for this present Year are found to Amount to 49023^lbs Tob°. being Levied upon 980 Tithables, at 50^lb Tob°. ℔ Poll, and there will be a Ball^s due from the Collector of 182^lb Tob° to be accounted for at the laying the next Levies ———

Thomas Dillard, & William Hare are appointed Church Wardens for the Ensuing Year, & Thomas Dillard is appointed Collector of the Parish Levy for this Present Year, Whereupon William Hare Enter'd into Bond with him as security & have acknowledged the same

Orderd with the consent of Col^l. Philip Rootes that the Money agreed to be paid him for the Glebe purchased of him, be paid unto Meſs^rs Capel & Osgood Hanbury of London Merch^ts or their Agents ———

Order'd that the Ball^s due from the Estate of the Rev^d: M^r: W^m. Robinson Deceased to this Parish be paid to the said Hanbury's or their Agents in part satisfaction for the said Glebe.

Absent the Hon Rich^d. Corbin

Order'd that Barbary Groom keep Charles McCarty the Ensuing Year. & that she have 700^lb Tob°. levied for the same at laying the next Parish Levies ———

Order'd that Charles Roane keep & find Mary Roffe the Ensuing Year and that he be allow'd 800^lb Tob° For the same.

Ordered that Dennis Brenin keep Mary Soward the Ensuing Year & that he be allow'd 600^{lb} Tob° for the same

Order'd that Thomas Bird keep his Mother the Ensuing Year and that he be allow'd 700^{lb} Tob° for the same

Order'd that Margaret Campbel keep Eliz* Brown the Ensuing Year and that she be allowd'd 600^{lb} Tob°. for the same

Order'd that John Kidd keep Mildred Evans the Ensuing Year & that he be allow'd 400^{lb} Tob°. for the same

Order'd that Mary Smith keep Clayton Jones Wilburne the Ensuing Year, and that she be allow'd 400^{lb} Tob° to be Levied at the laying the next Parish Levies

Order'd that the 300^{lb} Tob° & Cask which is Levied for Willis Wills be sold by the Collector with the other Tob° Levied to be sold for the use of the Parish

W^m. Hunt

N B on Examining the Lists of Tithables, I find 20 Tithes more then the Levy was laid upon, which @ 50^{lb} Tob° ⅌ Poll amounts to 1000^{lb} more to be sold & accounted for by the Collector at laying the next Parish Levy

[112]

At a Vestry held for Stratton Major Parish the 15th day of November 1769 To lay the Parish Levy

Present

The Rev^d. M^r. Willm. Dunlap

William Hunt	William Shack- elford
Francis Gaines	William Mere- dith
Thomas Dillard	
William Taliaferro	William Hare

} Vestry men

The Parish D*ʳ*. in lbs Tob°.	
To the Rev*ᵈ* M*ʳ*. Will*ᵐ*. Dunlap	16000
To ditto for Shrinkage of Notes 4℔ C*ᵗ*.	640
To Griffith Elrington Reader	1200
To Amey Adams Sexton	1000
To Frances Gaines for Perform*ᵍ*. the Office of Clk of the Vestry	700
To Barbary Groom for Charles M*ᶜ*.Carty	700
To Charles Roane for keeping & finding Mary Roffe	200
To Thomas Bird for keeping his Mother	700
To Margaret Campbell for keeping Eliz*ᵃ*. Brown	600
To Dennis Brenin for keeping Mary Sword	600
To John Kidd for keeping Mildred Evans	400
To 4 ℔ C*ᵗ*. for Cask	910
To Will*ᵐ*. Shackelford for Provid*ᵍ*. for the Comm*ⁿ*.	1000
To the Clk. for Copy of the List of Tithables	36
To Frances Rain's for her Support	500
To Unity Ellis for the Same	500
To Mary Brown for the Same	400
To Martha Coats for the Same	400
To Jane Peacock for the Same	400
To Eliz*ᵃ*. Guthrie for the same	400
To Ann Bowers for the support of her Children	300
To David Pearce for the Support of his daughter	400
To Mary Bowdric for her support to be laid out by the Ch Wardens	300
To Rob*ᵗ*. Brown for the Support of his Children the Same	400
To William Draper & his Wife to Buy Corn &c	500
To W*ᵐ*: Edw*ᵈ*. Waller to Buy him Corn for his Children	300
To Ann Sword to Buy her Corn & meat	250
To Judith Bunn to be laid out in meat by the Ch: Wardens	200

To Humphrey Garrett. for a lev'y over-paid last
    Year   50
To Edwd. Spencer fo his Acc^t. for 3 Barrels Corn
    found Robt. Brown and Boarding John Gard-
    ner 2 Months £3||10   312
To George Dillard for Boarding John Gardner 2½
    Months @ 50/   223
To Thomas Dillard for his Acc^t. Corn &c for the
    poor £2||13
To ditto for John Newcomb's Acc^t. Doctering
    John Gardner 9/   276
To Willm. Hare for his Acc^t. Corn &c for the Poor
    £1||6||2   120
                                                          ———————
                        Carried up   30917
    [113]   lbs Tob°.
    Parish Dr Brought up   30917
To John Lyne for Sundry goods dl^d. for the
    poor   £5|| 0|| 7   448
To William Shackelford ℔ Acc^t. ditto 4||19||11½ 445
To Lyne Shackelford ℔ his Acc^t. for 2
    Water Juggs   6|| 27
To Edwd. Walden for Inclosing &
    mending the Bellows of the Or-
    gan   £5|| 0|| 445
To William Shackelford for John
    Hookers Acc^t.   £1||13|| 3   147
To William Mure for Clearing the Church Yard   700
                                                          ———————
                                                           33129
To the Collecters Salary 6 ℔ C^t. on 33129^{lbs} Tob°   1988
                                                          ———————
                                                           35117
C^r. By 942 Tithables at 38 lbs. Tob°. ℔ Pole   35796
                                                          ═══════

The Levies being Settled for this Present Year are found to Amount to 35117 Pounds Tobacco being Levied upon 942 Tithables at 38^{lb} Tob°. ⅌ Pole and there will remain an Overplus of 679^{lbs}. of Tob°. in the Collectors hands, to be Accounted for. at the laying of the Next Parish Lev'y.

Richard Shackelford & William Taliaferro are Appointed Church Wardens for the Ensuing Year, and William Taliaferro is Appointed Collector of the Parish Levies for this Present year Whereupon W^m. Shackelford & Francis Gaines became Security & Acknowledged Bond for the Same

Ordered that Barbary Groom keep Charles McCarty the Ensuing Year & that she have 700^{lbs}. Tob° Levied for the same at the Laying the nex Parish Lev'y

Ordered that Thos. Bird keep his Mother the Ensuing Year & that he have 700^{lbs}. Tob°. Levied for the Same at the laying the Next Parish Lev'y

Ordered that Dennis Brenin keep Mary Sword the Ensuing year & that he have 600^{lbs}. Tob°. Levied for the Same at the laying the next Parish Lev'y

Ordered that Richard Bray keep Eliz^a. Brown the Ensuing year, & that he have 550^{lbs}. Tob°. Levied for the same at the Laying the Next Parish Lev'y

It is Agree'd by this Vestry that any Person who will undertake to keep John Gardner the Ensuing Year shall be Allowed 700^{lbs}. Tob°. at the Laying the Next Parish Lev'y

Ordered that the 250^{lbs}. Tob° Levied for Ann Sword do remain in the hands of the Collector & to be Accounted for, at the laying the Next Parish Levies

Ordered that the late Collector Settle his Acc⁽ᵗˢ⁾. of the Collection for the last year, with the Present Collector & Francis Gaines, and that the same be return'd to the Next Vestry.

W^m. Hunt

[114]

At a Vestry held for Stratton Major Parish at the Vestry House on Wednesday the 14th day of November 1770 to lay the Parish Lev'y

The Hon. Rich^d. Corbin Esqr.	William Taliaferro	
William Hunt	William Meredith	Vestrymen
Present Francis Gaines	Lyne Shackelford	
Thos. Dillard	William Hare	

The Parish is	D^r. in lbs. Tob^o.
To the Rev^d. Willm. Dunlap	16000
To ditto for Shrinkage of Notes	640
To Francis Gaines on Acc^t. of Griffith Elrington Serving as Reader 4 Months	400
To Thomas Va∫s for ditto 8 Months	800
To Amey Adams Sexton	1000
To Francis Gaines for Perform^g. the Office of Clk of the Vestry	700
To Barbary Groom for keeping Charles McCarty	700
To Thos. Bird for keeping his Mother	700
To Jane Didlake for keeping Elz^a. Brown ℔ Rich^d. Bray's Order	550
To Dennis Brenin for keeping Mary Sword	600
	22090
To 4 ℔ C^t. on d^o. for Cask	884
To William Shackelford for finding for the Comm^n.	1000

184   VESTRY BOOK OF STRATTON MAJOR PARISH

To the Clk of the County for two Copy's of List Tithables	36
To John Townley for keeping John Gardner	700
To Willm Taliaferro ℔ Acc^t. Poark & Corn found Thos. Lawson	230
To John Waller for Beef found Thos Lawson	18
To Doctor Hare for Physick Admin^d. to d^o.	45
To Lyne Shackelford for wheat, Beef & Corn for Thos Lawson	146
To Thos Dillard for Corn & meat found David ODear	86
To Rich^d. Shackelford: for Ball. Unity Ellis's Acc^t	47
To John Lyne ℔ Acc^t. Goods for the Poor. £7‖7‖4½	885
To Susanna Sykes for keeping Margaret Nettles 2 Mo^s.	120
To Lyne Shackelford for Saml. Metcalf's Levies for 1768	185
	26472
To Tob^o. to be sold by the Church Wardens to Raise Money towards paying for the Glebe	7000
To Frances Raines for her Support	500
To Unity Ellis for ditto	500
To Mary Brown for ditto	400
To Martha Coats for ditto	400
To Eliz^a Guthrie for ditto	400
To Ann Bowers for the Support of her Children	300
To Mary Bowdric for her Support	300
	36272
[115]	lbs Tob^o.
Parish D^r. Brought Up	36272
To Ann Brown for the Support of her Children	400

To W^m. Edwd. Waller to buy Corn for his Children	300
To Ann Sword for her Support	250
	37222
To Lyne Shackelford to be laid out in Neceſsarye's for the use of Thos. Lawson	700
To Eliz^a. Holderby for to Buy meat for Children	200
To Willm Bean for Burying & find^g. a Coffin for Jane Peacock	150
To Eliz^a Jones to buy her Corn	200
To James Guthrie for keeping Eliza Draper	400
	38872
To Salary for Collecting at 6 ℔ C^t. on 38872^{lbs}	2332
	41204
C^r By 898 Tithables at 46^{lbs}. Tob°. ℔ Pole	41308

The Levies being Settled for this Present Year are found to Amount to 41204^{lbs} Tob°. being Leie'd on 898 Tithables at 46^{lbs}. Tob°. ℔ Pole & there will remain an Overplus of 104^{lbs}. Tob°. in the hand[ ] of the Collector.

The Honble. Rich^d. Corbin Esqr. & Philip Rootes is Appointed Church Wardens for the Ensuing Year & Francis Gaines Jun is Appointed Collector of the Parish Levies for this Present Year whereup the Honble. Richd Corbin Esqr. became his security & Acknowledged Bond for the Same.— Absent the Hon: Rich^d. Corbin Esqr. —

Ordered that Barbary Groom keep Charles McCarty the Ensuing year at the rate of Seven hundred Pounds Tob°. ℔ Annum

Ordered. that Thos. Bird Keep his Mother Sarah Bird the Ensuing year at the Same rate

Ordered. that Dennis Brenin Keep Mary Sword the Ensuing year at the rate of 600^{lbs}. Tob°. ℔ Annum

Ordered that Esther Garrett keep Eliz^a Brown the Ensuing year at the rate of 550^{lbs} Tob°. ℔ An.

It is agree'd by this Vestry that 700^{lbs} Tob°. will be Allowed any Person who will Board John Gardner. untill the laying of the next Parish Lev'y

W^m. Hunt

[116]
At a Vestry held for Stratton Major Parish at the Vestry House of the Said Parish the 1st. day of October 1771.

Present

The Hon. Rich^d. Corbin Esqr.
William Hunt
Philip Rootes
Francis Gaines
Thomas Dillard

Willm. Taliaferro
Willm. Shackelford
Lyne. Shackelford
Willm. Hare.

} Vestrymen

Pursuant to an Order of King & Queen County Court dated the   Day of   1771 That the Vestry's of the Several Parishe's within this County, do Divide their Parishe's into so many Precincts as to them shall seem most Convenient for Procefsioning every Person's Land therein, & to Appoint Particular times for that Purpose between the last Day of September & the last Day of March Next, Ensuing, Pursuant to an Act of Afsembly in that Case made & Provided

Ordered that Lyne Shackelford Alex^r. Wedderburn & Corn^l. Livingston or any two of them do meet on the first Monday in January Next, and go in Procefsion of, & see all & every Person's Land between Poropotank Creek & Mattassip Swamp Plainly Marked, Continuing their Proceedings in all Suitable Weather untill the whole Precinct be finished, and all the Freeholders who are Inhabitants thereof are hereby required to Attend the said Proceſsioners According to Law. And the said Proceſsioners are further Ordered to make & return to this Vestry at their Next meeting after the last Day of March next, a true Acc^t. of what lands they have Proceſsioned, of the Persons Present at the same, of what Lands they have not Proceſsioned, and the Particular reason of Such Failure

Ordered that Rich^d. Anderson W^m. Taliaferro & Joyeux Collins, or any two of them do meet on the first Wednesday in Janary Next, & go in Proceſsion of. & see all & every Person's Land between Mattasip & Pepetico Swamps Plainly marked, Continuing their Proceedings According to law &c

Ordered that James Collier John Collier Jun. & Edwd. Walden. or any two of them do meet on the first Friday in January Next, & go in Proceſsion of & see all & every Persons Land, between Pepetico Swamp & Arracaco Creek. & the. Western Branch thereof Plainly Marked, Continuing their Proceedings According to Law &c.

Ordered: that James Didlake George Dillard & Thos. Bland, or any two of them do meet on the Second Monday in January Next, & go in Proceſsion of & see all & every Persons Land between the Eastern & Western Branch of Arracaco Creek Plainly Marked Continuing their Proceedings according to Law &c

Ordered that John Lyne Humphrey Garrett. & Chris^r. Steadman or any two of them do meet on the second Wednesday in January Next & go in Proceſsion of & See all & every Persons Land between the Western Branch & Arracaco Creek Plainly Marked &c.

Ordered that James Trice Thos. Brushwood & George Dillard or any two of them do meet on the second Friday in January Next & go in Procefsion of & see all & every Persons Land between Burgefses Swamp & the Monack Swamp, & from thence a Strait Course between Mary Hollenger's & the Land lately the Property of Doctor Joyeux Dec⁴. to Tarsatyan Swamp Plainly Marked &c.

[117]
Ordered that Thoˢ. Spencer Charles Roane & James Campbell or any two of them do meet on third Monday in January Next, & go in Procefsion of & see all & every Persons Land between the Monack Swamp & on a Strait Course down to Tarsatyan Swamp, & the Branch Next above Wᵐ. Hunts Plainly Marked &c.

Ordered that Isaac Ware Edw⁴. Ware & Spencer. Ware or any two of them do meet on the Third Wednesday in January Next. & go in Procefsion of & see all the Lands between the Branch Next above William Hunts & the Extent upwards Plainly Marked &c.

Ordered that Rich⁴. Garrett Chrisʳ Ware & Rich⁴ Walden or any two of them do Meet on the Third Friday in January Next, & go in Procefsion of & see all the Lands between Tarsatyan Swamp & Great Heartquake Swamp Plainly Marked Continuing their Proceedings According to Law &c.

The Parish is	Dʳ. in llds. Tobº.
To the Revᵈ. Willᵐ. Dunlap	16000
To ditto for Shrinkage of Notes 4 ℔ Cᵗ.	640
To Thomas Vafs Reader for	
To Willis Wills dº for	
To Amey Adam's Sexton	1000
To Francis Gaines for Performing the Office of Clk of the Vestry	1000
To Barbary Groom for keeping Charles MᶜCarty	700
To Thomas Bird for keeping his Mother	700

To Esther Garrett. for keeping Eliz⁸. Brown	550
To Dennis Brenin for keeping Mary Sword	600
To Joyeux Collins for keeping John Gardner	800
To 4 ℔ Cᵗ. on dᵒ. Cask	928
To the Clk of the County for Copy of List Tithables	36
To Frances Raines for her Support	500
To Mary Brown for dᵒ.	400
To Martha Coats for dᵒ.	400
To Ann Bowers for the Support of her Children	300
To Wᵐ. Ewᵈ. Waller for the Support of his Children	300
To Ann Sword for her Support	250
To Eliz⁸. Holderby for Support of her Children	200
To Eliz⁸. Jones for her Support	200
To James Guthrie for Eliz⁸. Draper	300
To John Kidd for keeping Mildred Evans two Year	400
To Tobᵒ. to be sold by the Collector to discharge the several Accᵗˢ due in Money to Sundry Persons, Pursuant to the Orders of this Vestry	3000
To Salary for. Collecting at 6 ℔ Cᵗ.	1825
Cʳ. By 900 Tithables at 36ˡᵇ Tobᵒ. ℔ Poll	32400

[118]

The Levies being Settled For this Present Year Are found to Amount to 32400ˡᵇ of Tobᵒ. being Levied upon 900 Tithables at 36ˡᵇ Tobᵒ. ℔ Poll & there will be an Over plus in the Hands of the Collector of 171ˡᵇ. Remaining to be Accounted For at Laying the Next Parish Levie

William Hunt & Fran⁸. Gaines are oppointed Church Wardens for the Ensuing Year & W^m. Hunt is oppointed Collector of the Parish Levies for this Present Year, Whereupon the Said W^m. Hunt has Entered into Bond with Fran⁸. Gaines Security & have Acknowledged the same

John Taylor Corbin Esqr. is Appointed Vestry Man in the room of John Whiting decd —

Order'd that Tho⁸. Dillard Collector for the Year 1768. Pay the Ball of the Money, due on the Settlement Made by Order of Vestry By Fran⁸. Gaines & W^m. Taliaferro being £4‖12‖9 Corr^t. Money unto David Ker as agent for Meſs^rs. Hanbury in part Payment for the Glebe

Order'd That Fran⁸. Gaines Ju^r. pay the Money in his hands for the 7000^lb. Tob^o., Levied last Year to the Said M^r. Ker on the Same Acc^t. being £57‖5‖8 Currant Money

Where as W^m. Taliaferro Collector For the Year 1769 Appears by his Acco^t to be Indebted, to this Parish A Ball of 957^lb Tob^o. it is Agreed by this Vestry that he be Indulged in the payment of the same untill the Laying of the Nxt Parish Levie ——

Order'd that the Church Wardens Apply to the Court for an Order to Bind Mildred Evans an Orphan According to Law ——

Order'd that the Collector pay James Mills 30/ for Blowing the Bellows of the organ in 1769 ——

Order'd that the Collector Pay the Several Acco: here after Mentioned After he has Made Sale of the Tob^o. Levied for that Purpose as followeth Viz^t.
To Matthew Anderson ⅌ Acco^t Store Goods
    for the poor   £ 2‖17‖ 4
To Fran⁸. Gaines ⅌ d^o. Shoos &c   1‖ 2‖ 6
To John Orburn ⅌ Acco.   2‖—‖—

KING AND QUEEN COUNTY, VIRGINIA, 1729-1783   191

To John Lyne ⅌ Acco. Store Goods for the Poor	3‖ 2‖	7
To W^m. Wright ⅌ Acco. Taylos work d°.	—‖10‖	—
To Edwd. Walden Acco. Steps Glazing &c at the Church	7‖10‖	—
	17‖ 2‖	5

Order'd that Barbary Groom Keep Ch^s. M^c.Carty the Ensuing Year & that she have 700^{lb}. Tob°. Levied for the Same at laying the Nxt Parish Levie

[119]
Orderd Thos. Bird Keep his Mother the Ensuing Year & that he have 700^{lb} Tob°. Levied for the Same at laying the Next Parish Levy

Order'd that Eliz. Garrett keep Eliz. Brown the Ensuing Year And the she have 550^{lb} Tob°. Levied for the Same at laying the Next P. Levy

Order'd that Denis Brining keep Mary Sweard the Ensuing Year & that he have 600^{lb}. Tob°. Levied for the Same at laying the Next Parish Levie

Order'd that Joyeux Collins keep John Gardner the Ensuing Year And that he have 800^{lb}. Tob°. Levied for the same at Laying the Next Parish Levie

Ordered & Agreed by a majority of this Vestry that W^m. Hunt Philip Rootes W^m. Taliaferro W^m. Hare & John Taylor Corbin Esqr or any three of them do Meet View & Consider Whether the Land Offer'd as a presant to this Parish by the Hon. Rich^d. Corbin Esqr or that Propos'd to be Sold by M^r. Jn°. Lyne, will be Most Convenient & agreeable to Erect a House on for the Reception & Acomidation of the Poor people of this Parish

And according to their determination the Same Gentlemen are directed to Proceed & EnGage a Workman to

192 VESTRY BOOK OF STRATTON MAJOR PARISH

Undertake the Building of A house Suitable for that Purpose Not Exceeding Seventy Pounds Courr^t. Money, to be Levied at the laying of the Next Parish Levie

Richard Corbin

N. B. Sarah Bird died the 8 Day of November 1771 And Mary Seward Died Janiary 23^d. 1772
W

[120]
At a Vestry held for Stratton Major Parish the 2^d Day of June 1772.

Present
William Hunt	William Taliaferro	
Philip Rootes	Lyne Shackelford	Vestry Men
Fran^s. Gaines &	William Hare.	
Thos. Dillard		

Where as the Honble. Richard Corbin Esqr hath been Pleas'd to offer to this Vestry at their Last Meeting to find & Provide Bread & Wine for the Use of this Church Gratis, it is agreed by the Said Vestry to Accept, of the Same as A favour, During his Pleasure.

Lyne Shackelford, Alex^r. Wedderburn & Cornelious Livingston, Procefsoners Returnd A Report of their Proceedings, Which is Orderd to be Recorded.

Richard Anderson & Joyeux Collins Procefsioners retund A Report of their Proceedings Which is Orderd to be Recorded. —

James Didlake & Thomas Bland Procefsioners returned a Report of their Proceeding, which is Orderd to be recorded. —

James Trice & Thomas Brushwood & George Dillard Procefsioners Return'd A report of their Proceedings, which is Orderd to be Recorded ———

Tho⁸. Spencer Charles Roane & James Campbell, Proceſsioners Return'd A Report of their Proceedings, which is Order'd to be Recorded ——

Edwᵈ. Ware, James Ware & Spencer Ware Proceſsioners Return'd A Report of their Proceedings Which is Orderd to be recorded ——

Richᵈ. Garrett Christopher Ware & Richᵈ. Walden, Proceſsioners Returnd A report of their Proceedings, Which is Orderd to be recorded

Where as it Appears to be Contrary to Act of Aſsembly For any Member of Vestry to be A Clark of the Same Vestry, Franˢ. Gaines Who hath been Clark for many Years Past, being one of the Vestry is willing to resign that office, and the Vestry do appoint Franˢ. Gaines Juʳ. to be Clark of this Vestry, to whom the Books & Papers is to be Deliverd at the Laying of the Next Parish Lev'y ——

William Hunt
Sepᵗ. 25. 1772 —

[121]
At a Vestry held for Stratton Major Parish 12ᵗʰ Day of November 1772 to Lay the Parish Levy

Present
| The Hon. Richᵈ. Corbin Esqʳ |
| William Hunt   William Taliaferro |
| Philip Rootes   William Shackelford |
| Francis Gaines   Lyne Shackelford |
| Thomas Dillard   John. Taylor. Corbin Esqʳ |

⎫
⎬ Vestry Men
⎭

Jnº. Taylor Esqʳ having Qualifyd According to Law is aded to this Vestry ——

Franˢ. Gaines Juʳ. this day Qualifyd as Clk for this Vestry

The Parish	D^r. in Tob°
The Rev^d. M^r. William Dunlap	16000
To d°. For Shrinkage Notes	640
To d°. Willis Wills Reader	1200
To d°. Amey Adams Sexton	1000
To d°. Fran^s. Gaines for Performing office of Clk Vestry	700
To d°. Barbary Groom for keeping Chas. M°.Carty	700
To d°. Esther Garrett for keeping Eliz. Brown	550
To d°. Denis Brenin for keeping Mary Sword 4 months	200
To d°. Thos. Bird for keeping his Mother 1 Mo: & 4 days	73
To d°. Samuel Fleming for keeping Jn°. Gardner	800
	21863
To 4 ℔ C^t. for Cask on 21863^{lb}. Tob°.	875
To the Clerk for Cop'ys List Tiths 40^{lb} Tob°. to be Paid in Cash at 12/6 ℔ C^t.	
To Tob°. to be Sold by the Collector for Raising Money to Pay for the Land & house for the Poor of this Parish & other Expences by Ord^r. of this Vestry	12000
To Me$\int$s^{rs}. Boyd & Browns Acco. for Store goods d'd for the *Poor *of *this Use of the Poor of this Parish from 1770	1668
To Thos. Walton for keeping Eliz. Guthrie one Year & 7 months, & Burying of her inclded	814
To Thos. Bird's Acco. for Burying his Mother	180
To James Campbell for a Coffin for Mary Sword	60
To Mary Edwards for her Acco. 10/	60
	37520

*Note! These words were scratched through in the original MS., but are still legible.—C. G. C.

[122]   lb Tob°.
D^r. Brought Over   37520
To Edwd. Walden for his Acco.   555

                                             38075
To Salary for Collecting on 41130^{lb} Tob°. at 6 ℔ C^t.   2467

                                             40542

C^r.
By a Ball. due from M^r. W^m. Taliaferro   957
By 914 Tithables at 45^{lb}. Tob°. ℔ Pool   41130

                                             42087

    The Levies being Settled for this Present Year are found to amount to 41130^{lb} Tob°. being levied upon 914 Tithables at 45^{lb}. Tob°. ℔ Pool & there will be an overplus in the hands of the Collector of 1545^{lb} of Tob°. which it is orderd that he Account for at the Laying of the Next Parish Levies ———

    William Shackelford & Jn°. Taylor Corbin Esqr. are appointed Church Wardens for this Present Year, & Fran^s. Gaines Ju^r. is Appointed Collector of the Parish Levys, Who Enterd into Bond with Fran^s. Gaines Security & they Acknowledged the same

    Orderd that the Collector pay Rich^d. Bray for Removing Francis O'Bland, his wife & four Children to the Church Warden of Petsworth Parish 40/ shillings

    Orderd that Amey Adams look after the house Preparing to accomidate the Poor people of this Parish in, and on her due Performance of the Care thereof that She Shall be allow'd Eight hundred pounds of Tob°. at Laying the Next Parish Levy.

Orderd that the Church Wardens agree with some careful person to take care of the Glebe House & all the other Houses on the said Glebe in the absence of the Minister of the said Parish

Absent the Hon. Richᵈ. Corbin Esqʳ. & Jnº. Taylor Corbin Esqʳ.

Orderd that the Collector Pay Mʳ. John Lyne Twenty Nine pounds ten shillings out of the Money Arrising on the Sale of the Tobº Lev'yd to Sold, in Consideration for Fifty Nine Acres of Land Purchased of him for to Build the Poor House on, Also forty one Pounds in Part for Building the said House ——

[123]
Orderd that the Collector Pay Susanna Walden ten Shillings for her Acco. of Work done for Chaˢ. Mᶜ.Carty

         William Hunt
 Register'd by
   Franˢ. Gaines Juʳ.

At A Vestry Held for Stratton Major Parish December 22ᵈ. 1772

    The Revᵈ. Mʳ. Wᵐ. Dunlap
    The Hon. Richᵈ. Corbin Esqʳ.
Wᵐ. Hunt Wᵐ. Shackelford
Philip Rootes Lyne Shackelford ⎱ Vestry Men
Franˢ. Gaines Jnº. T. Corbin Esqʳ
Wᵐ. Taliaferro

On the Petion of the Revᵈ. Mʳ. Dunlap to this Vestry Signifying that his Interest in the West Indies demᵈ. his immediate attention, It is agreed that he have Leave to be Absent for & During the Turm of Twelve Months, from the time of his Departure from hence Where upon Mʳ.

KING AND QUEEN COUNTY, VIRGINIA, 1729-1783   197

Dunlap Promises to Engage the Neighbouring Clergy to Officiate in his absence as frequently as Posibly they can

And we do hereby certify that during his residence among us, as rector of this Parish, his deportment has been regular & steady and the duties of his function he has Performd With Unshaken diligenc, & Constancy, thus diligent in the Discharge *of *his *duties of his duty, Constant & regular in his Deportment, we give this Testimony of it Under our hands ———

         Richd Corbin
  Register'd by
    Fran^s. Gaines Junr. Clk Vestry

[124]

At a Vestry held for Stratton Major Parish the 20 day of September 1773. to Lay the Lev'y.

Present
The Hon. Rich^d. Corbin Esqr.
William Hunt
Philip Rootes
William Taliaferro

Vestrymen
Lyne Shackelford
William Hare
Jno. T. Corbin Esqr.

	in lb^s. of Tob^o. D^r.
The Parish is	
To the Rev^d. William Dunlap (Salary)	16,000
To ditto for Srinkage of Notes 4 ℔ C^t.	640
To d^o. on Cask 4 ℔ C^t.	665

To Willis Wills Reader of the Church	£ 7‖16‖—
To Amey Adams Sexton	7‖12‖ 6
To ditto for Looking after the Poor House	5‖ 4‖
To Fran^s. Gaines Junr. Clk of the Vestry	4‖11‖
	25‖ 3‖ 6

*Note! These words were scratched through in the original MS., but are still legible.—C. G. C.

To Matt. Anderson ⅌ his Acco.	6‖14‖ 5½
To Meſsʳˢ. Boyd & Brown ⅌ Acco.	3‖10‖ 6
To Franˢ. Gaines ⅌ Acco.	3‖16‖ 3
To John Lyne ⅌ Ball for Last Year	10‖17‖ 9½
To Solomon Damm ⅌ Acco	2‖ 6‖
	52‖ 8‖ 6
To Cash for the Use of the Poor House	30‖.
	82‖ 8‖ 6
To the Revᵈ. Mʳ. Dunlap's Salary at 14/ ⅌ Cᵗ.	121‖ 2‖ 8¼
To Comm on £242 Ten Shillings	14‖11‖
	£218‖ 2‖ 2¼

The Levy being Settled for this Present year on 970 Tiths at 5/ ⅌ʳ Tith amounts to £242. Ten Shillings, & their will remain an over Plus in the hands of the Collector of £24‖7‖9¾ to be Accounted for at Laying the Next Parish Levy

Orderd that the Collector Pay the Hon. Richᵈ. Corbin Eſqʳ Sixty Pounds ten Shillings, out of the Money this Day Levied for The Revᵈ. William Dunlap, for the Use of Mʳˢ. Dunlap, his Wife & Children

[125]
Lyne Shackelford & William Meredith are appointed Church Wardens for this Present year, & Lyne Shackelford is appointed Collʳ. of the Parish Levy, Wᵐ. Taliaferro is his Security & They Acknowledg Bond for the same

A letter from the Revᵈ. Mʳ. Dunlap being read, desiring a further leave of absence for Six Months The Vestry having taken this Matter into Consideration, are of Opinion & it is accordingly resolv'd that the said Mʳ. Dunlap have Leave to be absent to the 24 Day of Next June, and if he should not return by that time the Vestry will think them selves at liberty to make Choice of another Rector, and as the Rev⁴. M'. Dixon has offerd to serve the Parish for that time & to officiate Every other Sunday for 4000¹ᵇ. Tob°., Col°. Rootes is desired to speak to him on that head

Orderd that M'. William Shackelford Settle with M'. Lyne Shackelford the Present Coll'., for the Ball in his Hands

                              Rich⁴. Corbin
    Registerd
        by Fran⁸. Gaines J'. Clk

[126]

At A Vestry held for Stratton Major Parish July 12ᵗʰ. 1774

          The Honᵇˡᵉ. Rich⁴. Corbin Esq'.
          Philip Rootes   Wᵐ. Shackelford
Present Francis Gaines   Lyne Shackelford   }Vestry Men
          Thoˢ. Dillard   Wᵐ. Hare
          Wᵐ. Taliaferro   John T. Corbin

It is agree'd by a Majorety of this Vestry that M'. Benˢ. Robinson be Appointed a Member of this Vestry in the room of Major Rich⁴. Shackelford dec⁴.

Ordered that the present Coll'. settle with Francis Gaines Jun'. the late Coll'. for the Balliance in his hands at Twelve & Six pence, or in Tob°. ——

Order'd that M'. Lyne Shackelford Pay M'. John Lyne the Balliance Remaining in his hands as far as his Accᵗ. amounts to

Absent the Honᵇˡᵉ. Rich⁴. Corbin Esq'.

                  Test. Philip Rootes
    Register'd
        By John Collier Jun. For Francis Gaines Clk

[127]
At A Vestry held for Stratton Major Parish Oct*. 7. 1774

The Rev⁴. Wᵐ. Dunlap
The Honᵇˡᵉ. Rich⁴.   Wᵐ. Taliaferro
  Corbin Esqʳ   Wᵐ. Shackelford
  Wᵐ. Hunt   Lyne Shackelford } Vestry Men
Present Philip Rootes John T. Corbin
  Thoˢ. Dillard   Esqʳ.

I. Benjamin Robinson do Promise to be Conformable to the doctrine & decipline of the Church of England as is by Law Established

       Banjamin Robinson

Benjamin Robinson having taken the Oaths appointed by act of Parliment & Subscribed to be Conformable to the Doctrine & decipline of the Church of England as is by Law Established is Aded to this Vestry

    Present Benjamin Robinson

The Parish is	Dʳ
To the Revᵈ. John Dixon	£ 43‖ 5‖ 2½
To the Revᵈ. Wᵐ. Dunlap	86‖10‖ 5
To Willis Wills Reader	8‖—‖—
To Amey Adams Sexton	8‖—‖—
To ditto for Looking After the poor house	7‖—‖—
To Francis Gaines Clk of the Vestry	5‖—‖—
To John Tunstall for Copy List Tithes	5‖—
To Cash for the Use of the poor house	30‖—‖—
To John Muires Accᵗ. for the Use of Wᵐ. Wyatt	10‖—
To Thoˢ. Dillard for ditto	1‖—‖—
To Wᵐ. Bland Jʳ: for ditto	1‖10‖—
To Benjamin Mores Accᵗ.	1‖ 5‖—
To Barbara Groomes Accᵗ.	1‖ 5‖—

To John Lynes Acc^t.	10‖ 3‖11
To Salary for Collecting on £242	14‖10‖—
	218‖ 4‖ 6½

By Lyne Shackelford	20‖ 2‖ 5
By Francis Gaines	1‖14‖10
	21‖17‖ 3

[128]

The Levy being settled for this present year on 968 tithes at 5/ ℔ tithe or 25^{lb}. Tob°. are found to amount to £247 there being a ball^{ce}. of Forty five pounds twelve Shillings & nine pence ½ to be Accounted for at *the Laying the next Parish Levy

Absent The Honble. Rich^d. Corbin, Esqr.

W^m. Hare & Benjamin Robinson are Appointed Churchwardins for this Present year & Benjamin Robinson is Appointed Coll^r. of the Parish Levy Who Enter'd into Bond with W^m. Taliaferro his Security & they Acknowledg the same

Ordered that the Church Wardens provide for Ann Seward with Cloaths ——

Order'd that the Churchwardens Provide W^m. Wyatt with such Neceſsarys as they shall think proper. ——

Order'd that the Churchwardens build a garden & hen house at the poor house.

Order'd that the Coll^r. Pay James Didlake one pound ten Shillings for his Acc^t. ——

---

*Note! This word is scratched through in the MS., but is still legible.—C. G. C.

Order'd that the Honble. Rich^d. Corbin Philip Rootes W^m. Shackelford John T. Corbin Esqr. & the Church wardens or any three of them be a Committee to meet at the Glebe to make such Repairs as they & The Rev^d. M^r. Dunlap shall think necessary & the Glebe being put in Such Repair the Rev^d. M^r. Dunlap agrees to take it upon himself dureing his incumbency

Order'd that the Coll^r. pay Edward Waldin one pound ten Shillings for his Acc^t.

W^m. Dunlap
W^m. Hunt

Register'd
  by John Collier J^r.
    for Francis Gaines Clk

[129]
At A Vestry of Straton Major Parish 7. day July 1775

Present {
The Rev^d. William Dunlap
Philip Rootes
Thos. Dillard
William Taliaferro
William Shackelford
Lyne Shackelford
William Hare
John T. Corbin Esqr.
Benjamin Robinson
} Vestry Men

Francis Gaines late Clk having Resign'd, John Collier is Appointed in his Roome ——

Philip Taliaferro is Appointed A Vestry Man in Roome of Francis Gaines dec^d.

Pursuant to an Order of King & Queen Court dated 10. June 1775 that the Vestry of the several Parishs within this County do devide there Parishes into somany precincts as to them shall seem most convenient for proceſsioning Every Persons Land therein, & to appoint particular times for that purpose between the last day of Sep.ʳ & the Last day of March Next Ensuing pursuant to an Act of Aſsembly in that Case made & provided

Order'd that Phil. Taliaferro, Alex.ʳ Weddeburn, & Stephen Field, or any two of them do meet the first munday in Jan.ʸ next and go in proceſsion of & see all and every persons land between porotopotank Creek & Mattasip swamp plainly markt Continuing there proceedings in all suitable weather untill the Whole precinct be finish't & all the freeholders who are inhabetants thereof are hereby required to attend the said proceſsioners according to law & the said proceſsioners are farther Order'd to make & Return to this Vestry at there next meeting after the last day of march next a true acc.ᵗ of what Lands they have proceſsion'd of the persons present at the same of what lands they have not proceſsion'd & the particular reasons of such failure ——

Order'd that Rich.ᵈ Anderson, Joyeux Collins, & Ben.ᵃ Robinson, or any two of them, do meet on the first wensday in Jan.ʸ next, & Go in proceſsion of, and see all, & Every persons lands between Mattasip & pepetico swamps, plainly Markt, Continuing there proceedings According to law &.C.

[130]
Order'd that James Collier, John Collier Jun.ʳ & Edw.ᵈ Waldin or any two of them do meet on the first fryday in Jan.ʸ next & go in proceſsion of & see all & Every persons land between pepetico swamp & Arrocaco Creek & the western branch thereof plainly markt Continuing there proceedings according to Law

Order'd that James Didlake, Geo. Dillard, & Tho.ˢ Bland or any two of them do meet on the second monday in Jan.ʸ next & go in proceſsion of & see all & Every persons land between the Eastern & Western branch of Arrocaco

Creek plainly Markt Continuing there proceedings According to law

Order'd that John Lyne, Christopher Stedman & Humphry Garret or any two of them do meet on the second wensday in Jany. next & go in proceſsion of & see all & Every persons land between the Western branch & Arrocaco Creek plainly Markt According to law ——

Order'd that Chas. Collier John Breshwood & Geo. Dillard or any two of them do meet on the second Fryday in Jany. next & go in proceſsion of & see all & Every persons land between burgeses swamp & the Monack Swamp & from thence a Strate Course between mary Hollengers & the land lately the property of Doc^r. Joyeuxes dec^d. to Tasatyan swamp plainly Markt

Order'd that Thos. Spencer, William Garret, & John Campbell or any two of them do meet on the third monday in Jany. next and go in proceſsion of & see all & Every persons land between monack swamp and on a Strate Course down to tarsatyan swamp & the branch next above W^m. Hunts plainly Markt ——

Order'd that Spencer Boyd, Isaac Ware, & Geo. Didlake or any two of them do meet the third wensday in Jany. next & go in proceſsion of & see all & Every persons land between the branch next above W^m. Hunts & the Extent upwards plainly markt ——

Order'd that Richard Garret, Christopher Ware, & Rich^d. Bray or any two of them do meet on the third fryday in Jany next & go in proceſsion of & see all & Every persons land between tarsatyan swamp & Great hartquake swamp plainly markt Continuing there proceedings According to law ——

                                        Philip Rootes
    Register'd
            by John Collier Clk

[131]
At A Vestry held for Stratton Major Parrish 21 decͬ.
1775

Present
{ The Rev͒. William Dunlap
The Hon͆͠. Rich͒. Corbin Esqͬ.
Phil, Rootes   Wͫ. Hare
Wͫ. Talliaferro   Wͫ. Meredith
Wͫ. Shackelford   Ben͒. Robinson
Lyne Shackelford } Vestry Men

The Parish is   Dͬ
                           lb Tob͒.

To the Rev͒. Wͫ. Dunlap	16,000
To Willis Wills Reader	8‖—‖—
To Amey Adams Sexton	8‖—‖—
To ditto for looking after the poor house	5‖—‖—
To John Collier Junͬ. Clk of the Vestry	3‖—‖—
To Expences for the use of the poor house	25‖—‖—
To Mͬ. John Lyne Accͭ.	4‖17‖—
To Mͬ: Matt͐ Anderson Accͭ	9‖ 4½
To John James Accͭ.	6‖ 6
To Mͬ. Geo. Dillard Accͭ.	15‖—
To Mͬ. Christopher Stedman Accͭ.	10‖—
To Mͬ. Wͫ. Bland Accͭ.	1‖—‖—
To Mͬ. John Muire for keeping Wͫ. Wyatt	2‖10‖—
To 8 ℔ Cͭ for Convenience on 16000͢ᵇ Tob͒. 1,280	
To Mͬ. Edward Waldin for Repairs of the Glebe	40‖16‖ 4
To John Tunstall for Copy List tithes	5‖—
	£ 100‖ 9‖ 2½
To Comi∫sion on 208‖9‖2½ at 6 ℔ Cͭ	12‖11‖—
To be laid out for the use of John Groome by the Church Wardins	3‖—‖—
	116‖ 0‖ 2½

The levey being Settled for this present year on 954 tithes at 5/ or 40 pounds of Tob°. p^r. pole amounts to 227 £ there being a balliance of two pounds nineteen Shillings & 9½ to be Accounted for at the laying the next Levey

Thos. Dillard and William Talliaferro Gen. are appointed Church Wardins for this present year

Ordered that Ben^a. Robinson pay the Balliance of £25‖4‖9½ in his hands To Edwd. Waldin

It is agree'd that the Rev^d. W^m. Dunlap appoint his Sexton

[132]
The Church Wardins are Directed to Agree with somebody to look after the poor house

Ordered that the Church Wardins do receive the sum of 5/ or forty pounds Tob°. p^r. pole within this Parrish in Case of nonpayment to levey the same by distreſs

M^r. William Griffin is appointed a Vestryman in the room of William Hunt dec^d.

Richd Corbin

Regestered by John Collier Clk

At a Vestry held for Stratton Major Parish on Tuesday the 14th of October 1777 ——

Present	Lyne Shackelford	John Lyne	⎫
	Richard Anderson	Richard Bray	Vestrymen
	George Dillard	James Didlake	
	Humphrey Garrett.	....	⎭

We Lyne Shackelford, Richard Anderson, George Dillard, Humphrey Garrett, John Lyne, Richard Bray & James Didlake do promise to be conformable, to the Doctrine and discipline of the Church of England, as by Law established

Lyne Shackelford   John Lyne
Richard Anderson   Richard Bray
Geo Dillard   James Didlake
Humphrey Garrett

John Shackelford is Chozen Clerk of y® Vestry and Sworn Accordingly

	D^r. in lbs. Tob°.
The Parish is	
To the Rev^d. W^m. Dunlap from 8th: of November 1775 to 1st: Janu^y. 1777	18419
To 8 ⏚ C^t. for Shrinkage of Notes and Cask	1472
	19891

To Willis Wills Reader 1 Year to the 1st: October 1776	8	0	0
To W^m: Dam Reader from 1st: of October 1776 to 1st: Janu^y: 1777 is 3 Months	2	0	0
To Thos. Wyatt Sexton from 22nd: Decr. 1776 to 1st: Janu^y. 1777 is 1 year & 9 days at 8 £ ⏚ y^r:	8	3	11¼
To John Collier Clk from 21st: Dec^r: 1775 to 25th: August 1776	3	6	8
To W^m: Bland for his Acc^t:	4	6	1½
To Lewis Walden for His Acc^t. for Keeping John Gardner	6	5	0
To Sarah Gramshill looking after the poor house 1 Month	0	10	0
	32	11	8¾

[133]

Brought up Tobacco and Cash 19891^{lb} & £	32	11	8¾
To Edward Walden for his Accompt	2	2	6
To Richard Tunstal Clk Court for lists of Tithables for 1776 & 1777	0	10	0

Ordered that Lewis Walden Keep John Gardner at 25/ ℔ Month and to be paid by the Church Wardens	15	0	0
To Mary Groom to be laid out by the Church Wardens in Corn & meat for herself and four Children	6	0	0
To the Church Wardens to Support the Poor	25	0	0
	81	4	2¾
19891 lb. Tob°. at 27/6	273	10	0
	354	14	2¾
To Salary for Collecting	21	5	9¼
£	376	0	0

The Levy being Settled for this present year on 916 Tithables at 8/3 or 30 lb Tobacco ℔ pole amounts to £377—17 and there will remain a balance of £1—17 in the Collectors hands to be accompted for at the laying the next Levy—

Lyne Shackelford and Richard Anderson are appointed Church Wardens for this present year ———

Ordered that the Church Wardens do agree with some person to put dead lights into the Church Windows & Grub up the bushes in the Church yard

Richard Anderson jun'. is appointed Collector of the parish Levies for the present year who entered into bond with Richard Anderson and Lyne Shackelford his Securities

      Test Lyne Shackelford
  Registered by
    John Shackelford Clk Vestry

[134]

At a Vestry held at the Church for Stratton Major Parish the 25th: April 1778

Present
Lyne Shackelford
Richard Anderson
George Dillard
Hum: Garrett

John Lyne
Richard Bray
James Didlake
....
} Vestry men

I William Hunt, do promise to be conformable to the Doctrine, & Discipline, of the Church of England as is by Law Established

Wm Hunt.

William Hunt having taken the oath appointed by Law; and subscribed to be conformable to the Doctrine, & Discipline of the Church of England, as is by Law established, is added to this Vestry.

Present, William Hunt.

Resolved, that it is the opinion of this Vestry, that the rev'd M^r. W^m. Dunlap, (by his Letter to Lyne Shackelford, & Richard Anderson, Church Wardens dated, the 16th. Febru^y: 1778) has resigned his right as rector to this Parish.

Ordered, that the Church Wardens, do Advertise Three times, in the Virginia Gazette, the resignation of the said Dunlap.

Test. Lyne Shackelford.

Registered by
John Shackelford Clk Vestry.

[135]

At a Vestry held for Stratton Major Parish on wednesday 23rd: Septr. 1778

Present
Lyne Shackelford
Richard Anderson
Humphrey Garrett.

John Lyne
Richard Bray.
....
} Vestry men

We, Philip Taliaferro, and Charles Collier, do promise to be conformable to the Doctrine, and Discipline, of the Church of England, as by Law established.
                    Philip Taliaferro.
                    Charles Collier.

Philip Taliaferro, and Charles Collier, having Taken the oath appointed by Law, and Subscribed to be conformable to the Doctrine, and Discipline, of the Church of England as by established; are added to this Vestry.

Present Phil. Taliaferro, and Charles Collier.

Ordered, that the Church Wardens make application to the rev^d. M^r. W^m: Dunlap, and the rev^d. M^r. Auther Hamilton about moving from the Glebe; and provided they refuse to move, the Church Wardens are hereby authorised to commence a suit against them.

                    Test. Lyne Shackelford.
    Register'd by,
                John Shackelford Clk Vestry.

[136]
At a Vestry held for Stratton Parish the 9th: day of December 1778.

	Richard Anderson	George Dillard	
	Hum: Garrett	James Didlake	
Present	John Lyne	Philip Taliaferro	Vestry men
	Richard Bray	Charles Collier	
	Wm Hunt		

The Parish is   D^r:
To Lyne Shackelford, and Richard Anderson,
    for the money borrowed of Thomas Dillard
    the 1st: of May 1778   300‖00 0
Interest to the 15th: of June 1779   16 17 6

To Susannah Mitchel for Keeping Betty Brown, & finding her clothes 2 years	22	00	0
To Frances Williams for looking after and finding Judith Holeday	10	00	0
To Lewis Walden as ℘ʳ. account	3	00	0
To Elias Burton for 1 Levy over paid last year	0	8	3
To Jane Seward for keeping Ann Seward	16	00	0
To Rachel Garrett for keeping Patty Coats	6	00	0
To George Standard for keeping Eliza: Curtis	16	00	0
To Mary Walden, for her immediate support	8	00	0
To Mary Groom for her Dº:	10	00	0
To Ann Waller for her Dº:	10	00	0
To Elias Burton for his Dº:	10	00	0
To John Shackelford Clerk of the Vestry	10	00	0
To William Wyatt for his support	10	00	0
	448	5	9
To the Collectors, 6 ℘ Cᵗ. for Collecting	26	17	11
Cr	475	3	8
By the Balance in the hands of Lyne Shackelford, and Richard Anderson Church Wardens	55	11	0
	419	12	8

The Levy being settled this present year on 842 Tithables at 10/ or 50 lb Tobº. ℘ pole amounts to £421‖00‖0, and there will remain a balance of £1‖7‖4 in the Collectors hands to be accounted for, at the laying the next Parish Levy.

Ordered, that Jane Seward keep Ann Seward the ensuing year, and that she be allowed £8‖0‖0 at the laying the next Levy.

Ordered, that Susannah Mitchel do keep Eliza: Brown, and that she be allowed £18||00||0 the ensuing year, for which she is to clothe her, and to be allowed it at the laying of the next Levy.

Ordered that Frances Williams be allowed 15/ ⅌ Month, for taking care of Judith Holeday, which is to be levied for her, at the laying the next Levy.

[137]
George Dillard, and Humphrey Garrett are appointed Church Wardens, for the ensuing year.

George Dillard, and Humphrey Garrett are appointed Collectors of the Parish Levies, for the ensuing year; who entered into Bond with Richard Bray, their Security.

Test   Richard Anderson
Registered by
John Shackelford Clk of the Vestry.

At a Vestry held for Stratton Major Parish, on Tuesday the 16th: day of February 1779. ——

Present
Rich d. Anderson   William Hunt
George Dillard   James Didlake
Hum: Garrett   Phil: Taliaferro   } Vestry men
John Lyne   Charles Collier
Richard Bray

Resolved, that Susannah Sykes keep Thomas Ellis this present year, and that she be allowed 25/ ⅌ . Month, at the laying of the next Levy; for which she is to clothe him &c.

Ordered, that the Church Wardens wait on the Revd. Mr. Hamilton, & offer him the use of the Glebe House, Garden, & such Houses as they think necefsary, and a piece of Ground, for a Pasture: in consideration whereof the said Hamilton is to attend the Church once a Month to perform the offices, and to give Bond & Security that no waste shall be made on the said House &c, during his stay, and that he will remove himself & Family, from the Glebe, and give poſseſsion, when required.

Ordered that the Church Wardens rent out the Glebe Land, after laying of the Houses, and Land, for M^r. Hamilton: also the poor House.

Ordered that the Church Wardens Advertise, the vacancy of the Parish.

      Test Richard Anderson
 Registered by
    John Shackelford Clk of Vestry.

[138]
At a Vestry held for Stratton Major Parish on Tuesday the 28th: day of September 1779

Present
Lyne Shackelford	William Hunt
Richard Anderson	Charles Collier
John Lyne	& Philip Taliaferro
Richard Bray	
James Didlake	

} Vestry men

Pursuant to an Order of King and Queen County Court, dated the   day of   1779.

That the Vestrys of the several Parishes within this County, do divide their Parishes into so many precincts as to them shall seem most convenient, for proceſsioning every persons land therein; and to appoint particular times for that purpose, between the last day of September, and the last day of March, next ensuing; pursuant to an Act of Aſsembly, in that case made, and provided.

Ordered, that Philip Taliaferro, Alexander Wedderburn, and Stephen Field, or any two of them, do meet the first monday in January next, and go in procefsion of, and see all, and every persons land, between Poropotank Creek, and Matafsip swamp, plainly marked; continuing their proceedings in all suitable weather until their whole precinct be finished; and all freeholders inhabitants thereof are hereby required to attend the s^d procefsioners according to Law: and the said Procefsioners are further ordered to make return to this Vestry, at their next meeting after the last day of March next, a true account of what lands they have procefsioned, and the persons present at the same, of what Lands they have not procefsioned, and the particular reasons of such failure.—

Ordered that William Taliaferro, Joyex Collins and John Webly, or any two of them, do meet the first wednesday in January next, and go in procefsion of, and see all, and every persons land, between Matafsip, and Perpetico swamp plainly marked, continuing their proceedings according to Law. &c

Ordered that Edward Walden, John Didlake, and Robert Ballard Dudley, or any two of them do meet the first Friday in January next and go in procefsion of and see all and every persons Land between Perpetico swamp Arricaco Creek and the western branch thereof plainly marked continuing their proceedings according to Law &c

Ordered, that Thomas Bland, Thomas Dillard jun^r., and William Bland Son of William or any two of them do meet the second monday in January next and go in procefsion of and see all and every persons Land between the eastern and western branch plainly marked, continuing their proceedings according to Law &c

Ordered that John Lyne, William Shackelford, and John Sadler or any two of them do meet the second wednesday in January next and go in procefsion of and see all and every persons Land between the western branch and Arricaco Creek plainly marked continuing their proceedings according to Law &c

[139]
Ordered that Charles Collier, John Breshwood and William Halliard or any two of them do meet the second friday in January next and go in procefsion of and see all and every persons Land between Burgefses swamp and the monack swamp and from thence a straight course between Mary Hollengers and the Land lately the property of Doct^r. Joyex dec^d. to Tarsityan swamp, plainly marked, continuing their proceedings according to Law &c.

Ordered that Thomas Spencer, William Garrett, and William Hunt, or any two of them, do meet the third monday in January next, and go in procefsion of, and see all, and every persons Land, between the monack swamp, and on a straight course down to Tarsatyan swamp and the branch next above William Hunts, plainly marked, continuing their proceedings according to Law &c.

Ordered that George Didlake, Philip Sears, and Isaac Diggs, or any two of them, do meet the the third wednesday in January next, and go in procefsion of and see all and every persons Land between the branch next above William Hunts and the extent upwards plainly marked continuing their proceedings according to Law &c.

Ordered that Christopher Ware, Richard Bray, and Thomas Burk, or any two of them do meet the third friday in January next and go in procefsion of and see all and every persons Land between Tarsatyan swamp, and great Heartquake swamp plainly marked, continuing their proceedings according to Law &c.

Gregory Smith is appointed a Vestry man in the stead of Spencer Boyd dec^d. ———

George Lyne is appointed a Vestry man in the stead of James Collier, who is moved out of the Parish. ——

Ordered that the Church Wardens apply to Colo. Richard Corban for the plate belonging to the Church. ——

       Test. Lyne Shackelford
 Truly registered by
    John Shackelford Clk of the Vestry

[140]

At a Vestry held for Stratton Major Parish on the 9th: day of December 1779.

Present: Lyne Shackelford, Richard Anderson, George Dillard, William Hunt, Humphrey Garrett, Richard Bray, James Didlake, Charles Collier, John Lyne. — Vestry men

Ordered, that the Church Wardens rent out the Glebe, for the next year.

       Test, Lyne Shackelford
 Registered by
    John Shackelford Clark of the Vestry

At a Vestry, held for Stratton Major Parish on the 20th: day of December 1779.

Present: Richard Anderson, George Dillard, Humphrey Garrett, John Lyne, Richard Bray, James Didlake, Philip Taliaferro, Charles Collier. — Vestry men

The Parish is	D^r:	
To Susannah Sykes, for keeping Thomas Ellis	7	10
To Jane Seward for keeping Ann Seward	8	10
To Susannah Mitchel for keeping Eliza: Brown	18	00
To Frances for taking care of Judith Holeday	9	00

To Susanna Mitchel for keeping Patty Coats	12	00
To George Dillard as ℔ accᵗ.	69	4
To John Lyne as ℔ accᵗ.	16	00
To Samuel Livingston, for keeping Eliza: Curtis 12 Months	30	00
To Jane Seward for keeping Ann Seward to the 1ˢᵗ: of January 1780	50	00
To the Church Wardens for the support of the Poor House	1359	11
To John Shackelford junʳ. for performing the office of Clark	100	00
	1679	5
To the Collector, 6 ℔ Cᵗ. for collecting	100	15
	1780	00

The Levies being settled this present year on 890 Tithables at 40/ ℔ pole is found to amount to £1780‖00‖0.

John Lyne and William Hunt are appointed Church Wardens, for the ensuing year.

John Shackelford junʳ. is appointed Collector of the Parish Levies, for the ensuing year, Lyne Shackelford as next Friend to John Shackelford, had entered into Bond, & John Lyne became his Security. ——

Cʳ the Parish
By a balance due from George Dillard, and Humphrey Garrett late Church Wardens of £22‖13‖4 as by their accᵗ settled this day. ——

[141]
Ordered that George Dillard and Humphrey Garrett pay the balance in their hands of £22‖13‖4 To John Lyne and

William Hunt Church Wardens, which is to be applyed to the use of the Work House

       Test, Richard Anderson
  Registered by
    John Shackelford Clark of the Vestry

At a Vestry held for Stratton Major Parish on the 2nd: day of February 1780

Present {
Lyne Shackelford, Richard Bray,
Richard Anderson, James Didlake,
Humphrey Garrett, Philip Taliaferro,
John Lyne
} Vestry men

It is ordered, that the Collector receive for each Tithable 10 lb of Tob°., or forty Shillings according to former Order. —

Richard Bray, is appointed Church Warden, instead of John Lyne, who is about to move out of the Parish.

Robinson Shackelford, is appointed a Proceſsioner in the room of John Lyne.

Stephen Field is appointed a Vestry man in the room of Gregory Smith, who declines his appointment ——

Alexander Wedderburn is appointed a Vestryman in the room of George Lyne, who declines his appointment. ——

John Lyne has resigned his seat in Vestry, on account of his removal out of the Parish. ——

       Lyne Shackelford
 Registered by,
   John Shackelford j^r. Clark of the Vestry

[142]

At a Vestry held for Stratton Major Parish, the 24th: day of August 1780.

Lyne Shackelford	Richard Bray	Vestry men
Richard Anderson	Philip Taliaferro	
Present Hum: Garrett &	Charles Collier	
William Hunt	....	

George Lyne, Gregory Smith, William Griffin, & William Dudley are appointed Vestry men in stead of Stephen Field, Alexander Wedderburn, John Lyne, and George Dillard

          Lyne Shackelford
Truly registered by,
   John Shackelford j': Clk of Vestry

At a meeting of the Vestry for the Parish of Stratton Major, on the 24th: day of February 1781 —

Present

Richard Anderson	Charles Collier	Vestry men
James Didlake	Gregory Smith	
William Hunt	William Dudley	
Richard Bray	& George Lyne.	

James Didlake this day resigned his seat in Vestry, & Thomas Dillard j'. was appointed a Vestry man in his stead—

It appears by a letter of M'. Lyne Shackelford that he declined acting longer as a Vestry man upon which its resolved that M'. John Shackelford Sen'. be appointed a Vestry man in his stead.

On the information of Richard Bray one of the members of this Vestry it appears that M'. Humphrey Garrett declines acting any longer as a Vestry man therefore resolved that M'. John Kidd be appointed a Vestry man in his stead.

Philip Taliaferro, & Charles Collier are appointed Wardens for the present year, who are ordered to settle the last years account with John Shackelford the Collector & make return thereof to the next Vestry & if the said Collector should refuse to pay the balance in his hands they are desired to give notice that a motion will be made against him in King & Queen C‡. (naming the Court day) for the balance in his hands ——

[143]
Ordered that the Wardens pay I[   ]

Ordered that the Wardens purchase [   ]
Bray 174 lb pork ½ brushel of al[   ]
of Brown Sugar

Ordered that a half bushel of allum [   ]
chased and delivered to John Lyne

Ordered that one peck & a half of Salt be [   ]
& delivered to M͞rˢ: Frances Williams.

Ordered that the Wardens pay William Hunt   214 4 9

Ordered that John Lyne's accᵗ be paid   16 5 0

Frances Williams her accᵗ   32 10 0

Ordered that the Wardens purchase either beef, bacon, or Pork, for the use of the poor in the Work house to the amount of   2000 0 0

Ordered that the Wardens purchase Corn or meal for the use afsᵈ. to the amount of   500 0 0

Ordered that there be laid out by the Wardens for such clothing as the poor of the Parish stand most in need of money to the amount of   200 0 0

Ordered that the Wardens or either of them rent to the highest bidder the Glebe of this Parish until the 1ˢᵗ: of Janʸ. next to be paid for in corn & to be delivered on that day, at the said Glebe ——

KING AND QUEEN COUNTY, VIRGINIA, 1729-1783 221

Ordered that the Wardens collect from the Tythes of the Parish or the owners of them four pounds Virginia money ℔ poll to comply with the orders of this day.

R^d: Anderson

Truly registered by,
John Shackelford j^r. Clk of ye Veſtry.

[144]
[   ] Major Parish the 4th: day of April 1781

[   ] George Lyne
[   ] Gregory Smith } Vestry men
[   ] & William Dudley

[   ]rch Wardens pay the Clk of this Vestry two hundred [   ]ast years services

[   ]dens pay John Lyne eight pounds, fifteen Shill^s. for [   ]

Jonathan Hives is allowed to keep schooll in the Vestry house & if he should not keep the house & Windows free from damage, he is to make good the damage

R^d: Bray

Registered by,
John Shackelford j^r. Clk of Veſtry

*At a meeting of the Vestry for the Parish of Stratton on the 24th. day of February 1781.

Present
Richard Anderson Charles Collier
James Didlake Gregory Smith
William Hunt William Dudley } Vestry men
Richard Bray & George Lyne

James Didlake this day resigned his seat in Vestry & Thomas Dillard junior was appointed a Vestry man in his stead*

---

*Note! That part of the record on page 144 of the MS. included between the asterisks has been scratched through with a pen, but is still legible.—C. G. C.

*It appears by a letter of M^r. Lyne Shackelford that he declines acting longer as a Vestry man upon which it's resolved that M^r. John Shackelford Senr. be appointed a Vestry man in his stead—

On the information of Richard Bray one of the members of this Vestry it appears that Mr Humphrey Garrett declines acting any longer as a Vestry man, therefore resolved that M^r. John Kidd be appointed a Vestry man in his stead*

[145]
At a meeting of the Vestry for the Parish of Stratton Major on the 22nd: of Decr. 1781

Present
Richard Anderson
Philip Taliaferro
Charles Collier
George Lyne

Gregory Smith
John Kidd
Thomas Dillard
& William Dudley
} Vestry men

Gregory Smith, & William Dudley, are appointed Church Wardens for the ensuing year ———

The Parish is in specie	D^r.
To Richard Bray	£ 4‖ 8‖—
To John Lyne	15‖—
To Francis Williams	9‖—
To John Lyne	5‖—
To Frances Williams	10‖—
To ditto	3‖18‖ 3
To John Lyne	1‖ 2‖—
To Gregory Smith	6‖—
To Charles Collier	5‖10‖ 7
To Richard Bray	6‖10‖ 6

*Note! That part of the record on page 144 of the MS. included between the asterisks has been scratched through with a pen, but is still legible.—C. G. C.

To the Church Wardens for the support of the
   poor   36||17|| 6
To John Shackelford j^r. Clerk of the Vestry   5||—||—
To Commiſsions for collecting   3||18|| 8

                                                                                          69||10|| 6

   The Levy being settled this present year on 900 Tithables, at 15^{lb}: Tob^o. ℔ poll which is judged sufficient to discharge the above sum of £69||10||6. & the inhabitants are allowed to pay 1/10 specie in lieu of the Tob^o. ℔ polle

   Ordered that the Wardens let the Glebe to some person who will take care of the Houses & Plantation rent free, on condition that they will not tend the Land & remove from it to the Overseers house when required ——
                                                    Richard Anderson
   Registered by
                    John Shackelford C: V:

[146]
   At a Vestry held for Stratton Major Parish April the 13th: 1782

Present   William Hunt   William Dudley ⎫
               Richard Bray   Thomas Dillard ⎬ Vestry men
               Philip Taliaferro & John Kidd ⎪
               Gregory Smith ⎭

   Lyne Shackelford junior is chosen Clerk to this Vestry instead of John Shackelford who has moved out of the County —

                   Present   George Lyne

   resolved that the Church Wardens employ a general Court Lawyer to commence an action in their names against John Meredith to recover damages for his failing to comply with his contract in not repairing the Houses on the Glebe Land ——

Ordered that the Church Wardens give John Meredith notice that he is not to continue on the Glebe longer than the first day of January next ——

Joyeux Collins is appointed Collector of the Parish Levies

Ordered that Alexander Campbell clean out the Church & Vestry House for which he is allowed five pounds the same to be kept clear for a year ——

William Hunt

Registered by
   Lyne Shackelford Clk of the Vestry

At a Vestry held for Stratton Major Parish November the 30th: 1782

Present: Richard Anderson, Richard Bray, Philip Taliaferro & Gregory Smith

Vestry men: William Dudley, Thomas Dillard, John Kidd

George Lyne, & Thomas Dillard are appointed Church Wardens for the ensuing year ——

Ordered that Thomas Wyatt, John Hooker, John James, Elias Burton, Samuel Padget, Samuel Livingston, & James Webb, be excused from paying their Parish Levy ——

Ordered that the Church Wardens do give John Meredith notice that he is to move from the Glebe before the first day of January next ——

Richard Anderson

Registered by,
   Lyne Shackelford C. V.

[147]

At a Vestry held for Stratton Major Parish on Saturday the 18th: of January 1783 ——

Present {Richard Anderson, Richard Bray, Philip Taliaferro, Charles Collier, William Hunt} {George Lyne, Gregory Smith, William Dudley, Thomas Dillard, & John Kidd} Vestry men

The Parish is	D^r:
To John Lyne his account	£ 5‖ 7‖ 6
To the Church Wardens for the support of the Poor	15‖—‖—
To William Hunt for his old account	2‖12‖—
To Joyeux Collins for his account	1‖ 8‖ 1
To Lyne Shackelford j^r: Clerk of the Vestry	5‖—‖—
To Alexander Campbell for cleaning out the Church & keeping it clean	5‖—‖—
	34‖ 7‖ 7

The Levy being settled this present year on 732 Tithables at 9 lb of Tob°. ℔ Poll which is found sufficient to discharge the above sum of Thirty four pounds seven shillings, & seven pence, & the inhabitants are allowed to pay one shilling in lieu thereof ——

Alexander Campbell to attend to the Church to keep it clean & the doors shut, except when divine service is to be performed ——

Alexander Campbell is appointed Collector of the Parish Levies this present year ——

Ordered that the Church Wardens let the Glebe to some person who will take care of the Houses & plantation rent free on condition that they will not tend the Land except a cotton & potatoe patch, & remove to the Overseer's house when required ———

The Wardens for the last year having settled their accounts it appears there is a balance due them of two pounds fifteen shillings & three pence which they are to receive of Joyeux Collins Collector for the last year ———

         Richard Anderson
Registered by,
    Lyne Shackelford Clk of the Vestry

[148]
At a Vestry held for Stratton Major Parish on Saturday the 17th of May 1783

  Richard Anderson George Lyne
  Richard Bray   Gregory Smith
  Charles Collier   Thomas Dillard
  William Hunt & John Kidd
  Philip Taliaferro

Ordered that the Churchwardens cause a suit to be prosecuted against John Meredith to recover damages for failing to comply with his agreement in repairing the houses on the Glebe land

Order'd that the churchwardens likewise bring suit against John Meredith to recover the money for the last two years rent that he lived at the Glebe

         Richard Anderson
Registered by
   Lyne Shackelford Junr. Clk of the Vestry

[149]
At a Vestry held for the Parish of Stratton Major on Saturday the 25th: day of October 1783.

	Richard Anderson	William Dudley
	Richard Bray	Thomas Dillard
Present	George Lyne &	John Kidd Vestry men
	Gregory Smith	

Pursuant to an Order of King and Queen County Court dated August the 12ᵗʰ. 1783 that (Present Philip Taliaferro) the Vestries of the different Parishes do divide their Parishes into so many precincts as to them may seem most convenient for proceſsioning every person's land therein and to appoint particular times between the last day of December and the last day of March next ensuing agreeable to an Act of Aſsembly in that case made and provided.

Ordered that Philip Taliaferro, Stephen Field, and John Shackelford or any two of them do meet on the first Monday in January next and go in proceſsion and see all and every persons land between Poropotank Creek and Mataſsip swamp plainly marked continuing their proceedings in all suitable weather until the whole precinct be finished. And the freeholders inhabitants thereof are hereby required to attend the said proceſsioners according to Law. And the said proceſsioners are further Ordered to make return to this Vestry at their next meeting after the last day of March next a true account of what lands they have proceſsioned and the persons present at the same and of what lands they have not proceſsioned and the particular reasons of such failure.

Ordered that Richard Anderson, Joyeux Collins, and John Webley, or any two of them do meet on the first Wednesday in January next and go in proceſsion of and see all and every persons land between Mataſsip and Perpetico Swamps plainly marked and continue their proceedings according to Law.

Ordered that Edward Walden, John Didlake, and Robert B. Dudley, or any two of them do meet on the first Friday in January next and go in procefsion of and see all and every person's land between Perpetico Swamp, Arricaco Creek, and the western branch thereof plainly marked and continue their proceedings according to Law.

Ordered that Thomas Bland, Thomas Dillard, and Charles Roane, or any two of them do meet on the second Monday in January next and go in procefsion of and see all and every persons land between the eastern and western branch of Arricaco Creek plainly marked and continue their proceedings according to Law.

Ordered that William Bland, Thomas Lamboth and John Sadler, or any two of them do meet on the second Wednesday in January next and go in procefsion of and see all and every persons land between the western branch and Arricaco Creek plainly marked continuing their proceedings according to Law.

Ordered that Charles Collier, William Halliard, and Major Roane or any two of them do meet on the second Friday in January next and go in procefsion of and see all and every persons land [150] between Burgefses Swamp and the Monack swamp and from thence a straight course between Mary Hollenger's and the land lately the property of Doctor Joyeux to Tafsityan swamp plainly marked and continue their proceedings according to Law.

Ordered that Benjamin Faulkner, John Collins and William Hunt or any two of them do meet on the third Monday in January next and go in procefsion of and see all and every persons land between the Monack swamp and on a straight course to Tafsityan swamp & the branch next above William Hunt's plainly marked and continue their proceedings according to Law.

Ordered that Isaac Diggs, Philip Sears, and William Crane, or any two of them do meet on the third Wednesday in January next and go in procefsion of and see all and every person's land between the branch next above William Hunt's and the extent upwards plainly marked and continue their proceedings according to Law.

Ordered that Francis Gaines, Thomas Burk, and Thomas Collins or any two of them do meet on the third Friday in January next and go in procefsion of and see all and every persons land between Tafsityan swamp and great heartquake swamp plainly marked and continue their proceedings according to Law.

Ordered that the Clerk furnish the present Collector with a copy of the list of balances due in the year 1775 as returned by Humphrey Garrett. And the said Collector is Ordered to apply to the different persons for their respective balances and in case of nonpaiment to proceed according to Law.

      Teste. Richard Anderson
Registered by
    Lyne Shackelford j^r. Clk Vestry

[151]

At a Vestry held for Stratton Major Parish on Saturday the 13th. of December 1783

Present
Richard Anderson
Richard Bray
Philip Taliaferro
George Lyne

William Dudley
Gregory Smith
Thomas Dillard
& John Kidd
} Vestry men

It is agreed by this Vestry that George Bray shall live at the Glebe the ensuing year on the same terms that he did this present year.

Richard Anderson, and John Kidd are appointed Church Wardens for the ensuing year

Ordered that the Churchwardens do proceed by suits or warrants as the case may require against the different persons who are in arrears for Parish Levies due in the year 1775.

Gregory Smith's account of four pounds eleven shillings and eleven pence one farthing is allowed as discount against his Parish Levies due in the year 1775 except a balance of four shillings which he is to pay to the Collector.

Thomas Dillard's account of one pound nineteen shillings and three pence is allowed by this Vestry.

George Lyne's account of one pound three shillings and six pence is also allowed.

Ned Shepherd and his family are allowed to live at the poorhouse during the pleasure of the Vestry.

Ordered that the Wardens do call on Benjamin Robinson and William Taliaferro to settle their Wardenship accounts for the time they acted for the Parish.

Ordered that the Wardens do call on George Lyne and Thomas Dillard to settle their accounts also.

M^r. James Henry is appointed a Vestry man in addition to this Vestry.

Lyne Shackelford junior is allowed five pounds for his services as Clerk of the Vestry.

Order that the Church Wardens for the next year do order executions on the two Judgments obtained against John Meredith as soon as the time expires.

Stephen Field is appointed a Vestry man in stead of William Griffin who has never qualified.

Teste. Richard Anderson

Registered by
Lyne Shackelford j^r. Clk Vestry.

APPENDIX

CLERGYMEN

The following list contains the names of the ministers (Incumbents of the Parish and temporary supply preachers) who served Stratton Major Parish between 1729 and 1783. The numeral (in parentheses) preceding the clergyman's name indicates the number of the page on which the name first appears; the date (in parentheses) following the name indicates the year in which the clergyman is first mentioned in the volume.

(1)	Skaife, John (1729)
(29)	Reade, John (1736)
(55)	Yates, Bartholomew (1743)
(55)	Yates, Robert (1743)
(60)	Robinson, William (1744)
(173)	Dunlap, William (1768)
(199)	Dixon, John (1773)
(210)	Hamilton, Arthur (1778)

Notes

Reade, John. On Nov. 11, 1734 the Rev. John Reade was accepted as temporary supply Minister of Christ Church Parish, Middlesex County, until the arrival of "one of the Sons of our late worthy Minister Mr Bartho Yates." [*Vestry Book of Christ Church Parish*, page 238]. On Nov. 23, 1736 the Rev. John Reade informed the Vestry of Christ Church Parish of his "Intention to leave the Parish, being Chosen Minister of Stratton major Parish in King & Queen." [*Vestry Book of Christ Church Parish*, page 244]

Yates, Bartholomew. In *The Vestry Book of Christ Church Parish* (page 238) the Rev. Bartholomew Yates is described as "one of the Sons of our late worthy Minister M'. Bartho Yates." On Oct. 13, 1737 he was chosen Minister of Christ Church Parish [*Vestry Book of Christ Church Parish,* page 245]

Yates, Robert. The Rev. Robert Yates was probably a brother of the Rev. Bartholomew Yates above mentioned.

Dunlap William. On Feb. 6, 1778 a Rev. William Dunlop offered himself (unsuccessfully) as a Candidate for the incumbency of Kingston Parish, Mathews (then Gloucester) County [*Vestry Book of Kingston Parish,* page 110] On Sep. 23, of this same year, the Rev. William Dunlap was occupying the Glebe of Stratton Major Parish under protest from the Vestry, they being of the opinion that he had resigned the Parish on Feb. 16th of that year [See within, pages 209 and 210] Query: Were the Rev. William Dunlop and the Rev. William Dunlap one and the same man?

Dixon, John. The Rev. John Dixon was received as Minister of Kingston Parish, Mathews (then Gloucester) County on Dec. 10, 1750. He resigned the Parish Oct. 29, 1770 [*Vestry Book of Kingston Parish,* pages 43 and 91.]

Hamilton, Arthur. On Dec. 19, 1770 a Rev. Arthur Hamilton offered himself (unsuccessfully) as a Candidate for the incumbency of Kingston Parish, Mathews (then Gloucester) County. [*Vestry Book of Kingston Parish,* page 94]

CLERKS OF THE VESTRY

The following list contains the names of the clerks of the Vestry of Stratton Major Parish between 1729 and 1783

(1)	Pigg, John (1729)
(18)	Hill, Henry (1734)
(48)	Gaines, Francis (1743)
(193)	Gaines, Francis, Jr. (1772)
(202)	Collier, John (1775)
(207)	Shackelford, John (1777)
(223)	Shackelford, Lyne, Jr. (1782)

PHYSICIANS

The following list contains the names of the physicians mentioned in this book.

(32)	Strachey, John (1738)
(50)	Joyeux, John (1743)
(81)	Leith, Charles (1749)
(146)	Fercharson [Philip?] (1763)
(181)	Newcomb, John (1769)
(184)	Hare, ———— (1770)

Notes

Strachey, John. In Oct. 1744 Dr. John Strachey was "allow'd as p' Acco' .. .. .. 800" lb Tob. by the Vestry of Christ Church Parish, Middlesex County [*Vestry Book of Christ Church Parish,* page 263]

Joyeux, John. It does not directly appear from anything in the present volume that Dr. John Joyeux was practicing the profession of medicine in Stratton Major Parish during the period 1729-1783. He had probably retired from the practice of medicine before 1743, when his name first occurs in the Vestry Book

Fercharson [*Philip?*]. In Nov. 1761 Dr. Philip Fercharson was allowed "⅌ account £3‖3‖6½" by the Vestry of Christ Church Parish, Middlesex County. [*Vestry Book of Christ Church Parish,* page 317]

Newcomb, John. In Nov. 1769 John Newcomb was allowed 9/ by the Vestry of Stratton Major Parish for "Doctering John Gardner" [page 181 of the present volume]. However, under the heading "Pews Allotted to Families &c in the New Church" [page 170 of the present volume] he is listed simply as John Newcomb. He is nowhere in the book given the title of Doctor, and was probably not a regular physician.

Index of Names of Persons

Abbot (Abbott): John—124, 168; (M^r) Daughters—168
Adams (Addams): Amy (Amey) —119, 120, 121, 123, 128^2, 134, 137, 140, 145, 148, 151, 154, 162, 165, 176, 180, 183, 188, 194, 195, 197, 200, 205; Joseph (Jo)—81, 98, 99, 105, 110, 115
Alcock: W^m—2
Anderson:—2; Hansford—167; Matthew (Matt)—190, 198, 205; M^r—15, 29, 32, 37, 40, 42, 43, 45^3, 52, 55, 56; Mrs Mary (Widow)—167; Richard (Capt. Rich'd, Mr Rich'd)—5, 6, 8, 12, 14, 15, 16^2, 17^3, 19, 20, 22^2, 25, 26, 27, 28, 29, 33, 39, 40^2, 41, 45, 48, 59, 60, 64, 66^2, 67^2, 71, 72^2, 74^2, 75, 77, 79, 80, 82, 85, 92, 94^2, 95, 96, 98^2, 105, 113, 143, 160, 167, 173, 187, 192, 203, 206^2, 207, 208^2, 209^3, 210^2, 211, 212^2, 213^2, 216^2, 218^2, 219^2, 221^2, 222, 223, 224^2, 225, 226^3, 227^2, 229^3, 230; (Rich^d) Wife—167; Richard, Jr.—208
Atkins: Jno.—58, 149

Bagwell: Wm Kettle—42
Baker: W^m—170; (W^m) Wife—170
Banks: Jno.—171
Barker:—20; Frances—14, 15, 16, 18, 19; James Robertson (Roberson, Robinson)—18, 19, 62; Susanna (Susana, Susa)—13, 15, 18, 19
Barkley: Mark—3
Barram: Thos—115, 118^3
Barret: Mary—128

Bartlet: Mary—4
Basket: Abraham—96, 105, 107, 110, 112, 115, 118^4,
Bayly: Francis—4^2
Bean: W^m—185
Berry: Jno.—22, 26; W^m—34, 40, 49, 68, 76
Birch: Grace—56; Wid^w—45
Bird: Sarah—135, 148, 149, 151, 152, 155, 156, 185, 192; Thos—138, 141, 146, 147, 148, 149, 151, 152, 153^2, 155, 156^2, 162, 164, 171, 176, 179, 180, 182, 183, 185, 188, 191, 194^2
Blackgrove: M^r—3
Bland: Thos—187, 192, 203, 214, 228; W^m (M^r W^m)—125, 136, 137, 139, 140, 142, 144, 145, 147, 148, 149, 151, 161, 169, 173, 205, 207, 214, 228; (W^m) Wife—169; W^m Jr.—170, 200; (W^m Jr.) Wife—170
Bourne (Borne, Bourn): Thos—9, 24, 26, 35, 41, 51, 76
Bowden: George—90; Thos—41, 75; W^m—169; (W^m) Wife—169
Bowdric: Mary—177, 180, 184
Bowen: Jno.—142
Bowers: Ann—155, 163, 177, 180, 184, 189
Bowles: Jno.—77
Boyd: James—125, 168; (James) Wife—168; Spencer—88, 103, 109, 111, 125, 144, 161, 168, 204, 215; (Spencer) Wife—168
Boyd & Brown: Messrs—194, 198
Bradger: Ann—56; Margret—56
Bradshaw: Jane—100^2
Bray:—220; George—61, 69, 76, 87, 103, 109, 125, 169, 229;

(George) Wife—168; Jno.—46;
Richard—44, 169, 182, 183, 195,
204, 206ª, 207, 209ª, 210, 212ª, 213,
215, 216ª, 218ª, 219ª, 221ª, 222ª,
223, 224, 225, 226, 227, 229;
(Rich^d) Wife—168
Brenin (once Brining): Dennis
  (once Denis)—146, 155, 157,
  163, 165, 171, 176, 179, 180, 182,
  183, 186, 189, 191, 194
Bridges: Augustine—61
Briggs: Jno.—171
Broadway: W^m—175
Brooks: James—117
Brown: Ann—59, 184; Betty—
  211; Eliz^a (Elizabeth)—44, 46,
  47, 53, 54, 57, 59ª, 61, 62, 64, 66,
  72, 73, 78, 79, 80, 82ª, 84, 90, 91,
  93, 96, 97, 99, 101, 105, 107, 110,
  112, 115, 117, 118, 120, 123, 128,
  129, 131, 134, 136, 137, 139, 140,
  141, 142, 145, 147, 148, 150, 151,
  153, 155, 157, 163, 165, 176, 179,
  180, 182, 183, 186, 189, 191, 194,
  212, 216; Henry—17, 20, 27, 30,
  32, 37, 39, 42, 46ª, 47, 53ª, 55ª,
  57, 58ª, 60, 64, 72, 77, 80, 82, 90;
  Mary—90, 93, 94, 97ª, 99ª, 100,
  101, 105, 107, 129, 135, 138, 141,
  146, 148, 151, 155, 163, 176, 180,
  184, 189; Robert—44, 148, 151,
  163, 170, 180, 181; (Robt) Wife
  —170; Samuel—170; (Sam^1)
  Wife—170; Thos—70
Brownen: Susanna (once Susan)
  —94, 95, 98, 99, 119, 121, 123
Brushwood (Breshwood): Ann—
  137; Jno.—204, 215; Thos—118,
  120, 123, 128, 131, 134ª, 137, 144,
  161, 170, 187, 192; (Thos) Wife
  —169; W^m—9, 50, 61, 65, 69,
  99, 101, 105, 110, 111
Bunn: Judith—180

Burch: Nicholas—156, 170;
  (Nich^s) Wife—171; Thos—36,
  41
Burges:—9
Burgess: Matthew—137
Burk: Richard—170; Thos—24,
  51, 215, 229
Burnet: Eliz^a (Elizabeth)—15,
  116, 118, 119, 121, 123; Thos—
  15, 62, 90
Burton: Elias—211ª, 224; Jno.—
  147, 148

Camm: Rev. M^r—127ª
Campbell (Camel, Camels): Alexander—224, 225ª; James—94, 188,
  193, 194; Jno.—40, 42, 43, 44,
  46, 80, 82ª, 84, 90, 204; Margaret
  (Margret)—94, 165, 169, 176,
  179, 180
Cannon: Mary—110
Cardwell: Jno.—103, 109, 125,
  144; Thos—10, 24, 26, 36, 41, 51,
  60, 70, 77; W^m—93, 95
Carter: Ja.—38; Jno.—58
Cary:—8; Col^1—129; Henry (M^r)
  —4ª; M^r (Carpenter)—8
Clear (Clair, Clare): Ann
  (Anne)—6, 7, 12, 13, 14ª, 17ª, 20ª,
  27, 30, 32, 37, 39, 42, 46, 53, 57,
  58, 60, 64, 72, 77, 80, 82, 90, 92
Coats: Martha—117, 129ª, 131,
  134, 137, 139, 140, 145, 148, 151,
  155, 163, 176, 180, 184, 189; Patty
  —122, 211, 217
Collier: Mrs Anne—20, 32; M^{rs}
  Anne (Widow)—167; Capt.—
  18; Charles (Mr Charles)—3, 7,
  13, 42, 43, 44, 45^t, 46ª, 48, 57,
  59, 60, 63ª, 64, 67ª, 72, 73, 168,
  204, 210⁵, 212, 213, 215, 216ª,
  219ª, 221, 222ª, 225, 226, 228;
  Mrs Fra^s (Widow)—167; (M^{rs})

Daughters—168; George—99, 105, 107; Henry—22, 26, 68, 76, 86, 102, 109, 169; (Henry) Wife —169; James — 102, 109, 124, 135, 139, 143, 157² 161, 168, 174, 187, 203, 216; (James) Wife— 168; Jno. (Mr Jno., Capt. Jno.) —1, 2, 3, 5, 6, 8, 10, 11², 12, 14², 16², 17, 18, 19², 122, 129, 134, 161 168, 202, 204, 207; (Jno.) Wife — 170; John, Cob^r—170; Jno. J^r—124, 143, 187, 199, 202, 203, 205, 206; (Jno. J^r) Wife— 168; M^r—4, 5, 6, 11, 42, 45³, 52, 55, 56; Thos—15; W^m—102, 108, 113, 114, 116, 117⁵, 120, 121, 124², 126, 127, 131, 133, 139, 157

Collins:—19²; Cath^a (Widow)— 168; George — 170; (George) Wife—170; Jno.—23, 228; Joyeux (once Joyex)—168, 187, 189, 191, 192, 203, 214, 224, 225, 226, 227; (Joyeux) Wife—168; Thos —9, 19, 23, 27, 35, 40, 47, 50, 53, 63, 229

Cooke: Thos—171; (Thos) Wife —170

Corbin: Coll.—1, 3, 5, 6, 11, 28, 29, 30, 44, 45, 46², 48, 52, 55², 56²; Gawin (Coll. Gawin)—2, 5, 6, 7, 8, 11, 12, 17, 19, 22, 25, 27, 28, 29, 42, 44, 48², 52, 55, 56, 57², 59², 60, 62; John Taylor (John T) Esqr—190, 191, 193, 195, 196², 197, 199, 200, 202²; Richard (Coll Rich'd, The Honble Rich'd Esqr)—62, 63, 66², 67, 72², 77², 89, 94, 95, 96, 98, 105, 109, 113, 114, 120, 126, 130, 131², 133², 134, 135, 136, 140, 147, 150, 152, 153, 154², 158, 159, 160, 166, 172³, 173², 174², 175³, 177, 178, 183, 185³, 186, 191, 192², 193, 196², 197², 198, 199³, 200, 201, 202, 205, 206, 216; (Rich^d) Family— 166

Corr: Jno.—169; (Jno.) Wife— 169; Thos—170; (Thos) Wife— 170; W^m—170; (W^m) Wife— 170

Costula: Bridget—47, 53; Lucy— 47, 53

Crane: W^m—228

Crawford: Andrew—167

Cristy: Samuel—42²

Crittenden: Richard—124, 143, 160, 168 (Rich^d) Wife—168

Crouch: Mary—19

Curtis: Eliza—211, 217

Daly (Daily, Dayly): Owen (Owin)—15, 18, 21², 28, 30

Damm (once Dam): Solomon— 90, 112, 170, 198; Solomon (Wife)—170; W^m—207

Dance: Mary—137², 138²

Daniel (Daniell): Alice—11, 15, 16, 18, 21², 28, 30, 31

Davenport (Devenport, Devonport): Amey—59; Ann (Anne) —33, 44², 59, 73, 119²; George— 119; Thos—119; W^m—73

David:—164

Didlake: Edward—30; Elizabeth —69, 112, 115; Frances—169; George—204, 215; James—103, 109, 125, 144, 161, 168, 173, 187, 192, 201, 203, 206², 207, 209, 210, 212, 213, 216², 218, 219², 221²; (James) Wife—168; Jane—116, 117, 136, 137, 139, 140, 141, 157, 163, 169, 183; Jno.—134, 168, 214, 227; (Jno.) Wife—168; Rebeckah—130, 134; Robert—50, 59, 70, 87

Diggs: Isaac—215, 228

Dillard: George (once Mr George)
—125, 144², 161², 168, 173, 181,
187², 192, 203, 204, 205, 206², 207,
209, 210, 212², 216², 217², 219;
(George) Wife—168; George Dr^a
—168; (George Dr^a) Wife—168;
Nicholas—22, 26, 34, 40, 49, 59,
68, 76, 86, 102, 109, 124, 143, 161,
168, 174; (Nicholas) Wife—169;
Thos—23, 26, 35, 40, 49, 57, 69,
76, 86, 103, 109, 136, 142, 145²,
153, 154, 158², 160, 163, 167, 172²,
174, 175, 178², 179, 181, 183, 184,
186, 190, 192, 193, 199, 200², 202,
206, 210, 222, 223, 224², 225, 226,
227, 228, 229, 230²; (Thos) Wife
—167; Thos J^r—214, 219, 221
Dowlin: Eliz^a—12
Dixon: The Rev. (M^r) Jno.—
199, 200
Draper (once Drapier): Eliz^a—
185, 189; W^m—156, 163², 180
Drummond: Jno.— 169; Thos—
168; (Thos.) Wife—168; Thos
J^r—169; (Thos J^r) Wife—169
Dudley: Capt.—1, 4, 5, 13, 14, 15,
18, 19, 29, 33, 39, 41², 42², 44²,
45, 52, 55, 56, 65, 67; Robert
(Capt. Robt)—1, 3, 4, 8, 11, 12,
13, 16, 17, 19, 20, 22, 25, 27, 28,
29, 32, 37, 38, 39, 41, 42, 45, 48,
57 59, 60, 62², 63², 64, 67², 71,
73, 77, 78, 113, 168; Robert
B(allard)—168, 214, 227; (Robt
B) Wife — 168; Thos — 167;
(Thos) Wife—167; Thos J^r—
168; W^m—168², 219², 221², 222²,
223, 224, 225, 227, 229; (W^m)
Wife—168²
Dugliss: Edward—51
Dunlap (once Donlap): The Rev
(M^r) W^m—173, 174, 175², 176,
178, 179, 180, 183, 188, 194, 196²,
197², 198⁴, 200², 202⁴, 205², 206,
207, 209², 210; M^rs—198

Edwards:—152; Ann—16; Charles
—169; David—13, 14, 15; Mary
—194; Sarah—152, 155
Eliza:—164
Ellis: Thos—212, 216; Unity—
124, 146, 148, 151, 155, 163, 176,
180, 184²
Elrington: Griffith—90, 95, 105,
110, 115, 120, 128, 134, 137, 140,
145, 148, 150, 154, 162, 176, 180,
183
Emmons: James—171; (James)
Wife—170
Eubank: Richard—119, 121, 128,
135
Evans: Jno.—18, 171; Mary—18;
Mildred—145, 152, 153, 155, 157,
162, 165, 176, 179, 180, 189, 190

Falkner: Jacob — 169; Richard—
148, 169; (Rich^d) Wife—169
Faulkner: Benj.—228
Fercharson: Doct^r—146
Field: Roger—69, 76, 86; Stephen
—203, 213, 218, 219, 227, 230
Fleming (Flemming): Samuel—
170, 194; (Saml) Wife—170
Forget: Charles—4²
Foster: Jno.—49, 59, 68, 76, 78,
83², 85, 86, 89, 90², 98², 108, 109,
111², 113, 115², 116, 120, 124²,
126, 127, 133, 134, 136, 140, 143,
153; M^r—6², 7, 11, 21, 29, 33;
Mr Thos—1, 3, 4, 5, 6, 7, 8, 11,
12, 14, 17, 19, 20, 21, 22², 25, 26²,
27², 28, 29, 32, 34, 37, 39, 40, 42;
Thos—29
Fox: Susan (Susa, Susana)—7,
13, 15, 17, 20, 21, 27, 30, 32, 33,
37

KING AND QUEEN COUNTY, VIRGINIA, 1729-1783 239

Gaines (Gaynes) :—12; Capt.—10, 16, 17, 18², 25, 29, 30, 32, 33, 36, 37, 40, 41, 42⁶, 43³, 44, 45², 48, 52², 55, 56², 57; Catherine—66, 79², 80; Francis—48, 52, 53, 55², 56, 57², 59, 60, 61, 62, 63², 64², 67², 71, 72², 74, 75, 77, 78, 79, 80, 81, 82², 85, 89, 90, 92², 95², 98², 99, 101, 104, 105, 108, 109, 110, 113, 114³, 115, 120², 124, 126, 127, 128, 130, 131, 133, 134, 136³, 137, 138, 140², 141, 143, 145, 146, 147, 148, 149, 150, 151², 153, 154², 156², 158, 159, 160, 162, 164, 165, 167, 172², 173, 174, 175, 176, 179, 180, 182, 183⁴, 186, 188, 190⁴, 192, 193², 194, 195, 196, 198, 199², 200, 201, 202³, 229; (Fraˢ) Wife & Daughters—167; Francis, Jʳ—168, 185, 190, 193², 195, 197³, 199²; Harry (once Genᵗ; once Major Harry)—43, 133, 141, 142², 150, 173; Henry—1, 3, 11, 12, 14; Robert (Capt. Robert)— 13², 14, 15, 16², 17, 19, 20, 22, 25², 27², 28, 29, 38, 39, 40, 41², 45, 48, 57, 59, 62
Gardner: Jno.—181³, 182, 184, 186, 189, 191, 194, 207, 208; Mary—110, 112, 115, 116
Garland: Robert—103, 109
Garrett (Garret): E l i z a — 191; Esther—186, 189, 194; Humphrey (Humphry)—2, 9, 24, 170, 181, 187, 204, 206², 207, 209², 210, 212³, 216², 217², 218, 219², 222, 229; (Humphrey) Wife—168, 170; Humphrey, Jʳ—162, 169; Mʳ—43; Mʳˢ Rachel (Widow)—168; Rachel—211; Richard—36, 41, 103, 104, 109, 125², 129, 144, 146, 162, 170, 188, 193, 204; (Richᵈ) Wife—170; Richard, Jʳ —144, 161, 169; (Richᵈ, Jʳ) Wife

—169; Robert—9, 44, 46, 47, 51, 53, 57, 70, 76, 88, 104, 109, 117, 122, 125, 129, 131, 134, 137, 139, 140, 145², 170; (Robᵗ) Wife—170; Robert, Jʳ—144; Thoˢ—41; Thoˢ, Jʳ—51; Wᵐ—169, 204, 215; (Wᵐ) Wife—169
Gill: John—73; P a t i e n t — 73; Thoˢ—171
Grameil: John—7
Gramshill [once Gramskill, but this was an error of the transcriber's] : Jno. — 171; Sarah—84, 93, 96, 110, 115, 120, 121, 123, 128, 131, 170, 207; Widʷ—33
Graves: Robert—15²
Green: Jno.—45, 65, 119, 121, 128, 135; Robert—170
Gregory: Mʳ—8; Mʳ Roger—3, 5
Griffin: Wᵐ—206, 219, 230
Grindley (once Gringley): Ann—131; Chris.—110², 115, 120, 121², 123², 128, 129, 131; Mary—131, 134, 136
Groom: Barbary—138, 139, 140, 142, 145, 147, 148, 149, 151, 152, 155, 156, 162, 164, 176, 178, 180, 182, 183, 185, 188, 191, 194, 200; Barbara (Widow)—171; Jno.—205; Mary—208, 211; Richard—136, 137; Robert—170; Zachʸ—152, 170; (Zachʸ) Wife—170
Guthrie (once Guthry; twice Guthrey): Ann—94, 110, 112, 115, 116, 118, 119, 120; Daniel—3, 84; Elizabeth—155, 163, 177, 180, 184, 194; James—122, 169, 185, 189; (James) Wife—169; Jno.—53, 171; (Jno.) Wife—171; Jno., Jʳ —99, 105, 107, 110², 118; Major —110, 112, 115, 116, 117, 118, 119, 120; Richard—94, 118², 119, 120, 170; Samuel—12, 27; Thoˢ —53; Wᵐ—18

Halliard: W^m—215, 228
Hallier: Thos—10
Hamilton: The Rev. Arthur—210, 212, 213²
Hanbury: Messrs.—190; Messrs Capel & Osgood—178²
Hannah: Molatto—94
Hare: Doctor—184; W^m—165, 167, 172⁴, 173, 174, 175, 178², 179, 181, 183, 186, 191, 192, 197, 199, 201, 202, 205; (W^m) Wife—167
Haynes: Richard—129; Stephen—56, 81
Hayse: Dan¹—2
Henry: Mr James—230
Herring: Arthur—17
Hickman:—28; Capt.—11², 15, 18, 19; Capt. Henry—1, 2, 3, 5, 6, 8, 11², 12²
Hill: Henry—18, 19², 20, 21, 25, 26², 27, 28, 29², 30, 31, 32, 33, 37², 39², 41, 42², 44, 45, 46², 48, 53; Liddy—75
Hives: Jonathan—221
Hodkins: Hannah—43
Holderby: Eliza—185, 189; Jno.—171; (Jno.) Wife—170, 171; Jno., J^r—171
Holeday: Judith—211, 212, 216
Holliday: Dorathy—12
Hollinger (Hollenger): Mary—50, 69, 81, 87, 103, 115, 117, 118, 120, 123², 125, 128, 129, 144, 145, 151, 161, 163, 188, 204, 215, 228; Mary (Widow)—170
Hooker: Jno.—39, 45, 155, 163, 171, 181, 224; W^m—171
Hunt: M^r—9, 10, 23, 24, 35, 36, 50, 52; M^r W^m—78; W^m—50, 59, 62, 63, 67², 70³, 71, 73, 75², 76, 77², 80, 85, 87², 88, 89, 92, 95, 97², 98², 99, 100, 102, 103², 104, 108, 109, 114, 115, 120, 124, 125², 126, 127, 131, 133, 135, 136, 137, 138, 139, 140, 143, 144², 147², 150, 152², 153, 154², 155, 157, 158², 159², 160, 161, 162, 165, 167, 172², 173, 174, 175², 179², 183², 186, 188², 190³, 191, 192, 193², 196², 197, 200, 202, 204², 206, 209⁴, 210, 212, 213, 215², 216, 217, 218, 219², 220, 221, 223, 224, 225², 226, 228², 229, (W^m) Wife & Daughters—167

Ireson: Jno.—163, 171; (Jno) Wife—171

Jackson: Elizabeth—94, 97, 99, 101, 105, 107; Job—18², 19, 20, 46, 47, 53², 54, 57, 71, 76, 107, 112
James: Anne—171; Jno.—171, 205, 224
Johnson: Capt.—1²; Capt. Richard—1; Major—3, 4², 5, 6, 7, 8, 11³, 14; Major Richard—2, 3, 5, 8, 12, 14
Jones: Eliza—151, 177, 185, 189; Jno.—46, 47, 53, 54, 57, 83; Mary—46, 47, 53, 54, 57; Thos—2
Joyeux (Joyeaux, Joyex, Joyuex): Ann—87; Doctor—50, 69, 125, 144, 161, 188, 204, 215, 228; Doctor Jno.—103

Kattle: W^m—84²
Kelley: Richard—73
Ker (once, Kerr): David—141, 177, 190²
Kidd: Jno.—145, 152, 153, 155, 157, 162, 165, 170, 176, 179, 180, 189, 219, 222², 223, 224, 225, 226, 227, 229²; (Jno.) Wife—170
King: Daniel—10, 24, 26, 56, 62, 76

KING AND QUEEN COUNTY, VIRGINIA, 1729-1783 241

Lambeth (Lamboth): Thos—175^2, 228
Lankford:— 3, Elinor—4; Jno— 41, 80; Thos—6, 8, 12, 14, 17, 20, 23, 26, 27, 30, 32, 35, 37, 39, 40, 42, 45, 49, 53, 57, 58, 60, 64, 69, 72, 76, 77, 80, 82, 86, 90, 92, 95, 99, 105, 106, 110
Lanktra: M^r—53
Lawson: Thos—184^8, 185
Leigh: Jno.—88, 104; W^m—137, 146
Leith: Doctor Charles—81
Lewis: Ann—84, 90, 91, 93^2, 94, 95, 97, 99^2, 100^2; George—84^2, 91, 94
Livingston: Cornelius—167, 186, 192; (Cornelius) Wife — 167; George—168; (George) Wife—168; Hugh—112, 129; Jno. (Mr Jno.)—8^2, 11^2, 12^2, 16, 19, 20, 22^2, 25, 26, 28, 29, 33, 37, 40, 45^2, 46, 48, 57, 58^2, 59, 60, 62, 63^2, 64, 67, 71, 74, 77, 80, 82, 85, 89, 91, 92, 93^2, 94, 98^2, 105, 108, 109, 111, 112, 113, 114, 115, 122, 124, 127, 128, 139; M^r—29, 32, 33^2, 38, 41, 52, 55, 56, 61, 65; Samuel—217, 224; W^m—48
Loe: Ann—106
Low: Francis—94
Lyne: Capt.—42, 45, 46, 47, 52^2, 54^2, 55^2, 56^6, 58, 65; George—216, 218, 219^2, 221^2, 222, 223, 224, 225, 226, 227, 229, 230^2; Henry—81; Jno. (once Mr Jno.)—139, 167, 177, 181, 184, 187, 191^2, 196, 198, 199, 201, 204, 205, 206^2, 207, 209^2, 210, 212, 213, 214, 216^2, 217^4, 218^4, 219, 220^2, 221, 222^3, 225; M^r —29, 31^2, 32, 33; W^m (Capt. W^m, M^r W^m)—16, 25^2, 29, 31, 32, 36, 37, 39, 41^2, 44, 45, 48, 57, 59, 60, 62, 63^2, 64, 67^2, 71^2, 74, 75, 77, 80, 81, 82, 83, 84, 85, 89, 95, 96, 98^2, 100, 102, 104, 105, 106^8, 108, 109, 110, 111, 112, 113, 114, 115, 117, 120, 122^2, 124, 125, 126, 127, 129, 131, 133, 135, 136, 137

Major: George—12, 18; Jrem^o—169; (Jrem^o) Wife—169; the Widow—169
Mallion: Patrick—45
Mansfield: Mary—33, 93, 96; W^m —171
Meddlicot: George—65, 90
Meredith:—Jno.—223, 224^2, 226^2, 230; W^m (M^r W^m)—154, 159^4, 160, 164, 166, 172, 174, 175, 179, 183, 198, 205; (W^m) Family—166
Metcalfe: Jno. — 117; Samuel—154, 165, 167, 184; (Samuel) Wife — 167; Thos — 119, 167; (Thos) Wife—167
Milbey: James—170; (James) Wife—170
Mills: James—190
Minion: Robert—116, 128, 129
Mitchel (Mitchell, Mitchel): Dorothy—30, 31^8; Gab^l—6, 9, 12, 14, 17; Jno.—169; (Jno.) Wife & Sister—169; M^{rs}—27; Nicholas —168; Susannah—211, 212, 216, 217; Thos—170; (Thos) Wife—170; Wid^w—28, 32
Moore: Ben (Benjamin) — 122, 171, 200; (Ben) Wife—170; Jos. (Jos^h)—53, 58: Mary — 142; Turner—142
Morris (Morrise): Ann — 119, 121, 123, 128; Elenor—75; Jno.—15, 119^2, 171; (Jno.) Wife—171; Sally—119^2, 121; Sarah — 15; W^m—4

Muir (Muire): James—6, 13, 20, 32², 143; Jno.—169, 200, 205; (Jno.) Wife—169; W^m — 169, 173², 177, 181; (W^m) Wife—169

Myry: Morgan—69

McCarty (Mcarty, MCarty, M^c-Karty, MacKarty): A m e y— 122, 123, 128, 129; Charles—38, 40, 42, 47, 53, 55, 57, 58, 60, 62, 64, 66, 72, 73, 78, 79, 80, 81, 82, 84, 90, 91, 92, 94, 95, 97, 99, 100, 101, 105, 107, 110, 112, 115, 117, 118² 120, 123, 128, 129, 130, 134², 136, 137, 138, 139, 140, 141, 142, 145, 147, 148, 149, 151, 152², 155, 156, 162, 164, 176, 178, 180, 182, 183, 185, 188, 191, 194, 196; Eliz^a —46, 75; Jno.—123, 129, 131, 134, 135, 171; Jos.—171; Nathaniel—123, 128, 131, 134, 135; W^m—24, 36, 41, 62, 64, 66, 72, 73, 78, 79, 80, 81, 82, 84, 90, 91, 92, 94, 95, 97, 99, 100, 101, 105, 107, 110, 112, 115, 118², 120

McKendree (MCandree, MacKendree, M^ckendree, M^candree, M^c-Andree): Dennis—46, 54, 57, 115; Jane—45, 53, 61, 65, 78, 81, 83, 90, 93, 96, 99, 101, 105, 107, 110, 111, 112, 115, 118, 120, 123, 128, 131, 134, 138

Needler: Benj^a (Mr Benj^a)—6, 7³, 8, 22, 26; M^r—11², 28
Nettles: Catherine—123, 129, 135, 137, 138; Margaret—184
Newcomb: Jno.—170, 181; (Jno.) Wife—170
Newton: Ann—137; Alice—141², 146, 147, 148²
Nichols: Jno.—144

Norman: Jno.—8

O'Bland: Francis—195
O Dear (once, O Deer): David—184; Isabel—75, 129, 135, 138
Orburn [Probably a mistake of the Clerk for Osburn]: Jno.—190
Orrill (Orrell):—2, 3; Saml—8
Osburn (Osborn): Jno.—110, 171
Overstreet: E l i z a b e t h—97, 99, 101, 105, 107, 110, 115; Gabriel—170; Jno.—50

Padget: Samuel—224
Palmer: Jno.—66
Peacock:—152; Jane — 151, 155, 163, 177, 180, 185
Pearce: David—170, 177, 180
Pendleton: Capt. Jno.—158, 172; Jno.—167; (Jno.) Wife—167
Philis (a Negro woman):—66
Pigg: George—32, 48, 65, 68, 76, 85, 99, 102, 108, 168; (George) Wife—168; Jno.—1, 2, 5, 6², 7, 11, 12², 13, 14, 16, 17²; Mrs Jane —20
Power: M^r Ja^s—66
Pryor: Arthur—3, 90; Christopher—102, 108, 115, 120, 124, 128, 134; Croxton—169; James—86, 102, 108, 124, 137, 140, 143, 145, 148, 151, 154, 162; the Widow—169

Ragon (once, Ragan): Elizabeth —59, 61, 62, 64, 66, 72, 73, 78, 79
Raines (Rains): Frances — 146, 148, 151, 155, 163, 176, 180, 184, 189
Ransom: Jane—75, 93, 96
Ray: Richard—44
Reade: The Rev. Jno. (M^r, Jno., The Rev M^r)—29⁵, 30, 31, 32²,

33^2, 37^2, 39^3, 40, 41, 42, 45^3, 52, 53, 55, 57

Reid: Mr Robert—151; Robert & Co.—155, 163

Richards: W^m—34, 40, 49, 86, 121

Roane (Roan): Alexander — 155, 163, 177; Charles—35, 40, 49, 118, 129, 135, 153, 155, 156, 162, 164, 169, 176, 178, 180, 188, 193, 228; Major—228; Michael—76

Robinson: Benjamin (Mr Ben)—199, 200^3, 201^2, 202, 203, 205, 206, 230; Coll—30, 32^3, 33^3, 37, 38, 45, 52, 55^2, 56, 61; Major Jno.—5, 12, 14, 16, 20^2, 22, 25, 27^2, 29; Coll. Jno.—37, 39, 58; Jno.—83, 124, 127, 142, 153, 169; Jno. Esqr—59, 60, 62, 63, 64, 66^2, 67, 74, 75, 80, 82, 83, 85, 89, 90, 92, 95, 98^2, 104, 105, 109, 111^2, 113, 114, 115, 120, 126, 127, 131, 133, 136, 139, 140, 142^2, 145, 147, 150, 154, 157, 158^2, 166, 173; (Jno.) Family—166; (Jno.) Wife—169; Major—4^2, 6, 11, 13, 14, 16, 17; M^r. Jno.—28; The Rev. W^m (W^m, The Rev M^r, The Rev. Mr Commissary)—60^3, 62, 63^3, 64^3, 67^2, 71^2, 72, 74^2, 75^2, 77^4, 79, 80^2, 82^3, 85^2, 89^2, 90, 92^3, 94, 95^3, 98^5, 99, 101, 102, 104^2, 105^2, 108^2, 109^2, 110, 113^2, 114^4, 115^2, 120^3, 124, 126^2, 127^4, 128, 131^2, 133, 134, 136^2, 140^2, 143, 145, 147, 148, 150^2, 153, 154^3, 157, 158^3, 159, 160, 162, 165, 176, 178; (The Rev. M^r. Commissary) Family—168

Roffe (Roff): Mary—56, 75, 106, 118, 129^2, 135, 136, 137, 139, 140, 142, 145, 147, 148, 149, 151, 153, 155, 156, 162, 164, 176, 178, 180

Rollins (Rollens): Elizabeth—38, 43, 44, 46^2

Roney: Elenor—93

Rootes (Roots): Capt. 14, 16^2; Capt. Philip—12, 13^2, 14, 16, 17, 19, 20, 27, 28; Coll.—199; Coll. Philip—166, 174^2, 178; Major—32, 33, 38, 39, 42, 43^2, 44^2, 45^2, 52, 55, 56, 64, 65, 129; Major Philip—29, 38, 39, 48, 93, 94; M^r—29; Philip—59, 62, 63^2, 64, 89, 91^2, 98^2, 105, 113^2, 122^3, 126, 127, 128, 131, 133, 135, 136, 140, 143, 147, 149^2, 150, 153, 154, 172^2, 173, 174, 175, 177, 185, 186, 191, 192, 193, 196, 197, 199^2, 200, 202^2, 204, 205; (Philip) Family—166; Thos Reade—130, 133, 134, 135, 136, 137^2, 139, 141, 143, 147, 148, 150, 154

Roy: M^r—6; Mr Richard—1, 3

Rymer (Rhymer): Margaret — 136; Walter—121, 123, 128, 131, 134, 136

Sadler: Jno.—214, 228

Sambo, a "Negro fellow":—113

Satterwite:—32; James—27, 28, 30, 31

Scuddy: Jno.—73

Sears: Philip—215, 228

Seward [See Soward]

Shackelford: Ben.—167; Daniel—170; (Daniel) Wife—170; Jno.—22, 26, 33, 40, 48, 57, 65, 68, 73, 74, 75^2, 76, 77, 78, 79, 80^2, 81, 82, 85^2, 89, 92, 98^2, 100^2, 102^2, 104, 105^2, 106, 108^2, 123, 167, 207, 208, 209, 210, 211, 212, 213, 216^2, 217, 218, 220, 223^2, 227; Jno., J^r—217^2, 218, 219, 221^2, 223^3; Jno., Senr—219, 222; Lyne—122, 130, 135^2, 138, 141, 143, 149, 157, 158^5, 160^2, 164^2, 167, 172^2, 173^2, 174, 175, 178, 181, 183, 184^2, 185, 186^2,

192², 193, 196, 197, 198², 199³, 200, 201, 202, 205, 206², 207, 208³, 209⁴, 210², 211, 213, 216³, 217, 218², 219³, 222, 224², 225, 226; (Lyne) Wife—167; Lyne J'—223, 226, 229, 230²; M'—21³, 29, 32, 33, 37, 42, 55; M'ˢ Fran⁸ (Widow)—167; Richard (Major Rich⁴, M' Rich⁴)—10, 16², 18², 19², 20, 27, 28, 29, 39, 41, 89, 103, 109, 113, 114, 116, 117⁵, 120, 121³, 122, 126, 127, 131, 133², 136, 143, 146³, 147, 148², 150, 152, 153, 154, 158, 160, 165, 166, 172, 173, 182, 184, 199; (Rich⁴) Family—166; Robinson —218; Wᵐ (once, Capt. Wᵐ)—144, 148, 151, 152, 153, 154³, 155, 156², 157, 158², 159, 161, 163², 167, 172², 173, 174, 175, 176, 177, 179, 180, 181², 182, 183, 186, 193, 195, 196, 199², 200, 202², 205, 214; Zachʳ—59, 168; (Zachʳ) Wife—168; Zachʳ. J'—168

Shepherd (Shepard, Shapard): Ned—230; Samuel—34, 40, 49, 53, 65, 68, 76, 86

Shipton: M'—1, 6, 40; Tho⁸ (M' Tho⁸)—38, 61, 100, 129, 138

Shumack (Shomack): Moses — 45, 47, 65, 75

Simco (Simcoe): Ann—75; Joseph—33, 37, 73, 119

Skaife: The Rev. M' Jno.—1², 2², 3², 4, 5², 6³, 7, 8, 11², 12³, 13, 14², 16², 17³, 18, 19², 20², 21, 22, 25², 26³, 27

Skelton: Richard—3, 7

Skipwith: M' Wᵐ—63, 64, 84

Smith: Gregory (M' Gregory)—34, 40, 49, 59, 167, 215, 218, 219², 221², 222³, 223, 224, 225, 226, 227, 229, 230; Jno. (M' Jno.)—9, 17, 21, 89, 103, 109, 125, 144, 161, 167, 174; Mary—151, 153, 155, 165, 176, 177, 179; Mʳˢ Cathᵃ (Widow)—167; Robert—168

South: Smith—99

Soward (Seward, Sword, Sweard): Ann—147, 148², 151², 154, 155, 162, 176, 180, 182, 185, 189, 201, 211², 216, 217; Benjamin—90, 171; (Ben) Wife—170; Betty—135; Grace—6, 12, 14², 17, 20², 27, 30, 32, 37, 39, 42, 46, 53, 54, 57, 58, 61, 64, 72, 77, 80, 82, 90, 92, 95, 99, 105, 110, 115, 120, 128, 134, 135, 137, 138, 140, 141, 145; Jane—211², 216, 217; Mary—151², 153, 155, 157, 163, 165, 176, 179, 180, 182, 183, 186, 189, 191, 192, 194²; Tho⁸—24, 26, 35, 41, 51, 70, 76, 141, 146, 148², 150, 151, 153, 155, 171; (Tho⁸) Wife —170

Sowell: George — 85, 102, 108; Tho⁸—68, 76

Spencer: Edward—23, 35, 40, 50, 70, 76, 87, 103, 109, 125, 135², 144, 161, 168, 174, 181; Tho⁸—161, 169, 174, 188, 193, 204, 215; (Tho⁸) Wife—169

Sprigg: William—10

Standard: George—149, 160, 169, 173, 211; (George) Wife—169

Stears: Grace—78

Stedman (Steadman): Christopher—142, 145, 146, 169, 187, 204, 205; (Christopher) Wife — 169; Christopher, Jr—169; (Christopher, J') Wife—169

Stevens: Barbary—101

Stones: Richard—78

Strachey: Doctor—32, 33, 38, 43, 54², 55, 56, 58, 62, 107; Doctor Jno.—41, 44, 59, 73, 83, 84, 90, 92, 94, 96, 100; Henry—119, 167;

Jno.—57, 59, 60, 63², 64, 67², 71, 75, 77, 80, 81², 82, 89, 92, 95, 98², 102, 104, 105, 106², 110, 113; Mr Jno.—26, 27, 28², 29, 30, 31, 37, 39, 41, 45², 48; Mary—119; M^r—29, 32, 33, 42, 52, 56
Stratton: Rachel—134
Sykes: Susanna(h)—184, 212, 216; W^m—171; (W^m) Wife—171

Taliaferro: Capt.—30, 37, 42, 45, 47², 52, 53, 55², 56², 65, 67; M^r—21, 29, 32, 33, 63; Philip—167, 202, 203, 210⁵, 212, 213², 216, 218, 219², 222, 223, 224, 225, 226, 227², 229; W^m (Capt. W^m, M^r W^m)—19, 22, 25², 26, 27, 28², 29, 39, 41, 45, 48, 57, 60, 63², 64, 67², 71, 73², 74², 75², 77², 78, 79, 80, 85, 89², 92, 95, 97², 98², 99, 100, 102, 104, 105, 108, 109, 113, 114, 115, 120, 124, 126, 127, 130², 131, 133², 134, 135, 136, 139, 140², 143, 146, 147, 148, 149, 150, 154, 158², 160, 166, 172², 173², 174, 175, 179, 182², 183, 184, 186, 187, 190², 191, 192, 193, 195, 196, 197, 198, 199, 200, 201, 202, 205, 206, 214, 230; (W^m) Family—166
Taylor: Jno.—193 [This is evidently a mistake of the Clerk's for John Taylor Corbin]
Thach:—66; Jno.—66
Thack: Jno.—25², 36, 41
Thorpe: Thos (M^r, Mr Thos)—35, 41, 45, 47², 48³, 52, 53, 54, 55, 56², 57, 59, 60, 63², 64, 65, 71, 74, 75, 77, 78², 80³, 82, 84, 85, 89, 90, 93, 95, 96, 98², 100², 102, 104, 105², 109, 113,. 115, 120, 130
Tibbs: Mrs Mary Ann (Widow)—167

Townley: Jno.—168, 184; Jno. (Wife)—168
Trice: Edward—35, 40, 50, 69, 76, 87, 103, 109, 125, 169; (Edward) Wife—169; James—50, 69, 76, 87, 103, 109, 125, 144, 161, 168, 187, 192; (James) Wife—168; James, J^r—169; (James, J^r) Wife—169; Mrs Jane (Widow)—168
Tunstall: Capt.—46, 53, 61; Jno.—200, 205; M^r—38; Richard (Capt. Rich^d, Major Rich^d)—42, 58, 65, 72, 93, 96, 99, 116, 207
Tureman: Ben.—171; Eliz^a (Widow)—170; George—30, 32, 54, 58, 59, 61, 62, 64, 66, 72, 73, 78, 79, 80, 82, 83, 84, 90, 91, 93; Ignce—10; Jno.—54, 58, 59, 61, 62, 64, 66, 72, 73, 78, 79, 80, 82, 83, 84, 90, 91, 93; Thos—93; W^m—93

Underwood; Richard Philip—19, 63

Vass: Thos—183, 188; Vincent—88, 90, 92, 95, 99, 105
Venus (a Negro woman):—106
Vernon: M^r—17

Walden (Waldin, Walding): Edward—138, 168, 177, 181, 187, 191, 195, 202, 203, 205, 206, 207, 214, 227; (Edwd) Wife—168; Jno.—45, 56, 79, 80, 81; Jno. Senr—23, 26, 41; Lewis—170, 207, 208, 211; Mary—42, 211; Richard—141, 170, 188, 193; (Richard) Wife—170; Susanna—196; W^m—110
Waller: Ann—211; Edward—148; Jno.—22, 26, 68, 76, 129, 169,

184; (Jno.) Wife—169; W{m} Edmond—137; W{m} Ed—141; W{m} Edward—146, 147, 148, 164, 180, 185, 189
Walton: Tho⁹—194
Ware:—2; Arthur—103, 109, 125, 144, 161, 168; Christopher—125, 144, 162, 168, 188, 193, 204, 215; (Christ{r}) Wife—168; Edward (M{r} Edward)—1, 2, 6, 7, 13, 28, 161, 170, 188, 193; Edward, J{r}—134; Fran⁹ (Widow)—170; Isaac —188, 204; James—193; Jno. (M{r} Jno.)—9, 16², 18, 19, 20, 21, 22, 24, 25, 26, 27, 28², 29, 168; (Jno.) Wife—169; John, Drag{n} —170; (Jno. Dr⁹) Wife—170; Robert—36, 41, 51, 60, 70, 77, 88; Spencer—168, 188, 193; M{r} Valentine—2, 3, 4, 5, 6², 8, 9, 12; W{m}—24, 26, 36, 41, 51, 60, 70, 77, 88, 90
Warren: Tho⁹—151, 168; (Tho⁹) Wife—168
Webb: James—163, 224; Richard—16, 19, 26; Wid{w}—30, 31
Webly (Webley): Jno.—214, 227; W{m}—170; (Will{m}) Wife—170
Wedderburn: Alexander — 143, 148, 160, 167, 173, 186, 192, 203, 213, 218, 219; (Allex{r}) Wife—167
Wells: Elias—118
Whiting (Whitinge): Jno.—123, 136², 138, 140, 141, 147, 149², 150, 151, 153, 154, 158, 166, 190; (Whiting) Family—166
Whitsides: Isabel (Isabell) — 76, 81²; Tho⁹—79, 80, 82, 83
Wilburne (Wilburn): Clayton Jones—165, 176, 177, 179
Williams: Benj⁹—117, 129, 134, 151, 152; Frances—211, 212, 216, 220², 222²
Willis: Jane—39
Wills: Willis—162, 169, 176, 179, 188, 194, 197, 200, 205, 207; (Willis) Wife—169
Wilson: W{m}—10
Wotherspon: Dorothy—91, 93, 96
Wright: W{m}—170, 191
Wyatt (Wiatt): Richard—52, 71, 76, 89, 96, 103, 106, 107, 109, 112, 125, 144, 161, 169, 174; (Richard) Wife—169; Tho⁹—170, 207, 224; (Tho⁹) Wife—170; W{m}—200, 201, 205, 211

Yates: The Rev. Bartholomew—55, 57; The Rev. Robert—55, 57

Geographic Index

Arracaco (Aracaco, Arracaca, Arracacoe, Arricaco, Arrocaco) Creek (Swamp) :—8, 10, 23², 25, 34, 35, 37, 49, 50, 52, 68, 69, 71, 86, 87, 89, 103³, 125³, 143, 144², 161³, 187³, 203², 204, 214, 215, 228

Brushwood's (W^m) [Plantation] : —50

Burges(s)field :—9, 23

Burgess's (Burgeses, Burgesses, Burgises) Swamp:—35, 50, 69, 87, 103, 125, 144, 161, 188, 204, 215, 228

England :—66, 126, 150

Goliahs ("Old field" belonging to the Honble. Richd Corbin Esqr) : —131

Great Heartquake (Hartquake, Harquip, Hartquip) Swamp :—9, 24, 36, 51, 70, 88, 104, 126, 144, 162, 188, 204, 215, 229

Hollinger's (Mary) [Plantation] : —50, 69, 87, 103, 125, 144, 161, 188, 204, 215, 228

Hunt's (Mr. or W^m) [Plantation] : —9, 10, 23, 24, 35, 36, 50, 52, 70², 87, 88, 103², 125², 144², 161, 162, 188², 204², 215², 228, 229

Joyeux's (Ann) Lands :—87

Joyeux's (Joyeaux, Joyex, Joyuex) (Doctor John) Land :—50, 69, 103, 125, 144, 161, 188, 204, 215, 228

Little Hartquake (Harquip, Hartquip) Swamp :—9², 24², 35, 36, 51²,

London :—178

Matasip (Matassip, Mattasip, Mattassip) Swamp :—22², 33, 34, 48, 49, 68², 85, 86, 102², 124², 143², 160², 186, 187, 203², 214², 227²

Monack (The) Swamp :—50², 69, 70, 87², 103², 125², 144², 161², 188², 204², 215², 228²

Myry's (Morgan) Corner :—69

Old Field (Goliahs) :—131

Overstreet's (John) [Plantation] : —50

Pepetico (Pepettico, Perpetico) Swamp :—22, 23, 34², 49², 68², 86², 102, 103, 124, 125, 143², 160, 161, 187², 203², 214², 227, 228

Petsworth Parish :—195

Portopotank (Poropotank, Porotopotank) Creek :—22, 33, 48, 68, 85, 102, 124, 143, 160, 186, 203, 214, 227

Richmond County :—129

St. Stephen's Parish :—130

Tarsatyan(s) (Tarsatian, Tarssatyan, Tarsityan, Tasatian, Tassityan) Swamp :—9, 10, 24, 25, 35, 37, 50, 51, 52, 69, 70, 71, 87², 88, 89, 103³, 104, 125³, 126, 144⁴, 161², 162, 188³, 204³, 215³, 228³, 229

West Indies :—196

York County :—127
York Hampton Parish :—127

Index of Topics

Absence of Minister:—197
Acknowledgment of Deeds:—64
Act (of Assembly):—102, 114, 124, 160, 193
  (of Parliament):—117, 122, 133, 136, 140, 154, 158, 159, 172, 200
  (Two Penny):—126
Administration of Baptism:—7
Agreement:
  Articles of, with workmen:—159
  Between Vestry and Contractor: —142
  Between Vestry and Minister:— 114
  For building the New Church:— 150
  To be Conformable (wording of):—116
  To build Church:—131
  To have new Church built:— 130
  To receive new Minister:—29
Aisles (of Church):—132
Allotment of Pews in New Church: —166
Allum (alum):—220
Altar Piece:—132
Appointment:
  Of caretaker of Glebe:—196
  Of Clerk of the Vestry:—19, 48, 193, 202, 207, 223
  Of Church Wardens:—4, 7, 11, 13, 15, 18, 21, 31, 33, 38, 40, 44, 47, 54, 58, 62, 66, 73, 78, 81, 83, 91, 94, 97, 100, 106, 111, 117, 122, 130, 135, 138, 142, 146, 149, 152, 156, 164, 178, 182, 185, 190, 195, 198, 201, 206, 208, 212, 217, 218, 219, 222, 224, 229
  Of Overseers of New Church:— 135
  Of Processioner in room of another:—218
  Of Sexton:—98
  Of Superintendent of Poor House:—195
  Of Vestryman (men):—6, 12, 13, 19, 26, 29, 42, 62, 78, 113^3, 123, 130, 136^2, 139, 153, 154, 157, 165, 190, 199, 202, 206, 215, 216, 218, 219^4, 221, 222^2, 230^3
Arrest:—18
Articles of Agreement:—133, 141, 159
Assembly:
  Act of:—102, 114, 124, 160, 193
  The General:—56, 113
Assignment of Church seating:— 16^2, 17
Attending a poor woman:—100
August Court:—55

Bacon:—220
Banisters (in Church):—133
Baptism, administration of:—7
Barn to be built:—5
Barrels of (Indian) corn:—16, 26, 148
Bastard (child, children):—13, 15^4, 18^2, 19^2, 20, 33, 44^2, 46, 56^2, 59^2, 73, 94, 96, 105, 110^4, 115^2, 119^2, 128
Bedd (bed):—81
Bedding:—76
Beef:—184, 220
Bellows of organ:—181, 190
Benches:—28, 53, 65, 129, 155

Binding out (children):—4, 10, 15², 18², 19, 31, 33², 42, 44², 54, 56, 59², 63, 73³, 94, 118, 119⁴, 131, 136, 142, 190,
Blacksmith's trade:—42
Black Walnut hand rails:—132
Blind Negro woman exempted from paying levies:—107
Blowing the bellows of the organ: —190
Bond:—53, 64, 114
Bond, acknowledgment of:—97, 101, 106, 111, 117, 122, 130, 135, 139, 142, 147, 149, 152, 156, 164, 178, 182, 185, 190, 195, 198, 201
Bond and security:—11, 31, 108, 118², 119, 213
Books, three:—29
Breeches:—28, 117, 155
Brick oven:—75, 79
Brown sugar:—220
Building the (New) Church:—129, 141
Burgesses of (King and Queen) County:—114
Burial service "read over" poor woman by the Reader (i. e., Clerk) of the Church:—46
Burying (poor people):—94, 112, 135, 137, 138, 148, 156, 185, 194²
Burying sheet:—84, 138
Bushels of lime:—14

Capitals (of columns):—132
Caretaker, for Glebe property:—196
Carpenter:—8
Carrying poor woman to the grave: —138²
Cash in lieu of tobacco for Parish Levy:—139
Certificate of Vestry to good deportment of Minister:—197
Chancery suit:—4

Chestnut (logs, shingles):—108, 159²
Child to be bound out:—19, 31, 33²
Choice made of Vestryman in place of deceased Vestryman:—73
Church:
 Agreement to build:—131
 And Vestry House to be kept clean:—224
 Cleaning out the:—225
 Furnishings (cushions, etc.) to be bought:—29, 150
 Man to keep it clean and the doors shut:—225
 Seating, assignment of:—16², 17, 21²
 Windows, cording:—100
 Yard(s), clearing, g r u b b i n g, railing:—1, 181, 208
Churches to be repaired:—21
Church of England:—7, 13, 25, 28, 31, 43, 47, 63, 74, 83, 117, 122, 134, 136, 140, 154, 158², 159², 172², 200², 206, 209², 210²
Church Wardens [functions, duties of]:—4³, 7, 10, 11, 12, 15⁴, 16², 18³, 19⁴, 21³, 28², 29, 31⁴, 33², 37², 38³, 39, 40³, 42, 43², 44², 47, 54⁴, 55³, 56, 59⁴, 60², 62², 63, 66³, 73³, 75, 79, 82, 89, 91, 94, 101, 107², 108, 112, 118², 119⁵, 131, 133, 136, 142, 150, 158, 159², 165, 172, 173, 175², 177², 180², 184, 190, 196, 201³, 202, 205, 206, 208⁴, 209, 210, 213², 216² 217, 218², 223², 224², 225², 226², 230
Church Wardens (of Petsworth Parish):—66
Clearing the Church Yard:—181
Clerk, of (King and Queen County) Court:—42, 72, 81, 83, 91, 106, 111, 121, 129, 134, 137, 141,

145, 148, 151, 155, 176, 180, 184, 189, 194, 207
Clerk (i. e., Reader) of the Church:—90, 162
Clerk of the Vestry [appointed, qualifies, serves, etc]:—19, 48, 193^a, 202, 207, 223
Clerk's fee(s):—53, 65
Closet in Glebe House:—74
Cloth (for Reading Desk; for Communion Table):—150^a
Cloth, Clothes, Clothing (for the Poor):—18, 38, 41, 76, 80, 84, 112, 117, 152, 201, 211, 220
Cloth, Virginia:—117
Coffin:—30, 110, 138^a, 151, 156, 194
Commissary (title):—140, 143, 145, 147, 148, 150, 153, 154^a, 158^a, 160, 162, 168
Committee (of Vestrymen):—133, 157, 191, 202
Communion (finding—i. e., providing—the Elements for):—30, 46^a, 53^a, 58^a, 61, 64, 65, 72^a, 78^a, 80, 83, 90, 93, 96, 99, 105, 110, 115, 121, 128, 134, 137, 139, 140, 141, 145, 148, 151, 154, 162, 163, 176, 180, 183
Communion Table:—1, 21, 29
Communion Table Cloth:—150
Compass Windows:—132
Conformable, subscription to be:— 47, 63, 74, 83, 116, 117, 122, 133, 136, 140, 154, 158, 159, 172, 200, 209, 210
Conformity (wording of promise of):—7
Constable:—3
Contractor(s) ["Undertaker(s)"]: —130, 133, 139
Copy of the Law:—46
Cording Church windows:—100

Corn [for the Poor]:—16, 18, 19, 21, 26, 30, 31^a, 45, 56^4, 75^a, 76^a, 93, 96, 100, 106, 112, 117, 118, 123, 124, 129^4, 135^a, 138^a, 141^a, 146, 148^a, 149, 151^a, 155^a, 156, 163^a, 180^a, 181^a, 184, 185^a, 208, 220^a
Corn House (at Glebe; at Poor House):—89, 98, 159
Cornish (Modilion):—132
Cotton patch at Glebe:—226
County Clerk (of King and Queen):—81, 83, 91, 106, 111, 114, 121, 124, 129, 137, 141, 151, 155, 184, 189
Court (August):—55
Court, (the) General:—4, 66
Court (July):—39, 40, 55
Court (King and Queen County): —48, 85, 102, 124, 143, 160, 163, 176, 186, 202, 207, 213, 220, 227
Crown Glass (London):—132
Cushions:—29
Cypher'd plank:—132
Cypress:
  Boards:—159
  Plank:—132
  Shingles:—5, 11, 132, 159
  Timber:—132
Dairy:—5, 67
Dead lights in Church windows:— 208
Deeds [of bargain and sale, etc]:— 64^a, 66, 114, 177
Delapidations, Minister not liable for:—85
Delinquents:—46, 53, 58, 121, 148, 155
Deportment of Minister, certificate of Vestry to good:—197
Desks (Church reading):—133
Dial post:—65, 93
Digging grave:—84

KING AND QUEEN COUNTY, VIRGINIA, 1729-1783   251

Distribution:
  Of Corn to the Poor:—45
  Of Fines:—41, 56, 75,
Doctering poor man:—181
Doctrine and Discipline of Church of England:—172², 200², 206, 209², 210
Door:
  Step at Vestry House:—61
  Steps at Upper Church:—93
Doors (to Church, Glebe House, pews):—14, 74, 132, 175
Doric Order:—132
Dormer Windows:—3
Drawing Deeds:—66
Drawing up Articles of Agreement:—141
Dressers in closet to Glebe House: —74

Education (of apprentice):—42
Executions (on judgments):—230
Exemption from paying Parish Levies:—4, 43, 47, 62, 79, 84, 107, 113, 119
Extraordinary services:
  Of Reader:—58²
  Of Sexton:—58²

Failure (Refusal) to qualify as Vestryman:—157, 165, 218², 230
Family to be turned out of Vestry House:—175
Fee(s) (of Clerks, lawyers):—8, 28, 32, 53, 65, 66²
Finding [i. e., providing] the Communion Elements:—121, 139, 140, 141, 145, 151, 154, 162, 163, 183
Fines:—15, 16³, 28, 41, 54, 56, 62², 75, 77, 92², 94, 106
Firewood for poor woman:—135
Font:—6, 7, 29
Food for poor man:—28

Fourth Payment on New Church: —141
Gable Ends:—132
Gallery (in Church):—39, 132
Gallon of Rum:—30
Garden:—31, 108, 201
Gazette, Virginia:—209
(General) Assembly:—56, 113, 114
General Court:—4, 66
General Court Lawyer to be employed:—223
Gift:
  Of Font to Upper Church:—7
  Of fifty Acres of Land for Poor House:—159
Girders:—132
Glass:—5, 7, 44, 96, 132
Glazing:—5, 14, 191
Glebe:—1, 3², 5², 6³, 7, 30, 31, 44, 46, 47, 55, 56², 60³, 67⁶, 72, 74², 79, 89, 96, 98, 100, 101, 104, 107², 108², 112², 113, 114⁴, 173, 174, 175², 177³, 178², 184, 190, 196, 202², 205, 210, 212⁴, 213², 216, 220, 223², 224³, 225, 226³, 229
Goods for the Poor:—90, 106, 107, 122, 137, 141, 151, 155, 163, 181, 184
Grave, digging a:—84
Great house:—5
Guarantee for "Seven Years" given by Contractor:—12
Gum (tree):—50, 69

Hand rails (Black Walnut):—132
Hatch to Porch of Church:—79
Heart of Pine:—108
Hen house:—1, 5, 201
Horse block: 32, 58, 61, 81, 90, 99, 111, 129, 141
House to be built for Poor Woman: —11, 16
House (Necessary):—75

Houses on the Glebe Land:—224

Improvements at Glebe:—31
Indentures:—18, 63, 73, 118, 119⁴
Indian Corn:—26
Isles (aisles) of Church:—132

Jists (joists):—132
Judgments, executions on:—230
Jugs (Water):—181
July Court:—39, 40, 55

Kersey jacket:—18
King and Queen County Court:—
  48, 85, 102, 124, 143, 160, 186, 202, 213, 220, 227
Kitchen:
  To be built on Glebe:—67
  Oven in Glebe:—74

Lapp'd plank:—132
Lathing:—75
Law, copy of the:—46
Lawyer:—8, 28, 223
Lead:—7, 44, 132
Leave of Absence of Minister:—
  198, 199
Letter of Minister:
  Relative to leave of absence:—
    198
  Relative to Two Penny Act:—
    126
Lime:—14,
Lime and sand (for mortar):—
  133
Linen shirts:—18
List(s) of tithables:—13, 14, 17, 32, 46, 53, 58, 61, 72, 78, 81, 83, 91, 93, 96, 99, 106, 111, 116, 121, 129, 134, 137, 141, 145, 148, 151, 155, 163, 176, 180, 184, 189, 194, 200, 205, 207
London Crown Glass:—132

Lower Church:—1, 2, 3², 5, 6², 8, 11, 12, 14², 17², 20², 25, 27², 28, 29², 30, 31, 32, 37⁴, 38, 39, 41, 42, 44, 45, 48, 53², 55², 57², 60², 61, 63, 64, 65², 71, 72², 77, 79, 80², 82, 85, 90, 92², 94, 95², 96, 98², 99², 105², 108, 110², 111, 112, 115², 119, 120², 124, 127, 128², 129, 134², 137², 140, 145, 148, 154, 162, 176

Man:
  Allowed to keep school in Vestry House:—221
  And family allowed to live at Poor House:—230
  Refuses to have poor girl bound to him:—12
  To be given notice to move from Glebe:—224
Maner (Manor) house:—5
Marble Font:—7
Meal:—220
Meat [for the Poor]:—18, 19, 21, 31, 93, 117, 123, 124, 129⁴, 146², 148, 151², 155², 156, 163⁹, 180, 185, 208
Meat house at Glebe:—67
Medicines [for the poor]:—96, 100, 107
Mending:
  Benches:—28
  Horse block:—90, 141
  Church windows:—96, 163
Minister:
  (New) received:—29, 173
  Offered Glebe house, etc., in return for services once a month:
    —212
  Of parish not liable for delapidations:—85
  Petitions for leave of absence:—
    196

To appoint Sexton:—206
To be applied to to vacate Glebe:—210
To be paid tobacco in lieu of Glebe:—60
To remove from Glebe:—213
Ministers (to serve during vacancy of parish) engaged for weekly services:—55
Modilion Cornish:—132
Money value (price) of tobacco:— 94, 97, 100, 101
Money, Virginia:—221
Mortar (in Church building):—133
Moved, "people who are":—116
Moving (poor) woman:—134, 137
Mulatto:—56, 59, 73, 94², 119²

Nails:—108
Necessaries [for the poor]:—122, 129², 135², 137, 162, 163, 185, 201,
Necessary House, at Glebe:—75
Negro:
　"Fellow":—113
　Woman:—66, 106
Neighboring Clergy to officiate in absence of Minister:—197
New Church:—129, 130, 131, 132, 133², 135², 138, 139, 141², 142, 147, 150, 153, 154, 157², 158², 159
New Minister received:—29, 173
Next Friend:—217
Numbering Tobacco Plants:—2⁵

Oak:
　Boards:—5²
　Logs:—159
　Plank:—21
　Timber:—159
　(White):—5, 108, 132
　(White) scantling:—74

Oath of Conformability (form of): —158, 159, 172, 200, 206, 209, 210
Oath(s) of a Vestryman:—7, 13, 18, 25, 28, 31, 43, 47, 63, 74, 83, 117, 122, 133, 136, 140, 154, 158, 159, 172, 200, 209, 210
Offer to provide Communion elements gratis:—192
Officiating as Clerk (i. e. Reader): —95
Orchards at Glebe:—67
Organ:—181, 190
Orphan girl (binding out):—4, 119, 190
Out house at Glebe, to be fitted up as Study:—175
Oven:—74, 75, 79
Overseers for New Church, appointment of:—135
Overseer's house at Glebe:—223, 226
Owner of Negro woman excused from paying parish levies for her:—66
Parish:
　Sued in Chancery:—4
　To be kept "undamnified":—31

Parishoners to be allotted seats in New Church:—165
Parliament, Act of:—117, 122, 133, 136, 140, 154, 158, 159, 172, 200
Pasture at Glebe:—212
Payment:
　On New Church:—138, 139, 157
　For Poor House:—196
People, "who are moved":—116
Petition:
　Of Minister for leave of absence:—196
　Of Vestry to General Assembly:—56

That "Negro fellow" be exempt-
    ed:—113
To General Assembly for Act
    permitting sale of Glebe:—113
Pews:—14, 16, 21², 132, 166
Physician's bill for "means Ad-
    min^d to the Poor":—94
Physick:—184
Pillars (to Church):—132, 150
Pine:—74, 108, 132²
Pistole (Lawyer's fee):—66
Plank:—74, 132²
Plate belonging to the Church:—
    216
Plastering:—5, 12, 75, 107, 177
Poor:—4, 20, 28, 38, 44, 45, 46,
    47, 65, 73², 75, 79, 80, 81, 82,
    84², 90, 91, 93, 94, 96⁵, 100⁶,
    101, 106², 107⁴, 112², 117⁶, 118⁵,
    119², 122², 123, 124, 129¹⁰, 131,
    134, 135⁶, 136², 137⁴, 138³, 141⁴,
    142, 146², 148⁴, 149, 150³, 151⁶,
    152², 155³, 156³, 157, 162, 163¹¹,
    175, 177², 180⁴, 181⁵, 184⁶, 185⁶,
    190, 191, 194⁴, 195, 201², 208²,
    211, 220³, 223, 224, 225
Poor House:—157, 159², 191, 192,
    194, 195, 196, 197, 198, 200², 201,
    205², 206, 207, 213, 217, 230
Poplar (timber):—1, 132
Porch:—74, 79, 107
Pork [for the Poor]:—21, 28, 129,
    184, 220
Potato patch at Glebe:—226
Precincts:
    For numbering tobacco plants 2⁵
    For processioning:—8, 9, 10, 22,
        23, 24, 25, 34, 35, 36, 37, 48,
        49, 50, 51, 52, 68, 69, 70, 71, 85,
        86, 87, 88, 89, 102, 103, 104,
        124, 125, 126, 143, 144, 160,
        161, 162, 186, 187, 188, 203,
        204, 214, 215, 227, 228, 229

Price (money value) of Tobacco:
    —94, 97, 100, 101
Processioners' Returns:—25, 26⁶,
    40⁵, 41⁴, 57⁴, 59², 60, 76³, 77, 108²,
    109⁷, 150, 173³, 174³, 192⁴, 193³,
    218
Processioning orders:—8, 9³, 10²,
    22³, 23³, 24³, 25, 33, 34², 35³, 36³,
    48, 49³, 50², 51³, 52, 68², 69², 70³,
    71, 85, 86³, 87², 88², 89, 102³, 103⁵,
    104, 124³, 125⁶, 143³, 144⁶, 160²,
    161⁶, 162, 186, 187⁵, 188², 203⁴,
    204⁵, 213, 214⁴, 215⁴, 227³, 228⁵,
    229
Promise of Gift of 50 Acres of
    Land for a Poor House:—159
Prosecuting a suit:—66
Providing (the elements) for the
    Communion:—17, 46², 53³, 58²,
    61, 64, 65, 72², 78³, 80, 83, 90,
    93, 96, 99, 105, 110, 115, 128,
    134, 137, 148, 176, 180,
Pulpit:—21, 133
Pulpit Cloth:—150
Purlines:—132

Quarter at the Glebe:—108
Quartered pine plank:—132

Rafters (of Church):—132
Railing ye Church yards:—1
Reader (i. e. Church Clerk):—3², 6⁶,
    12², 14², 17², 20², 27², 30², 32², 37²,
    39², 42², 45, 46, 53², 57², 60², 64²,
    72², 77², 80², 82², 90³, 92², 95², 99²,
    105³, 110², 115², 120², 128², 134²,
    137, 140², 145², 148², 150, 154,
    162, 176, 180, 183, 188, 194, 197,
    200, 205, 207²
"Reading over" (reading burial ser-
    vice over) poor woman:—46

Rector:—2, 5, 6, 7, 11, 12, 13, 16, 17, 18, 19, 21, 25, 26², 114, 120, 150, 157, 158, 165, 209
Refusal (of man) to have poor girl bound to him:—12
Refusal (Failure) to qualify as Vestryman:—157, 165, 218², 230
Removing:
  Man to another county:—129
  Poor family to another parish:—195
Rent of Glebe:—72, 220
Repairs:—1, 12, 21, 38, 44, 46, 47, 55, 85
Resignation:
  Of Minister:—209
  Of Vestryman:—218, 219, 221
Roof (of Church):—132
Rug:—75
Rules and Discipline of Church of England:—158, 159²
Rum (gallon of):—30

Sacrament:—3, 17
Salivating poor woman:—81
Salt:—220
Sand and lime (for Mortar):—133
Sermon:—55
Scantling (white oak):—74
Schooling of (poor) children:—41, 65
School in the Vestry House, man allowed to keep:—221
Seating in Church:—21², 165
Seats:—74
Security to be given to keep parish undamnified:—19
"Send home to England":—150
Seven years guarantee on repair work:—12
Sexton:—3², 6², 12², 14², 17², 20², 27², 30², 32², 37², 39², 42², 46², 53², 57², 58², 60, 61, 64², 72², 77², 80²,
82², 90², 92², 94, 95², 98, 99³, 105², 110², 115², 119, 120², 128², 134², 137, 140², 145, 147, 148², 151, 154, 162², 165, 176², 180, 183, 188, 194, 197, 200, 205, 206, 207
Sheet, to bury poor woman:—100, 138, 151
Shingles:—1, 5, 11, 132, 159
Shirts:—28
Shoes, for poor people:—96, 100, 117, 118², 129², 134, 138, 141, 152, 190
Shrinkage of Notes:—92, 95, 99, 105, 110, 115, 120, 128, 134, 136, 140, 145, 148, 150, 154, 162, 176², 180, 183, 188, 194, 197, 207
Shutters:—14
Slaves, reference to under the words "owners of them":—221
Sleepers (white oak):—132
Soder (solder):—7
Specie, in lieu of tobacco:—223
Specifications (building):—5, 131, 132, 133, 142, 159²
Square glass:—5
Stairs, to gallery:—132
Steps:—21, 61, 65, 74, 93, 112, 138, 155
Stockings, for poor people:—96, 117, 118, 138
Store:
  Account:—148, 177
  The:—21⁸
  Goods for the Poor:—190, 191, 194
Stranger in the parish:—3
Study for Minister in Out House on Glebe:—175
Subscription to be Conformable:—25, 28, 31, 43, 47, 63, 74, 83, 117, 122, 133, 136, 140, 154, 158, 159, 172, 200, 209, 210
Sugar, Brown:—220

Suits (Law):—4², 8, 15, 66², 126, 127, 210, 223, 226², 230
Summers (in Church building):—132
Summoning:—12
Sundries for the Poor:—96², 100, 107, 117², 129, 177
Superintendent of Poor House:—195
Surplices (two) to be provided:—66, 79, 150
Surplice, washing the:—3, 7, 13, 14, 17, 20³, 27², 30², 32², 39², 42², 46², 53, 60, 61, 64², 72², 77², 80², 82², 92², 95, 99, 105, 110, 115², 128, 134, 145, 154
Supply clergymen engaged for weekly services during absence of Minister of the Parish:—55
Support of (poor) family:—42
Sypruss (cypress) boards:—1

Tar (Tarred, Tarring):—1, 5, 11,
Taylor's (tailor's) work: — 129, 151, 152, 163
Test (signed by Vestrymen):—18
Tithables (tithes), list(s) of:—13, 14, 17, 32, 46, 53, 58, 61, 72, 78, 81, 83, 91, 93, 96, 99, 106, 111, 116, 121, 129, 134, 137, 141, 145, 148, 151, 155, 163, 176, 180, 184, 189, 194, 200, 205, 207
Tithables (tithes), number of:—4, 7, 13, 15, 18, 21, 28, 31, 33, 38, 40, 43, 47, 54, 58, 61, 66, 73, 78, 81, 83, 91, 93, 96, 97, 100, 106², 111², 116², 121, 122, 130², 135, 138², 142, 146, 149², 152, 156, 164², 178², 181, 182, 185², 189², 195², 198, 201, 206, 208, 211, 217, 223, 225
Tobacco plants:
Numbering:—2⁵

Precincts for numbering:—2⁵
Tobacco, price (money value) of:
—94, 97, 100, 101
Two Penny Act:—126

"Undamnified," parish to be kept:
—31
Undertakers (Contractors): — 130, 133, 139
Upper Church:—1, 3³, 6³, 7, 12², 14², 16, 17³, 19, 20, 21², 27³, 29, 30², 32², 33, 37³, 39³, 42², 45, 46, 52, 53², 56², 57, 59, 60, 61², 63, 64², 65, 67, 72², 75, 77², 80, 81, 82², 89, 90, 92, 93, 95², 98, 99, 104, 105², 109, 110, 113, 114, 115, 120², 126, 128², 129, 130, 133, 134², 136, 137², 138, 140², 143, 145, 147, 148, 154, 162, 175, 176
Use of Glebe Plantation put up to Highest Bidder:—67

Vacancies on Vestry filled by appointment:—16
Vacancy of Parish to be advertised:—213
Vestry:
Agree that Minister be not liable for delapidations:—85
Agree to buy land (for a Glebe): 63, 174
Agree to receive the Rev. Wm Robinson as Minister:—60
Conclude that Minister has resigned the parish:—209
Grant Minister extension of leave of absence:—199
Vestry House:—61, 141, 142, 158, 175², 183, 186, 221, 224
Vestryman:
Appointed (chosen):—6, 16, 19, 62, 73, 78, 113³, 123, 130, 136², 139, 153, 154, 157, 165, 190,

199, 202, 206, 215, 216, 218, 219³, 221, 230²
Declines to act longer:—219², 222²
Fails (refuses) to qualify:—157, 165, 218², 230
Offers to provide Communion elements gratis:—192
Qualifies:—193
Refuses (fails) to qualify:—157, 165, 218², 230
Resigns:—218, 219, 221
Serves as Clerk of the Vestry contrary to law:—193
Virginia cloth:—117
Virginia Gazette:—209
Virginia Money:—221

Wainscot (to pews):—132
Walnut, Black:—132
Wardens:—219, 220⁷, 221⁸, 223, 226, 230²
Warrants:—230
Washing the surplice:—3, 7, 13, 14, 17, 20³, 27², 30², 32², 39², 42², 46², 53, 60, 61, 64², 72², 77², 80², 82², 92², 95, 99, 105, 110, 115², 128, 134, 145, 154

Water Jugs:—181
Water Table:—132
Wearing apparel:—15
Well (to be dug etc):—31
Wescoat (waistcoat):—117
Wheat:—184
White lead:—132
White oak:
  Plank:—5
  Posts:—108
  Scantling:—74
  Sleepers:—132
Whitewashing:—12, 107, 177
Windows:—44, 74², 96, 107, 163, 175, 208
Windows:
  Compass:—132
  Dorment (dormer):—3
Wood for poor woman:—118
Work done (at churches, at Glebe):—53, 61², 100, 112², 129
Work House:—218, 220
Workman (men):—1, 5, 21, 31, 39, 67, 75, 79, 159

Yard and garden to be fenced:—31

www.ingramcontent.com/pod-product-compliance
Lightning Source LLC
Chambersburg PA
CBHW062006220426
43662CB00010B/1242